LIFE ON THE STREETS IS FUN—UNTIL IT ISN'T

PRAISE FOR *OVER THE PEANUT FENCE*

"**A blend of memoir and sociocultural commentary analyzes the problem of teenage homelessness.** Eichinger had known Zach when he was just a child, the victim of his parents' chronic negligence and abuse. One day, her partner, Cory, spotted him on the street, wandering about shiftlessly and clearly ill. They invited him home and discovered that he had been living on the streets for four years, scrounging for money, food, and shelter and struggling with drug abuse. The author divides her book into several distinct parts: a remembrance of her experience with Zach; a reflection on the root causes of homelessness in the United States; a synopsis of the latest research regarding the functioning of a youth's brain; an homage to organizations that make a positive difference; and two short stories that dramatize ways in which adolescents can be effectively assisted. The author's account is lucidly written, both intellectually thorough and emotionally affecting. In addition, this isn't a work of ax-grinding political partisanship — Eichinger prefers cool-headed analysis to grandstanding. Further, at the heart of her 'part memoir and part storybook' is a profound reflection on the ailing condition of American society, withering from the widespread disintegration of the family and the grim plague of 'lovelessness.' **An astute and moving assessment of an urgent societal problem.**"

— *Kirkus Reviews*

"Marilynne Eichinger has woven her personal narrative and research together with her experience as a science center director to make recommendations for those of us who wonder about the people we see with all of their belongings closely held in parks and other public spaces. I share her confidence in the importance of kinesthetic (hands-on) learning as an alternative for those for whom reading is a challenge."

— *Phyllis Katz, Ph.D. Science Education, Associate University of Maryland, Founder of the National Science Foundation award-winning Hands-on Science Program*

"The machines of war roar past a family's muddy tent as the mother searches the garbage for something edible. A youngster here in the U.S. scans a dumpster with the same goal, wondering Why me? And we dare to turn away. Our country has left a trail of suffering in our well intentioned pursuit of 'democracy' in foreign lands; our nation pretends not to see the homelessness on our doorstep, save to complain about it. This stunning book requires you to ask what you can do to help turn trauma into something better."

— Jack Segal, Consul General of the U.S. (ret.), Chief Political Adviser to NATO's Commander in Afghanistan. Segal has worked to aid innocent victims in war zones from Gaza to Afghanistan.

[Eichinger] "provides a powerful glimpse into the trauma and abuse that forces young people to run to the streets. Homeless youth are often invisible in their struggle to complete school while caring for themselves. Under overwhelming pressure, they must surmount many obstacles on their path to adulthood. The lucky ones connect with caring adults—a librarian, a counselor, or a teacher. Their stories are a call for action to libraries, government, youth agencies, universities, parents, and volunteers to work together to solve this national problem."

— Pam Sandlian Smith, President 2017-18, Public Library Association, Director, Anythink Library

OVER THE PEANUT FENCE

Fun? Until it isn't.

Marilynne Eichinger

BUILDING BRIDGES

Building bridges between our divisions,
I reach out to you, won't you reach out to me?
With all our voices and all our visions,
Friends, we can make such sweet harmony.

— From Greenham Common Peace Occupation: 1981 protest to challenge the decision to site 96 Cruise nuclear missiles in Berkshire, England. Greenham Song Book. Old Trafford, Manchester, England

ALSO BY MARILYNNE EICHINGER

— Lives of Museum Junkies: The Story of America's Hands-On Education Movement

Over the Peanut Fence and *Lives of Museum Junkies* are available online in e-book and paperback.

Request them from your library or bookstore.

Subscribe to Marilynne's newsletter at
https://eichingerfineart.com/email-newsletter

email: eichingerbooks@gmail.com

TABLE OF CONTENTS

INTRODUCTION

THIS IS A TALE OF awakening, of learning to pay attention to shadows. It's a quest to understand the lives of youths who struggle to survive—neglected, abandoned, homeless—living in hidden worlds far from the guarded, landscaped communities of social convention.

These youths are present at the periphery but rarely at the center of attention. Over a long and multifaceted career, I frequently encountered homeless youths and, sometimes, their families. I worked to accommodate the family needs, so that they too could be included. More recently, I came face to face with the greater picture, the one in the shadows, the full immensity of the daily challenges faced by just one of these youths, and I began to ask questions—thus this tale.

As the former president of two museums and as owner of a catalog company, I interacted with people from diverse socioeconomic backgrounds and saw the many, and at times tragic, damaging effects of poverty. Even newly housed people face difficulties. Isolation behind closed apartment doors can be depressing for those used to socializing on the streets.

It was not until my partner, Cory, and I agreed to open our home to Zach, a 19-year-old boy who survived four years living on the streets, that I became aware of youth homelessness. Though we knew Zach as a child, and threw peanuts over a fence to amuse him and five other siblings locked in their yard, we lost track until we saw him wandering aimlessly in Portland. He was ill, so we took him home for a week to bring him back to health: he wound up staying for five years. Over time, he became more literate, gained self-confidence and developed skills as a journeyman industrial painter.

Zach's plight made me curious as to why youths are taking to the streets in record numbers. I wondered if stemming the growth of youth homelessness is possible. Teens run away for many reasons including poverty, drugs, mental illness, pregnancy, abuse, sexual orientation, and natural and man-made trauma. In each instance their developing brains are impacted. Care providers focus on interventions to help them become calm and improve their self-esteem.

Over the Peanut Fence is part memoir and part storybook about homeless youths, agency leaders and volunteers. Tales are personal, like that of Kate Lore who, as a child with her mother and sister, was locked out of a comfortable home and left to reside in poverty. Narratives explain how teens negotiate city streets in search of places to sleep, socialize and eat. The teens reveal how much fun it can be, at least initially, to be free from previous abuse at home and to meet others like themselves. They also tell of the depression that takes over when they come to recognize that their future prospects are poor.

As I shared information with friends, I soon realized how little most people know about youth homelessness. They, like I used to be, were quick to label street people as lazy, thieves, and drug abusers without understanding what brought them to their current circumstances. Fed by erroneous media reports, they believed that street youths are dangerous and commit violent crimes. This perception is far from the truth. Rather than perpetrating crimes, homeless adolescents tend to be victims of criminal behavior and neglect which, in turn, toughens them up in order to survive.

Accordingly, "*A recent study in Los Angeles puts a finer point on this information. Interviewing hundreds of street youth, homeless advocates found that 46 percent of boys and 32 percent of girls take part in "survival sex." Of that group, 82 percent prostituted themselves for money, 48 percent for food or a place to stay, and a small group for drugs. A Hollywood study also found that half of the street youths sampled sold drugs. But interestingly, only one-fifth of that group--or, one in ten of all street youths--sold drugs to support their own habit. The rest sold drugs as a means to earn money for food or shelter."*[1]

Living on the streets is a relatively new phenomenon. Though there has always been mental illness, addiction and domestic violence, widespread homelessness started in the 1970s, when the country stopped providing public housing for the mentally ill and the poor[2]. Policies initiated by Presidents Nixon and Reagan continued under both Republican and Democratic administrations. The situation worsened as the economy declined in 2007. Large numbers of unemployed adults began to self-medicate with alcohol and drugs. Often, depressed parents became abusive and neglectful of their children, causing the children to take to the streets in record numbers.

Government entities seem unlikely to provide adequate funding to help homeless youth, so the private sector will need to pick up the slack. Volunteers, schools, church groups and youth agencies will have to join together and coordinate their efforts. Four years of research have provided me with reasons to hope. We can end youth homelessness because there are a great many people involved who care. Though cautiously optimistic that this societal problem can be solved, it will only happen if you and I step forward. This book is a call to action.

SECTION I
FROM THE STREETS

THE STORY OF ZACH

CORY AND I ARE LIFE partners, sharing a home in Portland, Oregon. In 2011, I owned and operated Museum Tour, a national education supply catalog and Cory was employed in a handful of ventures that used his engineering and carpentry skills. Under our house in the woods, he set up a shop and outdoor area to carve totem poles and Northwest coast masks, which he sells to a burgeoning clientele. When not at work, I spent my hours painting in a sunlit studio located on the lower floor of our contemporary seven-level house. The two of us had few encumbrances as we freely traveled, worked and made art.

All that changed one blustery November day when Cory noticed a youth pass in front of his car while waiting for the light to change. When the boy stumbled, he caught Cory's full attention, for he recognized Zach, whom he knew as a child from a troubled family who lived in his old neighborhood. Pulling over to greet the youth, Cory immediately saw that the lad was ill. Fearing pneumonia, he phoned me and after a short conversation we invited Zach for dinner in order to assess his well-being. Within an hour of his arrival and learning that he lived in shelters, we suggested he stay for a few days to be nursed back to health.

Zach quickly improved after sleeping in a comfortable warm bed and eating nutritious meals and by the end of the week was ready to return to the streets. Winter started early that year, the weather was wet and bitterly cold, and we were reluctant to send him back only to become ill again. Zach appeared to be such a young, lost and confused youth that I felt tenderness for him.

It was an emotional week, for Cory and I were uncertain as to the role we wanted to play in his future. Friends feared for our safety and were quite worried about us getting deeply involved. A few neighbors watched Zach moving about our yard and called to warn us of a vagrant trespassing on our property, advising us to call the police.

Zach certainly looked like a street transient. I must admit to my middle-class bias in that I did not like his appearance. He wore ragged clothing and had plugs in his ears. His reddish hair was greasy, straggly and unkempt, and he gave off a strong body odor. He walked hunched over, with a shifty look in eyes that never seemed to focus. Zach's appearance spoke emphatically of a downtrodden boy. Speaking softly when queried, his responses were a short yes, no, or I don't know. Though we certainly tried, it was difficult to get a complete sentence out of him.

Knowing that he came from a family that pilfered from one another, we feared he might steal so when we decided to let Zach stay we kept a constant vigil as he moved about the house, insisting he go to his room when we went to bed. My purse was always stored safely in our bedroom at night. This decision proved wise, for we suspect he took money one time when it was unguarded.

Once Zach agreed to our conditions, which required a haircut and removing the plugs in his ears, we let him remain for the winter. Zach was not happy to lose his straggly locks, but we insisted that if he was going to live with us he had to look like he belonged to our family. We took him to *Goodwill* and *Ross* Dress for Less to be outfitted from his feet up. Zach needed everything from undergarments to jeans, a warm coat, gloves and hat.

House rules included a daily shower, cleaning his room, and making the bed. As time went by, a daily exercise routine was added, and Zach was occasionally asked to help with chores such as shoveling snow and chopping wood. Our goal was to break up the hours he spent lounging aimlessly around the house or watching television. One activity he participated in without being

4

asked pleased us greatly—he continued to attend a drug rehab program. Thankfully, Zach had never been addicted to opioid drugs but was a light pot, molly, meth and occasional *shroom* (psychedelic mushrooms) user. While he was enrolled in the drug program, we never worried about him backsliding, and our trust has since been rewarded. We were concerned about his finances, however, because he had a large fine for possession of marijuana that had to be paid to a municipal district, and we wondered how Zach was going to meet his obligation without an income.

We decided to lend him money to keep the judicial system from compounding interest, but he needed to find employment. Fortunately, I was able to help, for my catalog company was in the middle of its busy retail season, and we needed workers to ship warehouse products. It was easy to provide a six-week seasonal job, though to keep it, Zach had to pass a drug test and prove he could do the work. He was somewhat concerned about the test. When we discovered there was a pill he could take that would purge his body of narcotics, we took him to a head shop to purchase it. Before we spent a lot of money, the proprietor suggested Zach be tested and thankfully the results showed that he was clean. I was especially glad of the outcome because I was uncomfortable with the idea of helping him disguise an addiction. In addition to becoming an enabler, I would have been a hypocrite for ignoring my own employment requirements.

But Zach's work habits amazed us all. He always arrived early and was purposefully the last one to leave, making sure there was nothing that needed attention before closing. Surprisingly, he was highly competitive, setting a goal of being the fastest packer with the fewest mistakes. Our warehouse manager spoke highly of his work ethic, and we soon realized there was something special about him. I was delighted.

After the busy holiday season ended, Zach was once more unemployed. Though he received a good recommendation from his boss and registered at many temporary agencies, he could not find work. I observed first-hand how brutal the job market is for an unskilled person. The Great Recession that started in

2008 put many qualified people in a job-seeking mode with few opportunities for those without training. During this time of unemployment he told me why he left home. By then we had a more trusting relationship that allowed Zach to share his story of his years on the street. Though I believed most of his tale, there were times when I was dubious, for he occasionally bent the truth. All that follows has not been 100 percent fact checked, but for the most part, it rings true.

TURNING TO THE STREETS

When nearly 16, Zach left home during a vicious family fight and never returned. The following four years he lived on his own, moving from one friend's house to another, occasionally sleeping in shelters, under bridges, in paper trash bins or in doorways. As a high school senior, his favorite sleeping spot was under a bush near the local McDonalds and close to school where he went in the early hours for warmth, a shower and breakfast. Being homeless was the beginning of an education in self-preservation that forced him to use his mind in frugal, clever pursuits. Zach described life on the streets as brutal but also as an adventure, for he was free from his family and their constraining demands.

At first, the local mall became Zach's hangout. "I got to know all the vendors," he said, "and was often given free food at the end of the day. I cleaned the tables even if I wasn't asked to and chatted with servers if they weren't busy. I guess the managers felt guilty not paying me, for they usually gave me food. They are still friendly when I return for a visit and want to know how it goes. Best was when a friend took me to his house for a few days. When that happened, I always tried to do something for his mother, like vacuum, wash dishes or even babysit so I wouldn't be a burden."

Zach learned that a smile and positive attitude went a long way toward putting money in his pocket. "I traveled light, only carrying a backpack, and depended on friends to store a suitcase with the rest of my belongings. When panhandling, I'd get a piece of cardboard from a dumpster and make a sign with a funny slogan. The one I liked most was, *Throw a quarter and see if you can hit me.* Though no one ever threw money at me, they laughed and I walked away with $20 within fifteen minutes," he said with a sheepish grin.

"As soon as someone approached, I put on my most serious face, neither smiling nor frowning, but one that was open to conversation. Also, I always tried to stay clean — locking myself in public bathrooms so I could take off my shirt, wash under my armpits, brush my teeth, and put on deodorant."

It did not take long for Zach to walk from his begging spot with a pocket full of change. "I learned not to be afraid of being broke since it was easy to beg, return empty soda cans or find change at the bottom of vending machines. I had a pretty good reputation among the other kids. They wanted to know my secrets. Most of the time I didn't tell them. Let them figure it out for themselves."

"You have to be smart to get by on the streets. You start by picking up free books or clothes (sometimes Nike will give out shirts and shoes), then sell them immediately to a place that buys used clothing. Another thing you do right away is get a food card. To get stuff that is not covered by food stamps, you use the card to purchase an expensive item like olive oil for $50, then, the next day, you return what you bought at customer service. They put the money back on an in-store card that will let you buy anything. I always bought cigarettes that way, but I know a lot of girls who use the trick to buy diapers for their babies. Before I was twenty-one I could sell the cigarettes to someone in exchange for beer. Then, with beer, I could always bargain for pot."

Zach continued with his lesson. "Never carry more than one bag. A backpack is best, but you have to make sure it's secure so you can run immediately in case someone chases you. Don't say anything bad about anyone, even if to a friend. It almost always gets back to the person and you'll have made an enemy. You have to learn to lie. I used to get extra train passes by going into different places that give them away to the homeless. It's easy to sell them to people waiting for the next train. For a while, I lived in a house with six friends, each with food stamps. That meant that we had $1,200 in stamps for the month which was plenty of food. Sometimes I had to travel a great distance for a place to sleep but it was worth doing if it was safe and warm."

Though he lived on the streets his senior year, Zach surprised family and teachers by actually graduating from high school at 17 with math scores at grade level, though a notation on his diploma said that he did not meet state standards in English. When informed of his graduation, Cory and I took the occasion to visit the old neighborhood and take Zach out for a Mexican dinner, surprising him afterward with a small monetary gift. He looked worn out and pale, sniffling during the entire meal, but happy to see us. That week he was sleeping on a sofa at a friend's house on the edge of town, so we dropped him off rather than make him walk the hour and a half to get there. We were saddened by his condition but did not think that we could do anything about his situation.

Zach later told us that after shifting around town for several years and occasionally finding work for a few days, he managed to get summer employment on the coast working in oyster beds. A bus picked up workers in the morning and at day's end returned the exhausted men to their homes, arriving late at night. The job demanded long hours spent in the cold Pacific coastal bay where newly seeded shells were distributed and mature oysters harvested. "I built a lot of upper body strength from lifting bags that exceeded my weight."

"One day I had an extra hour to spare, so I decided to take a walk on the beach, and met a woman who turned out to be my relative. After comparing family history we found out we had the same father. Crazy, huh? I have more brothers and sisters than I ever imagined. I have no idea how many are roamin' round the country."

Zach realized he was not getting anywhere living the way he was. "I had no hope for the future. Every day was a repetition of the one before. I spoke to the same friends, sat for hours in the mall playing cards, begged for money and food, and rode around town on my skateboard. I was tired of always wondering where my next meal would come from or if someone would give me a couch for the night."

Though he varied house stays with nights in the park, he began to feel that he was wearing out his welcome when staying with local friends. So one August day, after getting an invitation to visit a friend in Portland, he decided it was time to move on. A few nights in her apartment were enough to get him oriented, though not off to a good start.

"At first I wandered around town or skateboarded to parks where there were forty to fifty kids hangin' around. It was fun to hang with so many kids my age. They come from all over the country, and many of their stories were worse than mine. There was always someone who had a volleyball, so we all joined in a game to see who could slam the ball the hardest into some slow-moving slacker."

"Parks were good spots for playing cards or chess, bumming pot, and finding free meals or a couch for the night. Sometimes there were over 500 kids playing ball or just chillin'. I learned how to survive by paying attention. After a big night in the park, I would get up early looking for money that dropped out of peoples' pockets. My best day, I picked up $60. Sometimes kids forgot their jackets or skateboards. Other times boxes of books were placed in the park or on the streets with a free sign on it. Whatever—I would gather it up and sell it at a second-hand shop or barter with it for cigarettes or drugs."

"I figured out pretty quick how to get an Oregon ID card and food stamps. *Outside In* (a local youth agency) provided me with a mailbox, which helped. To survive on the streets you have to be smart, pay attention to what goes on. There were days when it was cold and all I did was ride the train back and forth. Most of the time I got by all right, but some days it was rough. I had no money."

"About midnight, some kid would shout, 'you can spend the night at my place.' Fifteen of us *couch drifters* might follow the invite. We would get there and party. When we got tired, we would find a place to sleep on the floor. If we got lucky, we got a piece of

9

a bed or the sofa. Lots of times other people in the building would knock on the door or walls complaining of the noise."

One evening, Jenny, a friend of Zach's, had an apartment that became such a place. Jenny and two girlfriends shared the cost of rent, but when ten kids arrived for the evening, her roommates were not at all happy. As a party got underway and became increasingly raucous, they became angry and told them to leave. No one paid attention. Drugs and alcohol were passed around making the roommates even more upset. Finally, they called the police.

"Me and a friend were outside smoking at the time enjoying fresh air when we seen a police car approaching. We ran inside to clean up."

When asked why he went back and didn't run he said, "You never leave your friends hangin'. It is the first law of the streets."

The two boys returned to gather up the remnants of pot, bongs, pipes and related drug paraphernalia, hiding them under mattresses or in holes covered by toilet paper stacks. By the time the police started pounding the door Jenny had decided not to let them in, but her roommates shouted that they were the ones who had called the police, so there was no stopping them. Two officers entered and started searching the house, first finding nothing. They put everyone in a back room except for his friend, the three apartment dwellers, and Zach who stupidly talked back to the cops. The boys were told to sit on the sofa and remain still.

"All of a sudden I realized," Zach said with a crooked grin, "that we had cleaned the apartment but forgot about what we was carrying on our bodies. I had a wad of pot in my pocket ready to be used in my soda-pop pipe. The bulge was so obvious that the cops cuffed us immediately. That's when they found that my friend was carrying heroin and I got really scared. The police grabbed us roughly, ready to take us to the station and charge us for possession of illegal drugs."

"I went crazy and screamed that I never used heroin. Luckily, I was backed by Jenny. The only thing the policemen had on me was possession of a small amount of marijuana so I was let go, but they were angry because I was belligerent. I was given a $1,200 ticket while my buddy was pushed out the door and taken to jail."

The fine was staggering for a person with no income. Plus, not able to stay in Jenny's apartment any longer, he was back on the streets, varying nights in doorways with visits to someone else's couch and occasional youth shelters. During those first months in Portland's center, he was nicknamed *Streetwise* by quickly learning how to handle himself in the city. Lots of kids are known by street monikers, rather than their given names.

"It was different from being homeless in a small town where many people knew me," he explained. "In the city, if there was a shady group of men at two or three in the morning, I opened my pocketknife and pretended to be studying the blade. I made sure they saw it and knew that I was ready for action. I always kept it sharp and knew what was going on around me. I slept on top of everything I carried, with my backpack under my head, making sure no one would take my stuff."

Outside In was one of the youth shelters Zach visited since it provided food, an overnight bed, counseling and a health clinic. Long-term accommodations were available for youths who committed to a career plan, but the applicant list was extensive with a waiting period of over six months. My impression is that the staff did what they could for Zach given their limited resources. During the intake process, he was assigned a personal counselor. For temporary nighttime accommodations, he was sent to Street Light Youth Shelter, a sister facility. Zach described the place as being packed, decrepit, but warm. Boys stand in long lines at seven in the evening hoping to obtain one of the available beds.

"You had to be lucky to get an empty spot," Zach said, "and when you did, you made sure you kept it. The rule is that if you made your bed you were guaranteed a place the next night."

In the morning, the shelter served an early breakfast and sent the boys back to the streets. Doors reopened for dinner, followed by a few hours of lounging and TV in a crowded breakroom. They were then taken to a large dorm crammed with twenty-four beds for twenty-four smelly youths, many of whom were ill. It was easy to catch the latest circulating disease.

"I spent cold and rainy days in the library and in coffee shops. One cup would last for hours. Sometimes I went to the mall to play cards." The library interested me as his choice for hanging out because I knew he was a reluctant reader. He said he watched videos on library computers if the librarians weren't paying attention or looked at picture books. It was a good place to go to check emails.

"Before TriMet got strict about collecting fares, I would just ride light rail for half a day when it rained. After I started drug rehab, I got a monthly TriMet pass from the center." He smiled sheepishly before adding, "I didn't really need to go to rehab. I wasn't an addict, but I wanted the pass. Then I would go over to *Outside In* and get two more passes to sell on the street."

Though he did not admit it to me immediately, Zach was quite involved in buying and selling drugs. It was not until he was almost charged the third time for possession that he decided to change his ways. He managed to evade the police while carrying a large stash in his backpack. If Zach had been caught, it probably would have resulted in a long prison sentence. As of this writing he has not touched drugs for over seven years and is unlikely to do so again.

MEETING POVERTY

You might wonder why Cory and I became so deeply involved with a homeless youth who passed our car at a stoplight. Zach was not an unknown entity, for we had some involvement with his family when he was in the third grade.

My partner, Cory, loved his grandmother. She raised him after his mother and sister died, cradling him in her arms and soothing his sadness until his father's grief healed enough to take over his care. When his grandmother was elderly, Cory became her caregiver, traveling three hours to her small home in the state of Washington; I often accompanied him on weekend trips.

After dinner, Cory and I often took a stroll taking us past a tumbledown two-story house. Neighbors expressed disgust at the dwelling's peeling paint, scattered trash, car parts, and uncut weedy lawn that added to the slumlike atmosphere. The two-bedroom house was home to six of nine of the parent's children. Three of the older sons, including Jim and Robbie, had been out of the house for years. Jim was halfway through a fourteen-year federal penitentiary term and Robbie had ongoing conflicts that eventually landed him in a state facility. The third boy, John, managed to eke out a subsistence living. In nice weather, the younger children were often seen running around their dirt yard with little to do.

When not in prison, Robbie visited his mother and became a role model for the younger boys. He played guitar, told tales of his wandering exploits, and brought with him one or another of the many children he fathered during his travels. To the younger children, his exploits were exciting. Since Robbie was without resources, he would plead for food and shelter, which his mother had difficulty denying. During visits home he demonstrated his adeptness at stealing by taking things that could be hocked for cash to pay for drugs. Toys, metal objects and wire routinely disappeared to pay for his vices. To get by, he impregnated young girls who became eligible for government subsidies once the baby was born. Over a ten-year period, Robbie fathered five children with three women. He lived with each woman for several years before being kicked out of their apartments. Drug trafficking and petty theft augmented his meager income and enabled him to survive.

Zach's parents did not regard formal education as necessary and did not push their children to graduate from high school. Area teachers were painfully aware of the family, however, and did their best to motivate the children. I know how hard they tried because I met several of their counselors and teachers. By the time I visited their school, I was invested in helping four of the younger children—but, I get ahead of myself.

During one of our summer walks, Nancy and Don (the parents) were smoking on their porch with six children crammed close-by.

By this time I was biased against the family, for neighbors had shared too many heartbreaking stories. As I curiously studied the scene, I mentally applauded the couple for not smoking in the house. Sitting on lopsided rockers, the group appeared to be enjoying the pleasant evening breeze. Cory greeted them and we stayed to chat for a few minutes. It was obvious that the children craved attention from their parents, for they jumped up and down, shouting over one another to be heard. The young ones seemed fond of their father and were crawling over him.

I later discovered that Don could be quite jolly when not drunk and was an excellent storyteller when partially sober. Unfortunately, most of the time the children were subjected to a darker side of his personality. After stopping at the pub he visited regularly after work, he would stumble home to collapse on the living room sofa. If he wasn't ready to pass out, it could be dangerous for a child accidentally in his way. One girl told me, "When my dad was sober he was like another person. He talked to us kids and even gave us advice. So we forgave him when he was out of it. We kept hoping it (his drinking) would not happen again."

As a sheltered woman from an upper-middle-class suburban neighborhood, I had not been exposed to poverty or drug abuse and was horrified by what I saw. I found it difficult to believe parents could be mean and negligent towards their own children. Over time, my naiveté gave rise to curiosity and I wanted to understand how the family survived from day to day. I stopped to speak to Nancy more frequently and got to know the children better.

Religion was a defining part of their lives. Don was a nonbeliever, but he never interfered with his wife who played the organ in a fundamentalist church. The religion was against most everything I was brought up to cherish. Close communication was discouraged with those not associated with the church, as was television, secular music, movies, sports, dances or parties. A five-foot blackberry fence around the family's barren yard kept the children separated from neighbors. Church members feared

14

that contact with nonbelievers would contaminate their values and way of life. They were not happy when Cory and I took the children out for occasional excursions.

Church elders see the primary function of marriage to be "go forth and multiply" so birth control is strictly forbidden. Don and Nancy's family of nine children was small by church standards where women averaged twelve babies, though fourteen was not uncommon. I was informed that one woman had given birth to seventeen children. It is not unusual for teens to marry second cousins. The town was inundated with the uncles, aunts and cousins of this clan.

Zach later mentioned how bored he and his siblings were so they invented their own way of having fun. During rainy or cold weather, when confined to their second-floor loft, the children would sneak down the stairs when their parents were not paying attention. Eventually, they were caught and sent screaming and laughing back to their sleeping quarters. Though rarely violent, from time to time slaps would send a young-one flying across the room. Both parents were occasional drug users though only the father abused alcohol. Each time their mother gave up drugs the church welcomed her back. This was not an issue for their father since he never joined. Prone to shouting matches, their commotion was heard on the sidewalk.

Cory was once asked to fix a plumbing problem near the children's second-floor bedroom. To do so, he had to climb over a carpet of dirty, smelly clothing flung throughout. Recently washed shirts and underwear were stacked willy-nilly like rags in a corner. The loft where the six children slept did not have closets or chests of drawers for storage. After the repair was finished, Cory vowed never to go inside the house again.

Occasionally, Nancy tried to be an attentive mother. One day she proudly told me, "I'm going to take the children out for daily walks." Her excursions, which lasted for several summer months, consisted of half-hour strolls around the block that defined the children's world. I observed the little ones hanging on to their mother's hand while skipping down the sidewalk. They were delighted to leave the backyard and their dirty faces beamed with happy smiles.

Don insisted Nancy prepare meals, though she was not much of a cook. For a short while she was determined to serve a healthy selection of food. The kitchen table was too small for family gatherings so it was primarily used for food preparation. As the dinner hour approached each child entered the kitchen carrying a spoon which he or she carefully guarded. Nancy scooped out the day's fare which was then consumed while sitting on the living room floor or couch. Dropped scraps were one of the reasons the place was covered with grime and reeked of odors. Unfortunately, Nancy's interest in fresh salads and vegetables faded after a few weeks.

Visits to a relative's home provided the children with a sense of what they were missing. Some of their more fortunate cousins enjoyed a normal, though extremely religious home life. "I used to try to stay overnight at my cousin's house as often as possible," Zach said."We went wild, speeding around on dune buggies and playing Nintendo. We could eat as much as we wanted. I was always hungry when I was a kid," he added.

A relative mentioned that church elders had long thought of Nancy as a problem, but since she attended services, she was accepted as a member. When her car wasn't broken, she accompanied the choir on the piano. Music was important to her, but her love of it was not passed on. In elementary school the children were taught to play a band instrument. One of the boys proudly practiced the trumpet, producing a racket heard throughout the neighborhood. The sounds at home must have been ear shattering. Once the children entered middle school, however, trumpets and saxophones had to be returned because they were not allowed to join the band. Their church did not permit them to attend sporting events, which was the primary location for band performances. Private lessons were not possible and the family could not afford to rent instruments, so music study ended in fifth grade.

In good weather, the children were permitted to go outside as long as they did not leave their barren yard. A chain-link fence built against head-high sticker bushes walled them in. Distressed by what he saw, Cory began throwing peanuts over the fence as he walked by. The kids responded gleefully, enjoying the hunt, jumping up and down to peer over the top of the bushes while shouting words of encouragement to throw more. Once in a while, Cory added packaged cookies to sweeten the game. Observing their lives made me wonder what would happen to them when they were old enough to leave home. What were their chances?

Cory visited the town more often than I and became deeply concerned by the children's plight. Whenever he passed by they would shout, "What are you doing? Can I visit?" Occasionally their mother did permit them to accompany Cory on an excursion to the school playground or nearby park. They even helped weed his grandmother's garden. We had frequent discussions about what we could do to help them. I suggested a visit to Portland to expose them to city life.

Trust was slow in coming but over time Nancy relaxed in our presence and let us spend more time with the kids. She seemed overwhelmed by the children and household chores. She rarely gave emotional or academic support to the kids but did not mind when we did. Nancy didn't seem concerned about what her church thought either, though years later I heard that she did get a lot of negative comments about letting her children spend time with us. We gained the children's trust by doing little things. If we were shown a report card with a passing grade, the child received a dollar. Very good grades would be rewarded with lunch at Pizza Hut. The new sights we introduced them to were greeted with an excitement and appreciation that was so contagious we wanted to do more.

Cory bought a basketball that he took to the playground for rounds of CAT or HORSE. He bought the children their first bicycles and taught them how to ride. We occasionally brought our bikes to town and formed a parade. Pedaling around the neighborhood must have been quite a sight with six young ones following us like ducklings. It was fun. Over a four-year period,

Cory purchased seven or eight bicycles because the old ones kept disappearing. When asked what happened, the children told us, "Someone stole them at night from our yard."

"Weren't they locked?" Cory asked.

"Yes, but they just cut the chain."

We naively believed the children and felt sorry for them, never questioning what happened. We later found out that Robbie had pilfered the bikes to sell for drugs. The most expensive gift he stole was the computer Cory gave the family. Each time something disappeared we vowed to stop buying gifts, but our resolution only lasted a short time. With each present, we gave a lecture on how to care for the gift. Hoping for the best, we were rarely rewarded.

The more we were drawn into the family's circle, the more concerned and fascinated I was by their actions. I was shocked, having little idea that survival could be so difficult. I was born into an educated middle-class family with parents who were attentive to my needs. They took me places and encouraged me to study. Enrolled in dancing and art classes during the winter and camp during the summer, I was busy and happy. When my children were born I carried in my parent's footsteps by being attentive to their needs, desires, and ambitions. We went on vacations, visited museums and attended plays and concerts. I assumed that my behavior was typical of all loving parents.

But in impoverished communities, the primary focus is not on how to enrich an offspring's life but on how to provide food and shelter. Don and Nancy's negligence and abuse was found throughout the neighborhood. When I called the local child protection agency to suggest intervening on the children's behalf, the woman I spoke to responded by saying, "These kids are not as bad off as other families in town. They at least have a roof over their heads. If I help them, I will have to support the entire community." Government assistance was unavailable and there were few charitable organizations dispensing aid. The town lacked service organizations, boys and girls clubs, after-school care, and homeless shelters.

Sometimes, well-meaning individuals stepped forward. For example, when several good samaritans decided to empty Nancy's house of all contents in order to fumigate and repaint it. One day a large dumpster arrived along with a group of volunteers who threw away everything they touched. After painting the inside walls, volunteers delivered clean, second-hand furnishings. Mattresses that previously had rested on the floor were replaced with raised beds. New clothing, bed linens, towels and kitchen utensils filled new storage shelves. For the next few months the house was kept clean but, over the course of a year, it went back to what it was before the intervention. The smell of dirty clothes once more reeked throughout the house. The children were responsible for washing their own clothes, which they did only occasionally. It might have helped if someone from a social service agency checked in from time to time to see that the children were fed and safe.

My five children were grown and out of the house, and I wasn't interested in getting involved with someone else's family. I was an *empty nester,* busy with a start-up company and enjoying freedom from the responsibility of caring for little ones. Walking away from this smalltown drama, however, was not meant to be, for Nancy was delighted when I took the children to Portland for days at a time. I am not sure why she didn't succumb to demands from unhappy church officials that she keep them home, but I assume she saw the visits as beneficial or, perhaps, she just wanted more peace and quiet.

I hoped to expose the kids to clean sheets, good food, nighttime stories and visits to cultural attractions. This may sound a bit pompous, but I wanted them to have some of the opportunities I had given my own children. I believed that visits to Portland would expand their world view and motivate them to want to increase their options for the future. For the children, exploring the city was like visiting a foreign country. Their smiles and willingness to try new things made us feel good.

Before the first trip to Portland, we established rules that included showering before getting into the car, wearing clean clothes and packing extra clothing in their backpacks. Since most of what they wore was frayed and stained, a trip to Goodwill was always the first item on the agenda. We purchased shoes, shirts, and pants and took the boys for haircuts.

Food was what the children mentioned most when thanking us. I have always enjoyed cooking. Seeing them ravenously devour what I made was a pleasure. They praised everything I put on their plates, and I encouraged them to eat all that they wanted. Bacon, eggs, fresh bagels and pancakes replaced their daily bowl of dried sugar cereal for breakfast. When visiting Portland the children were on their best behavior and, since we had a fine time together, invitations to return were repeated many times over a five-year period.

We took them on trips to the woods and to area museums, and let them splash in city fountains. Trail hikes and coastal treks added to their weekend delights. Though we were concerned that certain activities were against church rules, we decided not to worry since their parents never gave us a list of dos and don'ts. We took them to Timber soccer matches, went bowling, let them watch children's television programs, and visited movie theaters. Each night they huddled on my bed as I read a tale of intrigue and mystery before lights out. These emotionally starved children loved my attention and quickly settled down to sleep. On birthdays and holidays, Cory and I filled our car with toys, insuring that there would be more than pairs of socks or candy bars under the tree.

During his late fifties, Don became seriously ill, and we watched the family's situation go from bad to worse. Chain-smoking and bar visits were replaced by oxygen tanks and hours of restless sleep on the sofa. Sadness descended on Nancy and the children, distraught at seeing their father wear a mask while continuing to wheeze. Over the course of a year, they observed his slow, painful death. The six children still living at home were quite young.

Once their father was gone, days became increasingly intolerable. Food was scarce. Don's salary gone, Nancy received a small stipend, but rather than trying to stretch her money, she stopped cooking altogether, initiating a period of constant hunger. Nancy went into a deep depression and became apathetic. She slept day and night on a living room recliner, avoiding the bedroom she had once shared with her husband. Since she rarely moved, she gained an excessive amount of weight, stressed her heart, and ignored body hygiene. After several months Nancy was admitted to the hospital to stabilize her heart, further abandoning the children left on their own at home. When she was discharged, a disgusted nurse told Nancy's eldest daughter to cut her mother's toenails for they were so long that they curled inches over and around her toes. The nursing staff was surprised Nancy was able to put on shoes and walk.

The once bouncy children became melancholy, increasingly looking like abandoned street urchins. Zach later told me that when his mother did leave her recliner it was to lock herself in the garage to do drugs with friends. On those occasions, the children would knock on the door, shouting to be fed. Nancy would crack the door open and hand each child two dollars to purchase dinner at a corner convenience store. Constant hunger turned eleven-year-old Zach into a thief. He took money from his mother's wallet to purchase pizza. I drove past their house one trash pickup day and saw three feet of pizza boxes piled high. During visits to Portland, I noticed that my possessions started disappearing, most likely taken by Zach. Cory did not trust the boy and didn't like having him around our house. Zach remained my favorite though, for he was a survivor and the most inventive of the lot.

A few years later Cory's grandmother died and our trips to her town ended. By this time the children were in their middle and high school years and we lost contact with the family, with one exception.

Child number No.5, Pat, was difficult to abandon. He was a sweet boy who was intellectually challenged and needed extra help. For two years Cory continued to pay for an after-school tutor to help him graduate from high school. I helped Pat complete his school assignments as best I could. He would email his English papers to me so they could be corrected before he turned them in. We often spent hours in phone communication, discussing his homework.

Students were required to volunteer in the community in order to graduate from high school. We arranged for Pat to be a nursing home assistant, helping residents during weekly bingo games. When he was asked to call the numbers, at first he whispered them instead of shouting them out. Since it was difficult for hearing impaired elderly people to hear his calls, he was assigned to distributing cards and markers, a job he could do. Over several months, he learned to speak louder and was encouraged to try calling numbers again.

One day while Pat was running the game, an elderly man suddenly shot up from his seat and shouted to a nearby woman. "You birdbrain! You stole my walker." He started screaming, ready for a fight.

"I did not," the woman responded and walked away.

Instead of handling the situation, Pat stopped what he was doing and ran for the door. A very astute nurse observed his flight and grabbed his arm before he could exit the building. She pulled him back to the hall explaining, "We never leave in the middle of a task. Let me show you how to handle conflicts."

"Now, George," she said to the elderly man, "there was just a little mistake made."

The walker was quickly returned to its rightful owner and the bingo game resumed with Pat calling numbers in a shaky but audible voice. Experiences like this were important lessons to be learned and our hope was that when he graduated from high school he would work in a nursing home. He was a kind, compassionate boy whom residents liked. Unfortunately, Pat had other ideas.

He did graduate with fanfare as the school's most improved child. His photo was featured in the local newspaper alongside the valedictorian and those graduating with honors. Pat even received monetary gifts from several organizations for his achievement. We were proud and felt rewarded for our years of involvement. One gift was a stipend to attend community college where he enrolled in automotive technology. His decision concerned us for we were sure that the course would be too difficult.

Because the program was taught by an uncle, Pat was convinced he would sail through his classes. To ensure a good start, we purchased supplies for him including a four-foot high-wheeled box, automotive tool set and expensive textbooks. Since most of his assignments were completed in teams, a win-win situation quickly developed. Pat provided the needed tools while teammates did the mechanical work. Occasionally the other boys would let him turn a screw or attach a bolt but mostly he watched and benefited by receiving the team's overall grade.

Academic classes were more difficult. A psychology section run by a Harvard University graduate required a paper about transactional analysis. That's a difficult subject for any student let alone one who is challenged. Pat had no idea what to do or how to begin so I emailed an outline to get him started. Pat was confused by the outline, claiming it was too difficult to follow. Instead, we worked together by talking on the phone for an entire day. I would ask,"What is transactional analysis?" Pat would then look up the word in Wikipedia, copying, pasting and sending the information to me in an email. We then followed up at length by phone until he could write a sentence about the topic in a way that conferred meaning to him. This method of asking a question, copying the answer, following up with discussion, and final rewriting in his own words was repeated paragraph by paragraph until a semblance of a report was completed.

Cory jokingly told him that if the teacher asked him to talk about the assignment to just answer, *"I'm OK, You're OK."* Amazingly, he received a B for his grade. I thought it worthy of an A!

Pat must have reached the soul of this teacher because from that day on the man provided additional notes to Pat about his lectures and advised him on how to prepare for tests. Over the two years Pat was in community college, his language and writing skills improved greatly as did his appearance which benefited from physical education classes.

When it came to math, however, Pat was on his own because

testing was done on a computer in the classroom. He failed the required course three times in a row despite receiving extra tutoring help. One day when he called to give us a progress report, Zach happened to be in the room. When Pat told us that he had just come from the math lab and was then at the library studying, Zach later reported that that was a lie. Instead, "he was in the backyard messin' around,"

To our great disappointment, Pat started using black tar heroin. He never completed the automotive program and his drug habit got worse. Over the next five years, his language deteriorated, his posture returned to a slouch and his eyes developed a dull glazed look. A poor diet left him skinny with a chalky pallor. Learning about his addiction was the first of many similar stories I heard once I started to study the problems of homeless youth. They were dramas that often led to jail or serious illness.

Pat did the family some good, though, for he set an example that influenced the younger children to graduate. "I reasoned that if my retarded brother could graduate from high school, then I could too," Zach said. We are pleased that the four youngest children all graduated. One boy even maintained honor grades, taking community college courses when a high school senior. Over time and in part due to distance, we lost contact with the family.

TRANSITIONING

It would be four more years before we encountered Zach wandering the streets and another four before I was able to admit that the time we spent worrying about him was worth our efforts.

<hr>

"Don't talk. I want to finish this."

Our adopted son, Zach, sat across the counter while I fried onions for our evening meal. I was startled by his words and even more so when I looked up to find his dusty red head bent over Time magazine.

"Sorry, I don't mean to be rude," he continued,"but I want

to finish reading this article." I was both surprised and elated. I could hardly contain my joy. After years of trying to get him to read and pay attention to anything besides himself, the words he spoke were miraculous. Maslow's hierarchy of needs was finally clicking in and I celebrated knowing that he had just reached a higher level. How did it happen?

———————————

Cory, who spent most of his time in the studio under our home, was going crazy trying to keep Zach busy with odd jobs. We decided that if he was not employed, he would have to do volunteer work if he was to continue staying with us. Regular meals and a comfortable bed had ushered in a middle-class existence that Zach easily embraced and was reluctant to abandon. His grammar and speech even improved as he heeded my nagging corrections and strived to communicate with neighbors.

I presented a list of volunteer possibilities but he nixed them all. " Too boring," or "I don't want to work with poor people," were his most frequent responses. Since he could not come up with an organization, Cory decided to enroll him in his favorite charity, the Audubon Society. You might imagine Zach's reaction. *BIRDS*? It was almost comical to watch his face but life occasionally has surprises.

Zach reluctantly attended orientation at Audubon headquarters. He told us later that upon arrival he was immediately surrounded by high school and college girls who gravitated to his table since he was one of the few men in attendance. The Audubon staff were quite skilled at attracting and keeping volunteers and plied the trainees with plenty of food and soft drinks..

Upon returning from that first session, Zach came into our kitchen with a broad grin splashed across his face. It was the first time I noticed that he had a dimple. Over the next several months he helped clear hiking trails and even accompanied Cory, somewhat reluctantly, on bird-watching forays. Perhaps restaurant lunches following those expeditions made the trips more palatable. Cory gave Zach his first binoculars, a bird book, and a camera, and initiated an interest that continues to this day. Zach now pays attention to the many birds that visit our back porch to feed and bathe, even photographing them occasionally.

As an avid reader, I could not sit by and let Zach remain semi-literate so I encouraged him to spend time reading each day, an activity he rarely did without prodding.

"Reading just puts me to sleep," he complained. "I don't like it and never will. It is not important. I can watch YouTube to find out everything I need to know."

We did not let his reluctance dissuade us, however. Cory scanned the daily newspaper with Zach, taking turns selecting articles to read aloud. As with a beginning reader, Cory would read one line and Zach the next. Though I have shelves of books to interest most adolescents, Zach found nothing appealing. It was not until I pounced on his passion for skateboarding, discovering that he could name all of the top boarders, that I chose books that sparked his interest. He devoured the seventh-grade reading-level paperbacks I bought about skateboarders. It was a start that I followed with a series of adventure stories.

As spring turned to summer we discussed plans for a July Fourth celebration. During one conversation I asked, "Why do we celebrate the Fourth of July?" He answered with a grin, "because of fireworks and picnics."

When questioned further it became obvious that Zach had little knowledge of American history and did not know that the holiday was established to honor the birth of our nation. I was horrified by his lack of learning and could hardly believe that a person could graduate from school without a rudimentary knowledge of our country's beginnings. I wondered how to entice him to learn more of our country's history.

There is a superb series of graphic novels written by MIT historian Larry Gonick that I had given to my own son when in middle school. One was titled the *Cartoon History of the United States* and I thought it might be just the material to overcome Zach's reluctance. Zach did honor me by reading the book from cover to cover and surprised me by not complaining.

Still the task of finding work remained. Thankfully, Cory thought of Job Corps, a government training program, run military-style, for children just like Zach. Sites located throughout the United States specialize in a variety of vocational careers. Oregon alone has six centers, though getting accepted to one requires initiative, perseverance and knowledge of government systems. Cory drove Zach to an orientation meeting where he was instructed to apply online and explain why he was interested in participating in the program. He was also asked to identify the trade that interested him.

This was not easy. Zach was uncomfortable using a computer, plus it took weeks for our non-decisive youth to make a career choice. When asked what he wanted to do, his response was, "I don't know. I get bored after a week or two and will want to quit. You know, I'm ADD and need to move around a lot ... Nothing's interesting."

With our growing understanding of his abilities and interests, we prodded him to select commercial and industrial painting. The idea came after observing his fearless disregard for heights when helping to clean our roof of leaves and remembering his interest, as a child, when Cory let him tag along to help paint his grandmother's house. Zach can be careful and exacting when interested. He, like many ADD children, is able to hyper focus for hours at a time doing specific tasks. Industrial painting would require attention to repetitive detail and provide him with the excitement he constantly craved. Painting bridges, oil barges, and high water towers are a risky business requiring the worker to stay focused to avoid getting hurt. It is a trade requiring working in dangerous situations that raise adrenaline levels. Balancing his body while holding heavy buckets of paint on high platforms was an activity that seemed a perfect fit for our boy.

When accepted by Job Corps, Zach's initial words were, "at least I'll have a roof over my head and food in my stomach for the next two years." He shared that he had considered committing an illegal act in order to be sent to jail so he could have food and shelter. Job Corps turned out to be a better option and, once at the training center, he went through a dramatic transformation. While I was also excited, what transpired next was simply miraculous.

FINDING A CAREER

Tongue Point Job Corps is located in Astoria in a beautiful setting on the Pacific Ocean. Students spend the majority of their day in academic and hands-on career technical training. They are well fed and clothed, help with chores, join clubs and participate in team sports. Cory and I observed incredible growth during the year, starting with Zach's physical appearance. We noticed that he stood taller, with shoulders back, and smiled more easily. During visits, I saw energy in his steps and heard the excitement in his voice as he toured us around the campus and shared exploits of fellow students and teachers.

The Job Corps staff understands abused children and knows that emotional needs must be attended to as well as physical and intellectual concerns. In addition to vocational training, enrichment classes are offered in psychology, business and leadership skills. Mandatory sessions focused on compassionate communication and provided basic information about personal hygiene. Money management was another challenging subject and it took two years for Zach to trust banks with his savings and another two, after he was employed, to open a checking account. Each new skill required Zach to read training manuals before being tested. As a result, Zach became a better reader and even started perusing a few magazines for his own enjoyment. He told me later that if I had not made him read he would not have passed the competency test when he arrived at the center. He proudly let me know that he had aced it by two points, allowing him to skip remedial academics. This meant that he could immediately enroll in vocational training instead of doing English assignments for half the day.

Job corps has strict rules that have to be followed in order to earn privileges. Operating with a quasi-military model, it uses an effective tough-love approach to modifying behavior. Coupons are given to the trainees as added enticement for them to pay attention to on-the-job training and academic programs. Coupons could then be converted into tokens for purchasing clothing, snacks and free-time off campus. For any student, but particularly for those from poor backgrounds, these symbols of success are valuable commodities.

During the day, counselors patrol dormitories and randomly enter student rooms to make sure everything is as it should be. Drugs and alcohol are reasons for immediate dismissal but room searches also ensure that no one is ill or has committed suicide. Serious depression is a common occurrence among teens who have been marginalized most of their lives. Inspections also insure that rooms are thoroughly cleaned, clothing hung, and personal objects cleaned and stored properly.

In general, Zach played by the rules and took well to industrial painting. There may have been an incident or two when he strayed a bit while off campus but that is a guess on my part based on a few random comments from Zach about smoking pot. The most critical incident occurred after he fell in love with a young blond woman he met on campus. I think of as "Cutie." The two spent much of their free time together wandering the grounds. During one off-campus weekend, he even visited her at her grandmother's mobile home, learning for the first time that she had a child. The romance had been developing for several months when Cutie started a fight with another student, attacking the girl and threatening her with sharp scissors. Cutie's behavior was not a complete surprise to Zach because he knew she had grown up in a violent family. Her father is currently serving a life sentence for murder in a federal penitentiary.

Job Corps immediately suspended Cutie who promptly tried to persuade Zach to leave with her. "Come just for a week or two," she urged. Cory and I spoke to Zach and stressed that he shouldn't leave the program. "Don't worry," he responded, " it won't be a problem. If I do go with her, I'll come back."

Thankfully the staff knew better and was on our side. They told him that they had seen other kids in similar situations and none of them ever returned. Then they did something very astute to entice

Zach to stay. Knowing he wanted to get his license, they moved him forward on the waiting list for drivers ed. Once at the head of the line, he could start training immediately. The bribe did the trick and he elected to stay, though he was very lonely and called Cutie often. But as time went on he started to see that she was a drug addict with problems that required extensive treatment.

It took many months before he told Cutie that he didn't want to see her again, though she was unwilling to acknowledge his words. After he graduated from Job Corps, she moved near his work site and stalked him mornings and afternoons on the path where he rode his bicycle to and from work. Her behavior continued throughout the summer until the courts took her daughter away and Cutie was put in a drug rehabilitation center. It took another two years to completely end the relationship because she continued to call daily. During that period, her grandmother even called and tried to persuade Zach to return to her granddaughter. We later learned that Job Corps staff also struggled to keep Zach away from Cutie. It is an affirming demonstration of how well the staff work together on behalf of their students.

One of the key Job Corps staff members was Dewey who shared his personal story of going through Job Corps as a teen trainee. Now in his 50s, he became a staff member in order to give back to the organization that had so dramatically affected his life. The painting program is union-sponsored and teaches trainees how to apply paint safely, erect scaffolding, deal with hazardous material, administer CPR, drive a forklift and become a flagger. Dewey is a tough, cursing, imposing black man who knew all the tricks kids could devise. When they misbehaved he would sentence them to pushups or long runs up and down hillsides. One time when he was angry at Zach for not following instructions he threw an open bucket of paint at Zach. Zach was shocked when he caught the flying container as it sailed towards his chest. He laughs now when sharing that incident, telling how he spent the next few hours cleaning up the mess. Known to be a no-nonsense man, Dewey's sense of humor went a long way toward making him a popular teacher. His caring nature came through to those in need of parenting. Dewey holds the record for having the largest number of students graduate from any of the center's programs. Loved by students and mistrusted by colleagues he managed to get away with bending the rules a bit—quite a bit. He taught me the value of dispensing tough love.

As the year continued, Zach was promoted to hall and then dormitory monitor, which brought out hidden leadership abilities. Job Corps does an outstanding job rewarding students for each small achievement, thereby bolstering practices leading to good behavior. Zach told us proudly and in great detail about how he was singled out before his fellow students and acknowledged for accomplishments. Since he did not have to do remedial academic work, Zach finished the painter's program in just over a year instead of the usual two. He left with a big pile of certificates that he asked me to frame. I suggested putting them in a scrapbook instead.

Upon completing the program, Job Corps administers a final test. Zach was elated when he received 100 percent (a platinum) on his math and almost as good (a gold) on his reading test. During the graduation ceremony he was presented with a great many honors and certificates. Cory enjoyed watching the smiling faces of the graduates, though only a few had family members in attendance to celebrate their success. To my great disappointment, I had to work and could not attend.

Zach, nearing 21, left Job Corps standing tall, well dressed, without ear plugs, and full of smiles, bearing gifts of paint brushes and whites (painters clothing) to start his new career. With his energy and internal fire we were certain he would do very well. In just one year he had gone from no hope to a future with all sorts of possibilities. To me, he was a hero, as were the people who supplied meals for him in school, the counselors who helped when he lived in shelters, and the other committed individuals who touched his life in a positive way.

First Job

Some people are addicted to life on the edge. A 2002 IMAX movie called *Adrenaline Rush: The Science of Risk* explained how adrenaline levels spike when dangerous situations provide thrill seekers with a much-needed high. Rock climbers, skydivers, Indy-car racers, and competitive ski jumpers are among those who find legal ways to feed their cravings. Jails are filled with adrenaline junkies who travel, instead, in the risky criminal underworld.

Zach was such a person, often putting himself in dangerous situations. He enjoyed walking to the edge of a roof one hundred feet in the air and wanted to bungee jump and skydive. Given these interests, he discovered a good profession to meet his needs for adrenaline rushes. The work of an industrial painter is filled with dangerous situations that test intelligence, balance and ability to overcome fear.

Guaranteed a union job upon graduation from Job Corps, Zach's first assignment could not have been better. He was hired as an apprentice painter on the 250-foot high Astoria-Megler Bridge. Cory was thrilled with Zach's job. On visits to the coast he insisted on driving back and forth over the bridge to examine every inch of rigging and metalwork being painted. We studied the workmanship in minute detail and turned to the internet to learn the bridge's history. Built to withstand 150-mph wind gusts that batter the mouth of the Columbia River, it spans 21,475 feet end to end and is one of the most difficult and dangerous bridges in the nation to paint. While very proud, I also was worried that something horrible would happen to our risk-taking young man.

Zach also was proud of his employment though often exhausted. His upper-body strength grew over the summer which enabled him to do required tasks more easily. The Astoria -Megler Bridge is featured in some of his favorite movies including *Kindergarten Cop* and *Short Circuit*. "It is a movie star bridge," he beamed one bright Sunday afternoon. We learned that the bridge also appeared in *The Goonies* and stands in for the doomed fictional Madison Bridge in Irwin Allen's 1979 made-for-TV disaster movie *The Night the Bridge Fell Down*.

To prepare Zach for living in his first apartment, I purchased the dishes, silverware, bedding and household items needed to get him off to a good start. Cory bought him a bicycle since the

32

work site was nearby. We helped him locate a youth hostel not far from the bridge that offered rooms by the month with amenities including a shared kitchen, lounge and laundry room. It seemed like a perfect place, not overly expensive and allowing him to meet other young people.

On moving day we collected his meager belongings, loaded them in our car and drove to the hostel. We sent Zach to the front desk to pay the first month's rent with the allotment he received upon graduating from Job Corps. Much to our surprise, he returned a few minutes to say that a security deposit also was required. Zach did not have enough money and, despite his new union job, if I had not paid the amount for the deposit he would once more have been sleeping on the streets. That's what happened to several other graduates who tried to check in at the same time.

Zach's experience made me realize how tenuous it is to go from poverty to financial stability. Though there are many organizations helping homeless youths, they struggle for resources. Middle-class parents make sure their children are not put into failure situations at the start of their working careers, while poor children may be handicapped for many years.

My thoughts about how to help altered greatly during the time we assisted Zach. I began realizing that a cadre of adoptive "education-parents" are needed to help at-risk youths navigate crises during and after high school. Fulfilling that role for Zach, Cory and I gained an understanding of the heartbreaks and rewards of involvement with a needy child.

Zach had a lot to learn when we first took him in. He never had a bank account and felt uncomfortable with the idea. His family hid money under the mattress or in cracks in the wall. Since he didn't know how to arrange for payroll deposits, he had to pick up his weekly paycheck at the company's office which was only open during business hours. Not able to leave work early, he often went without cash for food while he waited for a rainy day to claim his salary.

In the Northwest, bridge painting starts in April and continues through mid-October. Unless it rains there is no such thing as time off to be with family, to rest, or to go to a doctor's appointment. To do so risks losing your job. Grocery shopping occurs after an exhausting day when all a worker wants to do is flop into bed. Apprentices do the heaviest jobs of mixing and carrying one hundred-pound cans in each hand, making trip after trip on precarious platforms to feed sandblasting equipment and spray guns.

On his first day, Zach was tested to see if he had the stamina and willpower to endure months of hard work. Directed to a nearby staging area, he was instructed to carry and stack heavy paint containers for an entire ten-hour shift. Most of the time he moved cans from one end of the lot to the other, finding no purpose to what he did. Though he was a runt of a youth, he complied without complaining. But that evening when he called at the end of a long day, Cory and I heard about his difficulties loud and clear. Over the course of the next few weeks, Zach shared that several new workers, submitted to the same tasks, walked away from the job. It was difficult for management to find willing workers with strength and stamina. But once Zach passed this grueling initiation period, the job became more interesting. He was sent high up on the bridge's pillars, satisfying his cravings for exhilaration.

Bridge work is exhausting. Painters rig, sandblast, prime and paint ten to fifteen hours a day, seven days a week. They walk on shaky three-foot platforms placed temporarily outside the bed of steel support beams. Each step creates a wave that undulates under the weight of the clipped-in men. Zach described what it was like to take his first step on the platform while peering over the side at a 200-foot drop to the water.

"I was pumped and wired looking over the edge," he bubbled enthusiastically. "What a charge! It's great being up so high, especially when the platform moves."

At times he worked misty, slippery mornings that later turned into 90-degree scorching afternoons. On those days, the inside of his heavy protective gear became damp with sweat streaming down his body, making him feel like he was in a warming oven. In

Astoria, there are also times when the wind blows so cold at these high elevations that the mens' clothing can't keep them warm enough. Hands are the first appendages to freeze since they must be free from coverings to do the required work. In the morning Zach was never sure how to dress for the day so he carried extra clothes in his backpack.

Observing workers moving on the bridge was like watching a circus act with performers scurrying up cables to the top of the two support towers. They hauled heavy hoses for sandblasting and carried ninety-pound industrial paint buckets. At the start of his employment, Zach was stationed close to the ground, working with the rigging crew to put up cables for the next day's work. He spent early mornings and late evenings on flag duty, placing cones to direct traffic to the center lanes. His muscles got stronger as the days passed but he was continuously plagued by sunburn of fair skin.

"I can't keep the lotion on," he said. "As soon as I start sweating it rolls off, and I start to burn."

After two months, fatigue finally overcame him. On a hot summer afternoon Zach collapsed and was hauled off by ambulance to the emergency room of the local hospital. His exhaustion and the intense July heat was more than his body could handle. A $2,500 hospital bill was his gift at the end of the visit. Weak and ready to give up, he was not sure that he was able (or wanted) to continue the job. But after resting for a week, and with a needed push from his Job Corps mentor, he went back despite misgivings. As the days cooled, he experienced less dizziness and started to enjoy work again. He certainly liked receiving high wages. And, without the time to spend his earnings, his financial situation improved.

It wasn't long before Zach befriended longterm staff who moved around the country with their employers, a painting company headquartered in the Midwest. The men were tough, fearless and hard working. They never stopped for breaks and only needed a half-hour lunch period to take care of hunger and bodily functions.

Because of the short summer season, wage and hour laws are bent for bridge repair to permit long hours and seven-day workweeks to continue for months at a time. Earnings are excellent, though, for not only do workers receive hazardous pay, they are paid time-and-a-half for over forty hours a week. An eighty-hour workweek is not unusual though the money is not enough to entice many experienced journeymen to spend their lives painting bridges. It was difficult for the company to find American painters willing to engage in such strenuous work. Most married men don't want to be away from their families for months at a time. Even though bridge painting goes to union shops, not all employees have to belong as long as a certain percentage of the positions do go to union workers. Zach said that some of the best painters were illegal immigrants who didn't mind a seven-day-a-week schedule since they could earn more money to send home to their families. During the months he was in Astoria, the Immigration and Naturalization Service looked the other way.

Meeting laborers from Central America was a cultural experience for Zach. The men liked him, for he was willing to be teased as the youngster of the group. After getting better acquainted, he was invited to a Mexican barbecue held in the back parking lot of their motel. We heard about one fantastic cook making more chow than the men could possibly eat. Zach was especially pleased because most of the food was gluten-free which allowed him to eat as much as he wanted without digestive issues. Hot sauce was liberally sprinkled on every kind of food to clear his sinuses.

"They were always swearing. I can't repeat their words in front of you," he said over dinner during one of our visits. "And they never stop joking or laughing after they've downed a few beers. They're funny and keep giving me advice like, 'Be sure to marry a Mexican woman because she will be loyal when you're away from home.' They speak broken English and use hand signals to communicate important stuff such as *pinche estupido!* (fucking idiot)." Zach did end the summer with an ample smattering of Spanish curse words.

By mid-July it was obvious that he needed a car. Over the Fourth of July weekend, workers were given a few days off because so many tourists were expected in Astoria that city officials did not want bridge lanes closed. We decided it was a good time to visit used car lots to see if we could find a pickup truck for a price Zach could afford. It wasn't long before he spotted a working man's vehicle, a white Dodge Ram with a toolbox on the back bed and a flashing signal light that beeped noisily when put in reverse. His eyes grew large, and I could see how excited he was as he bounded out of my car to inspect the engine and interior. Once he was given the keys for a road test he felt transformed. "I became a muscle man," he later confided.

The truck was in reasonable condition for a $5,000 vehicle, but it needed new tires. There also was a slight oil drip, and I prayed the transmission would last for at least a few years. The truck was a heavy, six-cylinder, gas guzzler. though I was appalled, both Cory and Zach were enthralled, so Zach went ahead with the purchase.

A word about finances. Though Zach earned a salary, because of past debts we still had to help with the $1,000 downpayment. Since it was a holiday evening and banks were closed, he was given a loan by the dealership for the remaining $4,000. The interest rate charged was 34 percent due to his lack of credit history. I was upset when I heard the terms of the loan and counseled against accepting such a bad contract. My apprehension was not heeded, however, and the purchase concluded with reassurance by Cory that it was the best way to build a credit history.

I do admit that the truck fit Zach, and the glow on his face was quite moving to behold. He returned to Astoria after a few days of practice driving a gearshift, was admonished to stay off the highways, and told not to use the vehicle frivolously. "It's old with a lot of miles that could give you problems at any time," Cory counseled.

Two days later Cory received a call from the dealership informing him that the truck was going to be repossessed.

"Why?" he asked.

"The loan officer decided that even with 34 percent interest and a good job it's too great a risk to take on a 20 year old with no credit." was the response. "Do you want to co-sign or should we pick it up?"

This became yet another instance in which we had to help financially. Rather than disappoint Zach, Cory decided to pay the $4,000 owed and let Zach repay him at a reduced interest rate. At first, everything went according to plan. Zach fulfilled his obligation to Cory with monthly installments. He took care of his rent, insurance, routine automobile upkeep and had enough money left over to purchase food. The cost of tires, though, had to be added immediately because it was too dangerous to drive to Portland on bald ones. Once more, the cost was covered by Cory, who added the expense to the loan.

Trouble began when bridge season was over and the hospital had not received payment for Zach's emergency room visit. His $2,500 hospital bill was sent to a collection agency that tracked him down and added 32 percent interest to the amount due. A repayment plan was eventually negotiated. Also hanging over his head was the remainder of the $1,200 fine levied during the pot smoking party at his friend Jenny's house, so it was going to be a long time before he could get out of debt.

When Zach first came to live with us we gave him an allowance in exchange for helping around the house. At Job Corps, he received a small stipend that he used to meet his monthly court payments. If he was unable to pay, we made sure he met his obligation by lending him the needed amount. We did not want him to accumulate additional fines and make matters worse. Though Zach tried to catch up, it seemed like no matter how much overtime he did, he could barely make ends meet. Paying for a car, insurance, rent, union dues, taxes, food and medical expenses added up.

Painters have many opportunities during warm weather but scramble for jobs in late fall and winter. As the summer ended, Zach had no immediate prospects and was ineligible for unemployment because he had not put in enough qualifying months. Though he immediately registered with the union whose job it was to find him employment, this was not easily obtained since most older journeymen are also unemployed during the off season.

Once more he returned to live with us. This time, however, he was less bored for there were weekly apprenticeship training sessions and monthly union meetings to attend. Before long ,he gained a reputation in class for speed and accuracy. But, for several months that fall and winter, we had to support Zach, feeding him and devising ways to keep him busy. Since he was not much of a carpenter or mechanic there was little he could do. He enjoyed chopping wood for the fireplace and participating in small home improvement and art projects. He had matured quite a bit in Job Corps and could be trusted around the house so I no longer had to keep my purse locked away.

We started to enjoy his presence at the dinner table for he had stories to share. When re-employed he planned to pay us rent for the bedroom and basement kitchen he occupied. We looked forward to that day, even though the amount would be below market value. Zach liked living with us, which was fine because he worked hard to become debt free. We wanted him to save for future needs and learn how to fend for himself without getting overly stressed. Each time Zach faced a crisis with his car or a work-related incident, he panicked and got sick. Confidence and problem solving-skills would need to be improved before he could live independently.

That fall Zach celebrated his 21st birthday, and we were determined to make it a festive occasion. The event Cory organized was as much an education for me as it was for Zach. For weeks we had been buying presents, silly ones along with those that were useful. To create drama we wrapped a great many boxes with fancy paper and bows and piled them in a visible place with instructions that they were not to be touched. We were determined to smother him with the attention he had never experienced. As a child, family birthdays were celebrated with a cake and, if lucky, a pair of socks, pack of cigarettes or a $10 bill.

This special year, as excitement mounted, we kept teasing

and goading him about becoming a man. On the evening of his birthday, loaded with nearly twenty packages, we went for dinner in a restaurant that featured belly dancers and delicious Middle-Eastern food. A gift-opening spree started a hoop-la that continued for several hours. After the meal, I discovered that Cory had something else in mind. When he was twenty-one Cory's father had taken him to a strip club so he decided to embarrass Zach with the same type of coming-of-age event.

I said, "Fine!" and was ready to leave for the nearby mall before returning home, but as much as I tried to get out of the outing, I couldn't. So the three of us entered one of the city's well known adult-only establishments. Once inside I was overwhelmed with the sights and shocked by what I saw. It was not the first time I had been in a nude strip club with dancers who hardly seemed to be out of the cradle. Those I visited in Las Vegas and New Orleans, however, were mild in comparison. The room had several locations where proportioned female contortionists were writhing on poles or gyrating their private parts in men's faces. Not allowed to touch the women, patrons sat stoically while women flung their legs over the shoulders of men who obviously enjoying have their space invaded. The women were acrobatic in the way they moved and quite talented. Many must have been gymnasts or dance students when younger. However, I could not get used to seeing women spread-eagle with their crotches fully exposed.

Cory and I found a sofa from which to watch the spectacle. I felt like the woman in the painting *American Gothic*, by Grant Wood. You know the one—a man is standing in front of a white farmhouse staring straight ahead holding a pitchfork next to his wife or spinster daughter. Uptight demeanor, domesticity and a hard-work ethic permeate the painting's message. As I stared at the dancers I knew I was living in the wrong era. My feminist emotions were scrambled. Once over the shock of seeing seductive women on display, I became both embarrassed and curious as a never-ending parade of girls gyrated before the crowd. I also was a bit jealous that I could no longer bend my body into near pretzel shapes.

While I was sitting next to him on a sofa, Cory was approached by several young women who came by to flirt and engage Cory in conversation, with barely a nod in my direction. Most told stories of putting themselves through college by working as a dancer. I wondered for how many women that was actually tale. Would they be living on the streets if they did not pursue this line of work? We left the club and returned to reality, leaving me worried that strip clubs might become a habit for Zach. That fear never materialized.

After six weeks, Zach found work again. This time his job was painting oil barges scheduled for delivery to Alaska by the end of the summer. It again meant working long hours, six or seven days a week.

I was concerned about his social life. He rarely went out with people his age since he had an erratic, work-filled schedule for ten to eleven months of the year. I began to understand why so many industrial painters stay single or, if married, don't want children. Divorce appeared to be an occupational hazard. To alleviate stress, quite a few turn to drink or drugs, putting other workers at risk on the job. Since there were frequent drug tests to insure workers were not taking narcotics, I decided not to worry. Zach was so tired at the end of each day that he came straight home, falling into bed early in order to be awake by five the next morning.

Another complication at this time was caused by the reemergence of Cutie. Each evening Zach spent an hour on his phone far away from our ears, knowing that we did not approve of the renewed friendship. We spoke of her often as a " bad-luck girl" and encouraged him to find a "good-luck woman." For six months Cutie called from her court assigned rehabilitation center, promising that if Zach would take her back, she would complete the program, get a job, and not be a burden. She was lonesome and desperate to be loved and taken care of, and I felt sorry for her. Thankfully she failed to entice Zach to continue the romance.

A UNION MAN

Zach completed his apprenticeship program and became a full-fledged journeyman. By twenty-five he was earning an excellent salary and had a bright future. The company he worked for sent him to various cities to paint bridges, water towers, and industrial machinery. Because it is a demanding profession that requires attention to details, strength, and balance, he stays fully engaged. He loves what he does and is good at it. His bosses recognize his loyalty and commitment to the company with frequent bonuses and praise.

Zach stopped distrusting banks and opened a checking account. He is a safe, though speedy driver, who cares for his car, and is on top of his laundry. He shops weekly for groceries, fills his lunch box, and even makes a meal for us once a week. Zach has become an outgoing conversationalist who doesn't gossip so people enjoy his company. When my grandchildren visit he is the one to organize Scrabble and card games. As an accepted part of my family, he participates fully during holiday gatherings. Sales girls smile flirtatiously wherever he shops and are eager to help with his order. So far, he has not collected phone numbers and says he'ss waiting for financial security before getting involved.

We continue to emotionally support Zach by helping him adapt to a middle-class way of life. His English has improved greatly, though he turns language on and off, embracing slang and curses depending on whom he is with. Over a period of five years we have provided financial support and a place to live. We helped him become a better reader and a less frustrated person. We arranged for vocational training through Job Corps, and stepped back proudly when he found employment in a profession he enjoys. We have also provided love and community. He came to us with intelligence, drive, and a commitment to improve his lot in life. He became a participating member of our household and a good neighbor to our friends.

Cory and I also became something I never thought we would — helicopter parents. We hovered over his every need, texting and calling each day, fretting and worrying when he was late. It became time to ween ourselves, setting him free to embrace his own successes and mistakes. He is not likely to fall back into bad habits, in part, because of dietary restrictions. Zach has a severe intolerance to dairy and gluten products, turning beet red with one bite of bread or glass of beer. As a result, he watches his diet, rarely touches alcohol and never smokes marijuana. I do worry about cigarettes, however, since his father died of emphysema. It will be interesting to watch him continue to evolve. He is a survivor who should be able to handle the hurdles life will continue to throw his way. I am so very proud of him.

A Few Facts about Homeless Youth

According to New Avenues for Youth, "Each day there are as many as 400 homeless youths living on the streets of Portland. Each youth has a different story — a unique set of needs and challenges. Some are teen parents, many are drug addicted, and others have mental health issues. Quite a few spent their childhood in the foster care system. There are youths who were forced from their homes or abandoned by parents. The strongest, fearing for their lives, have the courage to run away from abusive situations. Most street kids distrust authority and adults. Forced to leave childhood behind and adapt to street life they learn to survive on their own."

The National Coalition for the Homeless provides the following statistics for those under the age of 18.[3]

Each year there are between 1 million and 1.7 million homeless youth who run away or have been asked to leave their homes.

- According to the U.S. Department of Health and Human Services, 61.8 percent of homeless youths reported depression, 71.7 percent reported experiencing major trauma such as physical or sexual abuse, 79.5 percent experienced symptoms of post-traumatic stress disorder for more than a month.

- According to the US Interagency Council on Homelessness, in 2014, 11-37 percent of former foster youth reported having experienced homelessness and one-quarter to one-half experienced housing instability of some sort after aging out of the foster care system.

- Homeless youths are evenly male-female, although females are more likely to seek help through shelters and hotlines.

- According to the National Conference of State Legislatures, between 6 percent and 22 percent of homeless girls are estimated to be pregnant.

- 75 percent of homeless or runaway youths have dropped out or will drop out of school.

- Between 20 percent and 40 percent of homeless youths identify as LGBTQ.

Youth homeless shelters sprinkled throughout the nation can only house a small number of wandering teens. For those fortunate to gain access, a case manager is assigned to make connections to counseling, mental health facilities, education and housing.

I do not want to disparage the good work done by youth counselors who toil diligently to provide jobs, internship placements and transitional housing, but what they do hardly makes a dent in eliminating youth homelessness. These adolescents need assistance over a long period of time if they are to overcome years of childhood neglect and abuse. Patience is needed, along with long-term resources, to tackle their problems.

SECTION II
CAUSES OF YOUTH HOMELESSNESS

A Little History, a Bit of Hope

T HE STORY OF ZACH MOTIVATED me to want to understand the plight of homeless youth so I embarked on a three-year study. I suffer a bit from elitism and had a hard time grasping the skills needed to survive a street environment. Those raised in poverty grow up with a different set of priorities and values than those of us who have never lacked life's necessities. It is easy to look down on poor people, to call them an underclass, and to berate them for their situation. Over time, I came to admire their stamina and survival skills and discovered how even the poor have moments of great happiness. It still distresses me to see childhood trauma, whether caused by ignorance, substance abuse or poverty, so I set out to discover if it is possible to alleviate some of the dire situations defining the universe of so many young people.

Throughout my investigations, as I walked through town and observed the number of young people living on the streets, one burning question remained at the forefront of my mind: Is it possible to reverse the flow? I keep looking for signs of hope even as today there seems to be hundreds of tents erected on sidewalks, grassy highway hills, and in public parks, contributing to an appearance of neglect. Sleeping figures, shopping carts and mountains of trash create an eyesore for all who pass. Adolescents sit on cardboard, smoking dope and begging for handouts, blocking congested sidewalks and making shoppers and businesspeople uncomfortable.

When I speak of this to friends outside of Portland, they commiserate and share stories of their own, seemingly trying to outdo me in how bad things are. The problem is especially sad in those areas of the country with a mild climate. It is a local disgrace for Portland — an embarrassment. And, it is a national catastrophe.

How did our country end up with 32 million illiterate people without job-ready skills?[4] Why are so many of our youth addicted to drugs, without goals, and incapable of holding on to a job? When and why did we abandon the mentally ill, shoving them from hospitals to fend for themselves? Are we less caring than our parents' generation? Are we worse off than other first world countries or do they too face a growing population of street people? Politicians tell me that millions of dollars of private and public funds are spent to help those living in poverty but I couldn't help but wonder how these funds are allocated. These initial musings sent me thinking about the changing nature of family life.

The benefits of marriage are many. In addition to better health and finances, committed couples provide stability for their children. They even enjoy more sex. Yet, despite these advantages, marriage rates in the United States continue to decline, especially among middle and single parent lower class families.[5] And, unfortunately, children are hurt the most by the breakdown of family life.

Although the Great Depression brought with it tremendous economic hardships, families tended to remain together. The divorce rate fell because it was expensive to separate and live alone. Those who tried it often returned home to live cooperatively with their family. Everyone was expected to work including children who took part-time jobs. My father told tales of how he and his brothers sold apples and newspapers, bequeathing prime street corners from one child to the next. His older brothers quit high school so they could help their younger siblings stay in school. They worked hard and eventually earned enough money to pay my father's way through medical school. Today, many of the jobs held then by children would not be sanctioned by the Occupational Safety and Health Administration. Though I'm glad that we have

48

child labor laws, I suspect they contributed to the demise of the family as a self-sufficient economic unit.

When the country went to war in the 1940s, women went to work, filling positions previously held by their husbands. Grandparents and extended family members helped with childcare. My aunt and her two children moved into our small home while the men fought in Europe.[6] When the war ended and husbands returned home, moms went back to their domestic roles as cook and homemaker. Times were good, the economy boomed and incomes rose. Prices at the gas pump were low. Children came home from school to the smell of baked goods in the oven. Instead of needing children for economic reasons, friendships and emotional ties strengthened between parents and their offspring.

It wasn't until the 1960s, that the family, with its extended community of aunts, uncles and grandparents, started to decline. Some of the changes were brought about by the growing number of better-educated women entering the workforce. By the 1960s a third of middle-class women had full- or part-time jobs. Families became smaller and less stable.

Women from low-income families entering the labor force for the first time often did so because they were abandoned by their husbands and were suddenly thrust into the position of sole breadwinner. Struggling, they were forced to take low-paying jobs due to lack of education and training. Before the war, their plight would have been addressed communally through strong extended family contacts and church affiliations, but these social safety nets have disappeared for many.

Today four in ten births occur to women who are single or living with a nonmarital partner.[7] Instead of remaining home to raise their children as 87 percent of moms did in the 1960s, only 69 percent are able or willing to do this today. Dual-income families are more common with parents sharing household responsibilities. In black households, 54 percent of children live with a single parent and only 22 percent with both mother and father. Those fortunate enough to reside in a two-parent family often are neighbors with families that have been affected by divorce, remarriage and cohabitation. Because of a changing economy and shifting workplace demands, separated parents may have to find employment in other states, adding additional instability to their children's lives. The Department of Labor reports that women make up approximately 50 percent of the workforce though 70 percent of women with children, residing in non-married households, are employed.[8]

Poor working parents commonly avoid the cost of childcare by leaving their children unattended. Latchkey children return to empty houses at the end of each school day. Without adult role models at home to teach them practical and social skills and to provide a modicum of discipline, these youths fend for themselves and grow up without commonly accepted social mores. It is easy to lie to a tired parent about activities that might evoke disapproval, making it difficult for the parent to maintain a position as head of the household. As a result, there is a growing trend towards child-dominated households in all levels of society. In wealthier, two-income households, computers and the internet contribute to diminishing parental authority, while in poor homes, neglect is the main cause, though poor children also may have access to unsupervised use of technological devices.

Parents who live in dangerous neighborhoods face additional challenges maintaining their authority. Concerned, they ask their children to stay home for their own safety with mixed benefits. Younger children tend to spend their time watching television, becoming bored and apathetic. As they get older, they escape to the streets to hang out on corners or join gangs. Since there are few available jobs for teens, they are not asked to contribute to the family's financial well-being. And, since food is not a major problem (very few people starve in the U.S.), children are not sent out to beg. A lack of need, concern and involvement weakens family bonds.

My grandmother's family exemplifies poor immigrants who arrived in New York in the early 20th century. As soon as they were able, each of eight children took after-school jobs. As a teen, Grandma worked at home and was paid by the piece for crocheting window-shade pulls. By pulling together, family members formed a strong unit that managed to stay out of poorhouses and orphanages. The children developed a work ethic and sense of belonging that united them in the face of bullying due to their immigrant status. Each child participated in assigned household duties without being nagged or reminded. Everyone helped during bad times and were there to celebrate the good. The siblings remained friends and supported their mother throughout their lives.

Relatives living nearby provided cross-generational support. Aunts, uncles, cousins and grandparents played an important role in stabilizing the family. If a child did not get along with his or her parents, a grandparent or aunt might intervene. My grandparents certainly made life easier for my parents by babysitting for us when we were young. They reinforced the adage "that it takes a village to raise a child." When I was a young mother in the 1960s, family support had already begun disappearing. Since my parents lived in another city, I became dependent on cooperatives and paid childcare.

Meanwhile, with each hit to the country's economy, family cohesion disintegrated more. Fathers moved in search of employment. Without relatives and churches applying pressure for parents to remain together and with the increased ease in filing for divorce, separations soared, leaving women alone with their children. Fallout from breakups lands most heavily on the shoulders of the children. Struggling and exhausted, the working parent returns home with little energy for cooking, shopping or cleaning. Even talking or reading a bedtime story can be a burden. It's difficult to deal with ordinary childhood problems that need attention.

Most parents love and struggle to care for their children as best they can. Those I write of here are the most vulnerable members of society, raising children who, because of circumstances, have to make their own way in the world. Stressed adults who drink, take drugs or engage in risky relationships are seeking escape. They are likely to abandon their children to violent videos and late bedtimes. They are not aware that their children are spending the school day half-asleep. And so, their numbers continue to grow.

If children learn at an early age that their parents can't take care of them, they may blame themselves for having been born. They may believe they were unwanted or that they are no good. Since their parents show little interest in their education, they don't care either. Zach's parents, for instance, never discussed their children's report cards and rarely attended parent-teacher conferences. They did not have enough energy to clean their children's bedrooms or to teach them how to help. Floors stayed dirty, dishes piled high in the sink, and broken toys were abandoned and scattered.

Poor people often live at the mercy of absentee landlords who do not maintain their properties. At work they may be treated as slaves by a disinterested boss or compelled to work two jobs to make ends meet. Their children, hearing complaints about being overworked in boring jobs, wonder why anyone would want to be employed.

These are the families of the underclass, the ones whose children are most likely to become dropouts, join gangs or engage in criminal activities. These under-educated youth lack the training needed to fill vacancies in today's technological labor market. With low prospects of employment, they wander the streets, get in trouble, and are lucky to receive assistance from health, human resources, or legal systems. The easiest way to employment can seem to be to join the drug economy, collect returnable bottles and beg. On the streets, they become victims of abuse, exploitation, human trafficking, thievery, gang activities and prostitution rings. These kids turn into *street survivors* instead of *family contributors*.

Barack Obama ran his presidential campaign on the "Audacity of Hope," but for large numbers of Americans that hope has evaporated. The poor are staying poor. In the 19th and first half of the 20th century, the United States was considered a land of opportunity. As a nation we believed that even if you were poor, with hard work you could rise to the top. Immigrants came to our shores ready to work for a better future. Men, like my grandfather, a farmer's son, came through Ellis Island with a friend at the age of 14. He immediately found a daytime factory job so he could go to school at night. By studying hard and setting goals he eventually acquired a seat on the New York Stock Exchange. Though Granddad arrived alone, he was helped by others in his immigrant community. As with most healthy immigrants, he was here legally and did not live in fear that he would get deported.

Today's immigrants worry about bullying, bigotry and poverty. They live in hiding and fear while trying to raise their families and put food on the table. Their legally born children are traumatized by the uncertain fate of their parents. Those who remain in the states without family often wind up in foster care. As they age, some join gangs and some become homeless when childhood benefits end.

Most taxpayers are unaware of the difficulties of the poor and believe they should be able to overcome adversity to participate in the American Dream. What they do know, however, is that they don't want taxes increased to pay for services for poor or immigrant communities. They register horror when passing tents or confronting unruly groups of youth. Reactions of the *haves* range from feelings of pity to believing the *have nots* should be incarcerated or at least separated from the community. Once home, people tend to forget the poor they passed on the streets. Meanwhile, income inequality continues to escalate and young people increasingly run away from home.

Before we can do something about this downward spiral of despair, one needs to understand the causes that lead youths to choose to leave home. It is my hope that this understanding will motivate more citizens to demand change. This book is a map for the many caring people who ask what they can do to help.

HIERARCHY OF NEEDS

A short time ago, a group of Unitarian lay ministers met to discuss the topic of gratitude. The first to contribute was Ellen Howard. Her words were inspiring.

"When I hear the word "gratitude," what instantly comes to mind is the totality of my privileged life; that I have always felt loved and valued: that my opinions and feelings have generally been listened to; that I had the sort of family who raised me to be grateful, to value love and truth and beauty and to care for others; that I have always had enough; That I have often had more than enough; that my life and the life of my mind and spirit have been rich and full; that I have never had to meet my challenges alone; that, so far, I have found the strength to face and deal with the losses of my life; and that my sorrows have never been more than I could bear."

Ellen came from a poor, working-class family that survived from paycheck to paycheck yet managed to do so with gratitude for all that they had. I consider Ellen to be a self-actualized woman. She is at the apex of Maslow's hierarchy of human needs. Despite being raised in a poor family, she had security from knowing that she would be fed, had a place to sleep, and was safe. As the first child in the family, she was well-loved and remembers seeing the faces of parents, grandparents, aunts and uncles peering over her bed. Every child deserves this type of love and attention. Unfortunately, that is not what many receive.

The causes of youth homelessness are many and varied. A combination of factors coincide to determine who runs away and whether the runaway is resilient enough to overcome his or her set of circumstances.

In the 1940s, Abraham Maslow published *A Theory of Human Motivation* where he proposed that healthy people have needs that are arranged in a hierarchy.[9] He believed that human beings are compelled to satisfy certain biological needs and that it isn't until these are met that a person can move up the ladder to pursue higher callings. Maslow's earliest model was divided into five stages. The first two focused on basic physiological and safety needs such as food, water, breathing, sex, sleep security of body, employment, morality, resources, family, health and property. The third level, defined as love and belonging, involves friendships, family and sexual intimacy. Esteem, the fourth rung, carries confidence, achievement, respect for and by others, and self-esteem. At the apex of the pyramid is self-actualization giving life its meaning. It is the seat of morality, creativity, spontaneity, and problem solving. It is a place where prejudice is lacking and facts are accepted. Maslow called the bottom four levels, "deficiency needs" because people cannot fully ascend the ladder until they are met. Those at the bottom levels are likely to be anxious and unable to turn their attention to self-actualization. Only when basic needs are met, do qualities such as honesty, independence, objectivity and originality garner importance.

Maslow believed that every person has the desire and capability of moving up the hierarchy towards self-actualization. Though his theory is criticized for being overly schematic and not subject to vigorous scientific investigation, he presents a convincing intuitive idea that grew from his experience as a psychologist. It is an especially useful model when exploring the homeless population, for those who cannot satisfy their lower level needs appear to be stuck. Maslow goes on to mention that there can be fluctuations between one level and the next due to temporary situations. This is clearly seen when a job is lost that results in temporary homelessness. In later years, Maslow's model was expanded to eight levels to include cognitive, aesthetic and transcendence needs. Transcendence is now at the top of the pyramid and signifies that once a person reaches self-actualization, he or she is ready to help others. Most street youths have a multitude of "deficiency needs" that keep them hovering at the bottom of the pyramid. When their problems are addressed, they are set on a path to achieve a higher level of fulfillment.

THE BOTTOM RUNG - POVERTY

Those who are poor are ruled by basic deficiencies such as food insecurity and inadequate shelter, which can be passed on to the next generation. Children are quick to observe the family's deterioration that occurs when a parent loses a job. Boredom and depression from idleness take over and they might watch as their parent seeks relief through alcohol or drugs. Boredom was certainly part of the problem in Zach's family. His alcoholic father collapsed on the sofa each evening after returning from the local pub. His mother, overwhelmed by years of caring for nine children, could not stand up to her husband who occasionally became abusive, and at times violent. The situation went from bad to worse after her husband died, for she started taking methamphetamine in order to cope. It wasn't long before she depleted the small pension she had inherited. As income plummeted, the house was further neglected and the children were ignored.

Children born into such households are adversely affected by their parents' anger, violence and despair. When raised by poorly educated parents, problems are compounded. Since learning is not valued, the message children receive is that paying attention to the teacher is unimportant. By third grade many of these children cannot read at grade level. As school years continue, they are unable to follow what is being taught, don't complete assignments, and fall further behind. It's not unusual for such children to drop out of school as soon as it's legally possible. Unfortunately, without a diploma, they have little chance to learn a trade or pursue advanced education. The choice to leave high school perpetuates a cycle of poverty that gives rise to a high percentage of the next generation also winding up on the streets. According to the National Center for Children in Poverty, approximately 16.4 million children or 21 percent of all children under the age of 18 live below the federal poverty threshold.[10] In order to cover basic expenses, family income needs to be at twice the federal poverty level.

Poverty is the most prevalent underlying cause of youth homelessness. Though there has been a slight improvement over the past fifteen years, the numbers remain dismal. Millions of families are affected, with some socio-economic groups suffering more than others. Racial and ethnic disparities play a significant role in defining who lives below the poverty line. For example, in 2010, 38.2 percent of African-American children lived below the poverty line. The rate was 32.3 percent for Hispanic children, 17 percent for non-Hispanic white children, and 13 percent for Asian children. Four out of ten American youth experience some form of economic hardship.

Before effective strategies can be developed to keep them off the streets, it's important to understand what it's like to live in a low-income family. In Zach's case, there were days when his mother gave her children $1-2 each to purchase dinner at the corner convenience store. If it was not for school breakfast and lunch programs the children would have been continuously hungry. As it was, they often complained of having inadequate food. Many schools across the nation now send students home with bags of groceries to supplement weekend dietary needs.[11] A few socially conscious states also provide meals during vacations and on weather-related days off.

Poverty often includes substandard housing, inadequate nutrition, food insecurity, lack of childcare, limited access to health care, unsafe neighborhoods and poor schools. It is the main factor behind dropouts and juvenile delinquency, hindering successful transition to adulthood. Children in low-income families are 4.5 times more likely to leave school before graduation. They lose education and training opportunities affecting future livelihood and placing a tremendous economic burden on society. They are at great risk of having behavioral and emotional problems such as impulsiveness and difficulty getting along with peers. A high number get diagnosed as having ADHD and other conduct disorders.

Emotional problems escalate rapidly with anxiety, depression and low self-esteem. Parental problems caused by chronic stress and marital discord only serve to accentuate childhood agitation. Risky behaviors such as smoking, stealing and early sexual activity are likely to become the new norm. Poor, unsafe neighborhoods expose youth to violence and drugs that put them at risk for injury and even death. The more intelligent children learn early that the way to survive is to become violent. They often find their role models in the strongest and most abusive adults in their community.

Poverty also contributes to health problems resulting from

low birth weight, inadequate food and environmentally caused conditions such as asthma, anemia and pneumonia. News articles are awash with stories about poor communities exposed to environmental contaminants. Flint, Michigan provides a good example of what can happen when a government cuts expenses to save money and winds up polluting the water supply of an entire city.

Does poverty predict teen homelessness? Not necessarily, but it is a contributing factor. When survival is at stake, leaving home seems to be the safest thing for the child to do. Substance abuse, physically violent parents or step-parents can drive youth to become runaways. This is particularly so in the LGBTQ community.[12] Female-headed households with working mothers are especially vulnerable as are teen parents without a high school degree or job skills. Lack of affordable housing adds to their burden, since the jobs they do obtain pay poorly. It is not uncommon for a low wage earner to pay more than 50 percent of his or her income for rent or mortgage.

The cost to society for allowing homelessness to continue is incalculable. Being cared for in an emergency health clinic is the most expensive way to be served. Problems related to poor health, depression, hunger and violence make it almost impossible for those living in low-income neighborhoods to transition to well-paid jobs. Delinquent youths become half-buried with their feet stuck in the mud, unable to pull themselves up. When caught, they are treated by a system that can cause additional trauma. Though they may be put into an expensive retraining center, it may be ineffective because it doesn't deal with underlying problems. Government assistance to these youth is a burden shouldered by all taxpayers, many of whom are increasingly tired of having their dollars spent supporting the homelessness. During the Trump administration, subsidies for the poor have diminished, making matters worse.[13]

A word of caution. Though poverty may be a prime cause, children from wealthier households also are found on the streets. Hovering parents at times smother their children and make them crave freedom. Overworked parents in high-position jobs may neglect their children and pass them on to poorly trained caretakers. Youth may leave home because their parents fight, treat them violently or make them do things they don't want to do. They may be pushed out of their homes because of religious differences, sexual orientation or involvement with drugs. Wealthy children also suffer from mental illness, become victims of bullying or can be stressed by social demands and homework. Raising healthy children is not an easy task for anyone. It is just that poor families carry an extra burden of fear that comes from an inability to pay bills, making the job more difficult.

RACISM

Writing for the *Huffington Post,* Jeff Olivet, president and CEO of the Boston-Based Center for Social Innovation, suggests that homelessness is a symptom of racism.[14] Overall, the white population is six times wealthier than African-Americans. Even as the economy improves, people of color and their families tend to lag far behind. One of the most consistent drivers of racial inequality is lack of affordable housing. According to HUD, "people of color are shown fewer rental units and more often denied leases based on credit history compared to white renters." African-Americans are more likely to be unemployed. They receive 50 percent fewer job call-backs than those who have white-sounding names. Though they make up 30 percent of the population, they comprise 60 percent of those sent to prison. Once jailed, a felony record is attached to their profile making future employment and access to housing extremely difficult.

Racism is not new. It followed the Obamas to the White House with the "birther" movement and large number of racial threats. Denying that Obama was born in the United States was an expression of unease with having a person of color in a position of leadership. A great many white Southerners and numerous Northerners still question the right of black Americans to vote.

They lampoon black officeholders, and even condone murdering leaders. The Ku Klux Klan and other violent groups are at the forefront of the movement promoting disenfranchisement and segregation.[15]

In 2015, a study was conducted in response to Michael Brown, a young, unarmed black man, being shot dead by police in Ferguson, Missouri. Known as The Ferguson report, it gives a picture, based on hundreds of interviews, of how the police force and court system work together to ignore civil rights and to permit racism. And as recent as December 2016, Carl Paladino, Trump's New York campaign co-chair, said he wished President Obama would die of mad cow disease and that the first lady would turn into a man and be sent to live with a gorilla in Africa.[16]

As long as there is racism, African-American communities will likely continue to have staggering numbers of homeless youth. One of the strangest studies I read shows that though white Americans think racism is a problem, they believe it's actually worse for the white population than it is for African-Americans. They think that there is a bias against white people that is more of a problem than biases against African-Americans. The only area of agreement is that both black and white groups believe that relations between the races are deteriorating.[17] This growing negative attitude toward minority races does not bode well for youth of color.

NEGLECT

The federal Child Abuse Prevention and Treatment Act (CAPTA), (42 U.S.C.A. §5106g), reauthorized in 2010, defines child abuse and neglect as:[18]

"Any recent act or failure to act on the part of a parent or caretaker which results in death, serious physical or emotional harm, sexual abuse or exploitation; or an act or failure to act which presents an imminent risk of serious harm." The definition encompasses malnutrition, inadequate shelter and lack of supervision. Neglect also includes the failure to provide your child with medical or mental health treatment, to educate them, to ensure his or her emotional and psychological well-being, or to get your child into a substance abuse program.

Teachers and physicians are the first line of defense trained to look for sudden changes in performance and learning including signs of physical and sexual abuse, frequent absences from school, and begging or stealing food or money. But it is not unusual for abusive parents to blame the school for problems that emanate from home. Some describe their child as a constant problem and request that harsh physical discipline be applied at school. Neglect has long-term effects that put the child at risk for cognitive delays and emotional difficulties. It produces physical and mental wounds that can affect the nervous and immune systems, causing permanent damage.

Nutritional abuse is one of the most common forms of neglect, though more difficult to identify than a child dressed inadequately in cold weather. Those suffering from a poor diet are at risk of having lifelong health issues. According to a 2011 article in *The Urban Child,* "shortages of nutrients such as iron and iodine can impair cognitive and motor development and these effects are often irreversible. Similarly, there is growing evidence that DHA, an essential fatty acid, is a key component of the intensive production of synapses that makes the first years of life a critical period of learning and development. Many other nutrients— choline, folic acid and zinc, to name just a few—have been linked specifically to early brain functioning."[19]

The subject of nutrition and brain development is complex, affecting cell size and chemical processes. More than one-third of child deaths worldwide are attributed to malnutrition weakening the body's resistance to illness. An adequate amount of proteins, carbohydrates, fats, vitamins and minerals are needed to keep organs functioning well.

Though children in the United States do not suffer as much as those in developing countries, there are still many who experience food insecurity by being given cheaper, more filling provisions instead of a nutritious, varied selection. Their unbalanced meals not only are of poor quality but serving sizes can be small. Food-insecure children are likely to develop learning and developmental problems that lead to low academic achievement, poor health, and emotional problems.[20]

A common image of a poorly fed person is of a skinny body, but bad food choices may instead lead to obesity, which carries its own set of physical and psychological problems. Cheaper, more filling provisions contain an abundant amount of fat and sugar. Ostracism, low energy due to inadequate exercise, and health issues such as diabetes and cardiovascular diseases are more prevalent in obese children than those in the normal weight range, causing them to suffer throughout life.

It is expected that a child will grow and gain weight rapidly during his or her first two years. By receiving proper nutrients and ingesting adequate calories, the body builds a buffer for those times when energy and nourishment are lost due to illness. During well-baby visits, doctors are asked to identify children with poor weight gain. Unless there is an identifiable illness, low body weight is an indication that something in their home environment is wrong. It is the physician's responsibility to identify and report possible neglect to child welfare authorities. Not all do.

When conducting home visits, trained social workers pay attention to cleanliness. Water and food supplies should be clean and dairy products refrigerated, especially in hot weather. They look for adequate toilet and hand-wash facilities and want to make sure that children will not get worms and other sicknesses from their environment.

I know of two young children who were placed in a bathtub to play, eat and defecate while their parents were in a drug-induced stupor. Concerned neighbors called child welfare workers who found the children starving and filthy. The youngsters were removed and their father sent to prison. Their mother spent time in a rehabilitation center, later regaining custody of her offspring — for better or worse, I don't know.

Emotional deprivation is a devastating form of child abuse that can be worse than beatings, bruises, hunger and broken bones.

Children ignored by parents become unresponsive. They suffer both emotionally and physically when treated with verbal or corporal hostility. This type of home produces children with low self-esteem, poor ego control and negative feelings which makes them easily angered, hyperactive and impulsive.[21]

TRAUMA

Abuse, violence and naturally occurring disasters such as war are traumatic, but so are painful medical procedures, the loss of a loved one, neglect, verbal put-downs, being treated like a slave and starvation. These situations can cause debilitating reactions, often leading to dysfunctional behavior patterns that affect the youth's ability to grow into a balanced thoughtful adult.

"Sara" was in a horrendous boat accident when she was eleven. On a sunny summer day a waterspout developed that suddenly hit the family's boat from behind. The small craft was capsized and her mother lost a part of a finger as she floated out to sea. Her father's leg was partially severed while he held on to "Sara" by her poorly secured life jacket. fortunately, the family was rescued by a passing stranger and taken to a local hospital. After the accident, the girl's friends started calling her a jinx. Since she was physically fine, her parents did not realize that she needed psychological counseling to get over the incident. The emotional damage of the event stayed hidden and was one of several traumatic instances that led to a mental breakdown at the age of eighteen.

Negligent caretakers, even if naive as in the above case, keep children from developing into strong, healthy adults. Instead of developing confidence, their children grow up feeling that the world is unsafe. They may lose trust in older people and have problems regulating emotions. As they age, they draw into themselves and find it difficult to connect with other people their own age. As teens they are likely to have conflicts with authority and create unnecessary problems in school, at work or with law enforcement. Romantic relationships and friendships tend to be sparse and unhealthy.

The stress from growing up in an abusive environment contributes to impaired brain development plus chronic or recurrent physical problems such as headaches, stomachaches, rapid breathing and heart-pounding. It is not unusual for a traumatized child to self-medicate with drugs, alcohol and overeating. Some children become hypersensitive and act out inappropriately while others are just the opposite and become disassociated from their senses. Constant anxiety and fear, more often than not, lead to severe depression.[22]

In school, a traumatized child tends to space out by daydreaming and not paying attention to assignments. Childhood trauma and neglect can affect the child's ability to learn to read. It is hard to pay attention when your home problems are of more immediate concern than schoolwork. Their wandering minds lose track of time and, in many cases, impulsive behavior replaces rational thought, making the youth unpredictable, volatile, and extreme. Believing they are powerless in the face of adversity, traumatized youth compensate by becoming defensive and acting aggressively when feeling blamed or attacked. A great many move toward high-risk behaviors like self-mutilation, unsafe sex or high-speed auto races.

Since abused children have difficulty thinking and reasoning clearly, they are unable to plan ahead and anticipate their future. Their fight and flight reactions take precedence over rational thought and problem-solving. Without hope or purpose life has little meaning and is without value. Without the ability to influence their lives, they operate in survival mode.

Though it may take years to turn around negative feelings of self-worth, with the right intervention, it can be done. My friend, Caroline, shared her upbringing with me. As a child, she was raised in poverty in a small Appalachian community. Though loved, her young life was traumatized by poverty and illness. As the eldest of four children, she was called on to care for the younger ones and assist her mother in household chores. Daily activities were especially cumbersome, for her mentally unstable mother was hospitalized frequently. When Caroline was in fifth grade, her father developed tuberculosis (TB) and was hospitalized at the same time her mother was committed to a distant mental hospital. In those days there were limited ways to treat TB and most patients spent years in a sanatorium. The family thus was without a bread winner and facing starvation. At eleven years, Caroline became responsible for her younger brothers and sister.

When the state finally learned of the situation, a social worker found Caroline foraging by herself in the woods. She and her siblings were separated by the state, with two boys sent to one orphanage and the two girls to another. Caroline wondered if she would ever see her young brothers again. Describing her feelings at that time she said, "I believed that my family was no-good trash. After all, we were poor with no chance of improvement. I thought that since things were so horrible, we must be bad people who got what we deserved. I was sure that I too would come down with TB and suffer from mental illness as I got older. I assumed that all of our misfortunes were inherited."

Fortunately, Caroline was taken in by a loving couple, both doctors, who dedicated themselves to caring for the homeless children of Appalachia. The two adults were inspirational role models for the young girl. With scarce finances to operate their orphanage, but with an infectious can-do attitude, they impacted the lives of thousands of children. Their perseverance and positive outlook attracted help from others in the nearby city of Charlotte, North Carolina. At one point the doctors decided to build a clinic. Without the necessary money to do so, they relied oncommunity help and organized the children and mountain neighbors to help dig river rocks for the building's foundation. To earn additional revenue, they collected used clothing from wealthy in-town donors and started a thrift shop that is now over fifty years old. Their actions and positive attitude were role models for young Caroline.

Most importantly, they showered her with attention and love. They convinced Caroline that tuberculosis and her mother's mental state had nothing to do with her. As an adolescent, her self-esteem grew and she began to believe that the tragedies she had experienced could be surmounted. Upon graduation from high school, Caroline was awarded a scholarship to college where she studied nursing. She fell in love and married a physician who provided a comfortable home where she became a social force in the community as she raised her own five children. She later went on to direct a prestigious science center.

Caroline is still attached to the mountains of Appalachia and continues to support the orphanage that helped her become a successful businesswoman. The sister who had accompanied her to the orphanage also flourished under the tutelage of the two doctors. Unfortunately, her brothers did not fare as well in their group home and struggled throughout their lives.

Not only does trauma burden children, it causes economic and political repercussions that carry a high price. Medical, law enforcement and legal expenses are paid for by the rest of society.

Parents who leave their children alone for long hours, whether due to illness, drugs, or excessive work schedules, often are faced with unexpected consequences. In poor neighborhoods, children might play outside in a combative, primeval atmosphere similar to that described by William Golding in *Lord of the Flies*. They might move about in city jungles without adult guidance, join gangs and exist in survival mode. They might become unruly and unwilling to play by the rule of law, with little regard for the consequences of their actions. These youngsters add to the load on our courts, foster care, and juvenile detention systems, burdening the country with billions of dollars in long-term costs.[23]

VIOLENCE

Whether they are victims, perpetrators or observers of violent acts, children are tremendously affected by violence. In 2016 more than 700,000 youths between the ages of 10 and 24 were treated in emergency rooms for violence according to the National Institute of Health.[24] Violence takes many form—from physical and mental abuse to hunger, sexual abuse, malnutrition, and neglect. David Gill of Harvard University studies the social and cultural forces that lead to violence against children.[25] After looking at nearly 13,000 incidents, he concluded that violent behavior is deeply rooted in cultural practices of childrearing. Those in destitute, poorly educated and broken families with over four children are the most likely to experience serious abuse. Gill also comments that "American culture encourages the use of a certain measure of physical force in rearing children." The implementation of tough love can harbor negative consequences.

There are subsets of society that equate harshness with love. "Spare the rod and spoil the child" is a sentiment still embraced by many families. Only recently have teachers been prohibited from hitting children for misbehaving. As a child, I remember a storage closet used as a paddle room in elementary school. Periodically I heard the shouts of boys being disciplined behind the door.

The United States has one of the worst records among industrialized nations for child abuse.[26] More than 3 million cases are reported annually with over 6.3 million children referred to state child protective services. The most common side effect of such debasement are mental health disorders.

Life expectancy for abused children is twenty years shorter than for the average person. And 80 percent of deaths are of children not old enough to start kindergarten. Many begin their abusive journey while still in utero through exposure to drugs. Once born, their parents all too commonly ignore and often don't provide adequate nutrition. These children are likely to succumb to alcoholism and drug abuse in later years. It is not surprising that many become severely depressed and attempt suicide.

As teenagers, they subject their partners to the type of violence they witnessed as children. Once out of the house, they tend to have multiple sexual partners which commonly leads to sexually transmitted diseases and unintended pregnancies that have a higher than average chance of ending in fetal death. Fetuses carried to term have a high rate of chronic pulmonary and liver diseases.

Teenagers who escape from violence most often are the ones willing to fight for their lives. They demonstrate strength by leaving home and show a readiness to do whatever is necessary to survive. Often the healthiest child of the family, they recognize their abusive situation and understand that safety lies away from home. Sadly, they may go from one frying pan to another, for living by themselves on city streets and in local parks invites unimaginable dangers. They can be forced to engage in thievery, begging and bottle collecting, and naive adolescents become prey to drug dealers and pimps ready to lure them into the sex trade.

It is into these seemingly hopeless situations that agencies intervene with a variety of options for the youths. But more about that later.

LOVELESSNESS

As I wander around Portland, observing dozens of teens hanging out, I wonder who will have a productive, happy life and which ones will fail. If you're like me, you do not enjoy having homeless youths take over neighborhood parks or sit on public sidewalks begging for a handout as you pass. If you're like me, you don't enjoy descending the stairwell of city-center parking garages that smell like urine. And, if you are like me, you feel intimidated when a gang of youths walks down the street making lewd remarks.

Helping these adolescents is important, not only for their sake, but selfishly for mine. This is why I questioned whether street youth were permanently damaged. I wanted to know if they lost all sense of morality. What I discovered was that antisocial behavior is aimed at society at large and not their own peer group. Most follow a strict set of rules that define street-life values. They care for friends by sharing food, cigarettes, information and a code against "ratting".

These are hopeful behaviors because they can be exploited

and transferred to society at large. My questioning continued. When did they acquire a willingness to help others? Did lack of parental love affect their behavior? I had always assumed love is instinctual and that every newborn is a recipient of warm parental care. Without it, I reasoned, a helpless infant could never survive. I now realize feelings of love and responsibility are not a given.

The majority of us are fortunate in that we are surrounded by affectionate parents and relatives. As infants, we were held and cherished. And as adults, we find partners and form bonds based on fondness and mutual respect. But what happens to children who are never caressed or told they are special? What are the long-term effects of never having been touched or cuddled? What befalls those who are abandoned, left on doorsteps or placed in cribs and not attended to when they cry or their diapers need to be changed?

A cornerstone study about infant neglect was initiated in the 1980s when Dr. Nathan Fox and colleagues from Harvard Medical School walked into an orphanage in Romania.[27] Due to a recent ban on abortion, the number of orphaned babies had soared. some 170,000 children were placed in 700 overcrowded and impoverished facilities across the country, staffed with an insufficient number of caretakers. Though the facilities were clean, the infants were emotionally neglected. Left day and night in their cribs, the babies were changed periodically and fed without being held. The nurseries were eerily quiet places. Since crying infants were ignored, they stopped making sounds. No attention—no cries—only silence.

Dr. Fox followed the children for over fourteen years. During the early years, autistic-like behaviors such as head-banging and rocking were common. As the children got older, their head circumferences remained unusually small. They had difficulty paying attention and comprehending what was going on around them. Over time, 50 percent of the children suffered from mental illness. They displayed poor impulse control, were socially withdrawn, had problems coping and regulating emotions and were handicapped by low self-esteem. They manifested pathological behaviors such as tics, tantrums, stealing and self-punishment. Poor intellectual functioning caused them to have low academic success. Those youngsters fortunate enough to be put in a caring foster home before the age of two were able to rebound. Those who entered foster care at a later age were not so lucky and many became permanently damaged.

Between 1962 and 1967, the HighScope Perry Preschool Project, in conjunction with nurse-family practitioners ran another insightful study conducted with three and four year old African-American children.[28] The school had an average child-teacher ratio of 6:1 and their curriculum included decision-making and problem-solving activities as well as physical movement. Program directors asked parents to participate in weekly visits designed to bring them into the education process.

The project is important because it followed the children until the age of forty, proving the effectiveness of early intervention. In-depth analysis enabled educators to design successful curriculums. The study concluded that "without repeated acts of love, a child's brain doesn't make the growth hormone needed for proper mental and physical development." The child is left scarred and permanently affected. Their stress levels are high, setting the stage for elevated cholesterol levels, cardiovascular disease, metabolic syndromes and other conditions that pose serious health risks.

Even small insults of shame and rejection can impact a youngster's health. Adults who say "I can't believe you would embarrass me like that," or "You Idiot! Who do you think you are?" hurt the child by affecting his or her self-esteem. Many children act out by being cruel to animals, setting fires, taking drugs or simply withdrawing into themselves.

Warmth and love are crucial for a child's well-being. Writing for *Psychology Today*, athlete, coach, author and public health advocate Christopher Bergland concurs that "toxic childhood stress alters neural responses linked to illness in adulthood."[29] He writes of a 2013 study published in the *Proceedings of the National Academy of Sciences* where researchers examined the effects of abuse and lack of parental affection across the regulatory system. They discovered a biological link between negative experiences early in life and poor health in later years. The study documented what most healthy families have always known, that children need to be showered with love and kindness and live in a welcoming environment. Love helps youths develop defense mechanisms that provide a buffer from abuse and trauma.

Zach's story is a good example of the importance of attachment. Though often neglected and occasionally abused, he was loved by his parents. When they were high on drugs or alcohol he was occasionally smacked and at times not fed, yet those instances were not as important in the long-run as knowing he was wanted. Since he belonged to an extended family that lived nearby, when the situation became intolerable he found shelter with relatives. This minimal amount of support during difficult times helped him grow into a caring person.

Those who have never been the recipient of affection are not so fortunate. I was a mental health student when younger, and saw what can result from neglect. Baby Charlie was left in his crib for hours without attention from a caring adult. When he cried there was no one around to pick him up or to provide comfort, so he eventually became silent. His diaper was changed irregularly and rashes developed causing more discomfort. During feedings a bottle was propped on a pillow by his mouth while he lay silently in his crib. He rarely felt the warm arms of a loving adult. He remained listless and grew slowly, sitting and crawling months after what was developmentally appropriate for his age. By two years, he acted like a child half his age.

Bullying also is abusive in that it makes the victim feel inadequate. Feeling shame and humiliation, bullied children risk having toxic neural effects. Most keep silent about their abuse, not only because of fear of reprisal but because they think they are "no good." A bullied child subconsciously thinks, if no one loves me, then how can I love myself? The victim sees himself as undeserving and incapable of change. Even when completing a well-executed task, the person has difficulty being satisfied or accepting compliments.

Unloved children become detached and have difficulty having fun.[30] It is not unusual for them to withdraw and hide their anxiety when faced with aggressive or cruel behavior. Buried feelings may keep them from developing a sense of morality. Empathy for others stays dormant. When the child misbehaves, he or she is quick to blame others instead of accepting ownership of the deed. Most unloved children have difficulty recognizing emotions associated with happiness, anger and sadness so they respond in inappropriate ways. Since they don't trust others, they have problems developing in-depth relationships. Social workers I interviewed talked of lack of trust as being the most difficult problem they have to overcome before they can help their client.

Cognitive concerns are expressed by Dr. Joseph Castro, who writes about the effect a mother's love on a child's brain.[31] Without love, concepts of cause and effect, logical thinking, and future planning become impaired. The mind develops confused thought processes that make abstract thinking difficult. When a child is anxious it can cause both verbal expression and gross motor skills to be delayed. Children have a different time participating in ordinary social interactions if they have poor eye contact, are withdrawn or lack self-awareness.

Modifying behavior when the child is young is the best way for an intervention to be successful.[32] Parents who ask to keep their children at home rather than turn them over to court appointed foster care, need help to learn better ways of communicating. But a healthy environment requires much more. Families need assistance with housing, financial aid, counseling and healthcare as well.

With basic food and shelter needs alleviated, most parents want to provide a nurturing home environment. When they understand how their behavior affects their children, they seek ways to create a more demonstrably loving home. Shame and anxiety don't survive when love and compassion are given.

Children living in one-parent households where the adult is

not capable, willing or able to change his or her own behavior are at an immense disadvantage. These young ones grow up unloved and may be better off removed from the home.

SLAVERY

Youth Ending Slavery or YES is an organization founded in 2012 by five students from St. Mary's Academy, a private center city high school located in Portland, Oregon.[33] YES's mission is "to combat modern-day slavery by raising awareness about its prevalence in the world and empowering youth to be advocates for change." After operating for two years, it became a 501(c)(3) nonprofit organization, expanding YES chapters in partnership with dozens of other like-minded organizations. Today, YES raises funds for those helping victims of human trafficking. You might wonder why students became interested in the fight against youth slavery.

The Interstate-5 corridor, linking California to Mexico, turned Portland into a hub for sex trafficking.[34] The report, prepared by the International Human Rights Clinic at Willamette University College of Law, says that the city, aided by easy access to an international airport, sadly boasts having the second-highest rate of sex slavery in the country. Portland's culture continues to support the strip clubs and prostitution centers that blossomed during its early days as a lumbering town. Today, Portland has more sex establishments per capita than any other city in America. Young girls in the area are an easy target for exploitation.

UNICEF reports as many as 2 million children are subjected to prostitution in the global commercial sex trade.[35] The National Center for Missing and Exploited Children wrote in 2014 that 1-in-6 runaways are victims of sexual exploitation. Sex servitude has a long lasting impact causing psychological trauma and social ostracism. It contributes to diseases like HIV and AIDS, drug addiction, unwanted pregnancies, malnutrition and even death.

U.S. law divides slavery victims into three populations: children under 18 forceed into commercial sex, adults over 18 forced or coerced into commercial sex, and those made to perform labor or services through force, fraud or coercion.[36] Traffickers lure and ensnare children through clever manipulation. They recruit, transport, harbor, force, kidnap, threaten or use other psychological methods to get them to bend to their will. Violence and substance abuse are common methods of controlling their prey. Traffickers may be labor brokers or factory owners in need of free labor. Family members willing to exploit their own women and children also are known to be involved in the trade. Traffickers of the same ethnic or national background as those they exploit may work individually, as pimps often do, or in large gangs.

Kevin Donegan, when employed by Janis Youth Services, told me that teenagers are greeted on the streets within a few days of arrival by men on the lookout for naive adolescents of both sexes. These prowlers form an immediate friendship with their target and often become lovers of the youth who is in search of human kindness. He promises to keep her (or him) safe from other predators and, if attractive, may prostitute her or him to high-ranking men. In no time at all, the girls or boys are drugged and forced to work for their keep.

I observed this cleverness up close when an eighteen-year-old daughter of a family friend visited town. On her first day, a good-looking man of about twenty-five years old stopped to talk to her while she was resting on a park bench. He made her feel special and asked to see her again. On the second day, he tried to lure her into his car. Thankfully, because of several worried conversations I had had with her about sex trafficking, she wisely declined his offer. I do believe that if she had not been coached, she would have succumbed to the man's lures.

Forced labor is a common form of youth slavery imported, most notably, from South Asia where a bonded arrangement may be the result of parental debt. Though illegal in the United States, it does exist in many immigrant communities where involuntary domestic servitude is culturally accepted. Child enslavement by definition happens when a person benefits by making a child not belonging to the family perform work without the child having

74

an option to leave. This type of forced labor by unscrupulous and abusive employers is a direct result of poverty, discrimination, crime and political conflict. In migrant communities, acceptance of the practice is more common among parents who lack monetary resources. A blind eye is turned to slave labor if a family considers it to be a survival mechanism. It is especially hard on girls who are sexually exploited and sold as domestic servants. Sons tend to be more valued since boys are expected to take care of parents in their old age.

Housed in isolated communities, threatened with deportation, bullied, beaten, and charged outrageous fees, migrant families often find it impossible to get ahead. Children born into these households, even if citizens of the United States, inherit their family's overall situation —they too are trapped. They often are pulled out of school and sent to work in places where they are subjected to unfair wages and long hours. A few courageous youth do manage to escape, adding to the homeless population nationwide. human rights commissions working with at-risk communities offer free legal services with the hope of empowering abused youth to combat their situation.

LGBTQ

Lesbian, gay, bisexual, transgender, and questioning or queer are the words behind the LGBTQ acronym, representing up to 10 percent of the overall youth population. The majority are accepted by their parents and able to thrive at home during adolescence. Those who become homeless often do so because of family rejection. Several independent street studies of LGBTQ youths report that as many as 20 percent were physically or sexually abused at home, often before the age of 12. Once on the streets, LGBTQ youths are 7.5 percent more likely to be sexually exploited than their heterosexual peers.[37]

A disproportionately high number of LGBTQ youths come from African-American and Native-American communities in low-income areas composed of working-class and impoverished families. Once victimized, these rejected adolescents commonly develop mental health problems or physical disabilities resulting from unsafe sexual behavior. Inadequate shelters, lack of a high-school diploma, drugs and limited job opportunities add to their problems.

Prostitution quickly becomes their primary method of survival. Youth agencies commonly report that 40 percent of their clients are LGBTQ. Every major city has a desperate need for more crisis intervention sites, drop-in centers, and housing with supportive services. Gregory Lewis, executive director of Cyndi Lauper's True Colors Fund, works with gay, lesbian, bisexual and transgender adolescents. He sums up the situation up by saying, "transgender youth need us to stand with them so that they can stand on their own."[38]

DRUGS/ALCOHOL

A 2014 survey conducted by the National Institutes of Health states that, except for marijuana, the use of drugs, alcohol, cigarettes, and prescription pain relievers has gone down. This is encouraging news. Yet the numbers remain high, and among homeless youth and in certain parts of the country, they are still higher.[39]

Drug abuse is more extreme for those living on the streets than those in shelters or in their own homes. The consequence of involvement with illegal substances can mean years of incarceration or even death. A nationwide survey of 600 street youths revealed that 50 percent of those who attempted suicide were using drugs or alcohol at the time.[40] Over the past ten years, street youths are more addicted than ever to heroin and crack cocaine due to the ease and low cost of acquisition. These highly addictive drugs are more prevalent among males than females and among more Caucasians than African-Americans. "The high rates of abuse underscore the need for intervention and treatment services for runaway and homeless youths — and they are not being adequately met," says Dr. Christopher Ringwalt, doctor of public health, and Jody Greene, MS.[41] "The longer they remain homeless the more likely they are to have a substance abuse disorder." Childhood environment plays a big role, for those coming from substance-abusing families have a higher incidence of use than those who don't. Ringwalt and Greene suggest employing mobile vans and storefront drop-in sites in order to reach out to youths in street hangout areas.

Depression also puts youths at a high risk for substance abuse, creating dire consequences at great cost to society. Suicide is of particular concern since one-third of all street youths try to kill themselves.

Zach enrolled in a substance abuse program shortly after he arrived in Portland and before we took him into our home. His treatment was offered at no cost because of support from government grants and generous donors. Though he was one of the youngest in attendance, he went regularly, not only to get clean, but to receive free transportation passes, also subsidized. Paying for transportation may seem like a small bribe, but it went a long way towards ensuring that Zach attended sessions regularly. He attended as an outpatient because his use of drugs was minimal. Those seriously addicted have to be locked in treatment centers for long periods of time if there is to be any chance at rehabilitation. As of this writing, Zach has been drug-free for seven years. When offered marijuana, though legal in Oregon, he chooses to pass it on to someone else.

Books about drug and alcohol abuse fill a great many library shelves. Since the subject is so well explored, I recommend that those interested seek out some of the excellent publications that provide insight into causes and treatments.[42]

PREGNANCY

In 2015, women between the ages of fifteen and nineteen gave birth to 229,715 babies.[43] This number is historically low, suggesting that teens are less sexually active than their predecessors and use more birth control. Still, the U.S. rate for teen pregnancies is the highest in the industrialized world. Black, Hispanic, Native-American and socioeconomically disadvantaged women of all races show the highest rates for teen pregnancy and childbirth.

Nearly all teen pregnancies are unplanned. Poverty, education, irresponsible fathers, risky behavior, drugs, and alcohol contribute to the cause. If births were limited to those ready and able to care for children, there would be an impressive reduction in social problems.

The cost to taxpayers is tremendous. Over $9.4 billion is spent each year on health care, foster care, lost tax revenue and incarceration rates among children of teen parents. These children, like the parents, have health issues and low educational achievement. Only 50 percent of teen mothers receive a high school diploma by the age of twenty-two as compared to 90 percent of women in the general population. With poor skills and employment in low-level jobs, they remain in poverty throughout their lives.

Rather than expelling pregnant mothers as they did forty years ago, many schools provide programs that focus on issues related to pregnancy. The goal is to keep teen moms engaged in traditional degree-granting programs or in flexible GED options. This works especially well if the youth's parents continue to provide housing for their child and soon-to-be grandchild. Problems escalate quickly when the pregnant teen is kicked out of the house.

The curriculum for those enrolled in parenting programs includes information about communicable diseases, health, nutrition, use of condoms, personal values about sex, and how to avoid situations that might lead to unwanted sex. Lessons in child development and infant and baby care are also given.

A homeless youth who seeks agency help with a pregnancy may have a host of other issues that need attention. Illness, lack of housing, abusive relationships and addiction are just a few. Most youth agencies are connected to organizations that help young pregnant women remain in school. Many churches help by offering short-term family shelters for mothers (at times fathers) and their children. Some of the better-endowed agencies are able to provide longer term housing. The goal is to enable the parent (parents) to finish high school and to find a suitable apartment and employment that will allow the mother to support herself and her offspring. The biggest driver behind the dip in teen pregnancies started in 2010 under the Obama-era federal grant program. Unfortunately, the Trump administration cut funding to teen pregnancy prevention programs[44] and the positive trend is in danger of reversal.

GANGS

My first introduction to gangs was when my mother took me to see West Side Story. I still cry whenever I hear the song "Maria." It wasn't until I spoke to people engaged in getting youths out of gangs that I realized how prevalent they are in poor neighborhoods. I wondered why young people join such destructive groups and if it is easy to leave.

Gangs abound in rural communities, suburban enclaves and on city streets, with few areas in the country escaping their reach. Statistics vary on how many homeless youths join, but most of the reports I read say the average is about 15 percent. The Department of Justice defines gangs as an association with a gang name, symbols, leadership, a geographic territory, regular meetings and collective actions that carry out illegal activities.[45] Children as young as 5 years have been known to join but the average age is between 12 and 24. Most gang members use drugs, are involved in trafficking, and engage in violence for turf control against rival factions. It is difficult to know how many young gang members are homeless because once recruited, they are usually are provided with a place to live.

Gangs use a variety of recruitment techniques including the promise of money. These savvy marketers often misrepresent what the group stands for. They may claim that they are not really a gang but just a club that guarantees security. Once admitted, it is not unusual to be given a loan or a gift that establishes obligation. Coercion, another recruitment ploy, may result in death threats to family members if the recruit does not join the gang. Many youths, especially juveniles and younger siblings, see membership as glamorous so they are aggressively recruited.[46]

There are approximately 1.4 million gang members in the United States and two out of every five of them are under the age of eighteen.[47] Though activity and violence declined in the mid-1990's to 2000 it has since increased. Members are more likely to be Hispanic/Latino (50 percent) and African-American (32 percent) than white (10 percent) or all others (8 percent). Women compose about 10 percent of memberships but their numbers are rising.

The largest gangs are found in southern Californian, Southern Arizona and Chicago. In the north, youths are more likely to join gangs in rural communities than big cities. Members who roam streets, are active in prisons, or participate in outlaw motorcycle clubs are responsible for 48 percent of all violent crimes. Gang life is tough and life expectancy is not more than twenty years from the time a recruit becomes a member. Robin Petering, a UCLA social work researcher found that youth without traditional family support develop their significant relationships on the streets with peers who form a surrogate family.[48] Disconnected from the assistance of schools and family, they wander their neighborhood streets and witness a great amount of violence. Needing support from somewhere, they join gangs that give them protection, both real and perceived.

By the time a child joins a gang he or she has usually spent a great deal of time witnessing and living with exploitation. In addition to family abuse, they may have been victimized by foster parents, used drugs, lived with depression, were abandoned, experienced personal violence or had been sexually abused. Once in the gang, they continue to have a high risk of being victimized by perpetrators who roam the streets.

The police are most likely to be called first when a youth commits a crime. Sadly, detention centers are not the place to go to get your life back on course. They tend to narrow future job options and train delinquents to be more successful at managing life as a criminal. Rather than building skills and providing a career path forward, correctional facilities can tear down what little self-esteem the youth possesses, producing negative consequences. Arrest and incarceration is likely to keep a delinquent youth on the streets where they are accustomed to surviving under the radar of the law. Once the words "gang member" are stamped on their file, they are subject to increasingly harsh sentences forever after.

It surprised me to realize that gangs provide all that is needed to climb from the bottom rungs of Maslow's pyramid. Physiological needs are met with adequate food, water, sex and a place to sleep. Safety and security is provided by the morality of the "family," which is there to protect them. Many gangs have enough resources to provide healthcare and employment, though in the latter case it is usually illegal. Love, caring and a sense of belonging grow through multiple friendships and sexual partners. Over time members even begin to develop self-esteem and exhibit greater confidence. They learn to respect other members and, in return gain their respect, becoming more creative and better problem-solvers. On the other hand, though gang members are less prejudiced and more spontaneous within their own group, they usually are more hateful and bigoted to those on the outside. (And, as noted above, they tend to have very short lives.}

Once in a gang, it is difficult to get out. Leaders work very hard to keep members from leaving for they know too much about the group's illegal activities and can be a liability if they provide evidence to authorities. Members are kept loyal when moving to another city through reciprocal arrangements set up to keep them in the family.

Petering suggests that some of the good attributes learned while in the gang are a base of opportunity for case workers to use in redirecting behavior toward more socially acceptable activities. Unfortunately, gang and homeless services are not administered through the same agency in most cities. Their effectiveness would increase if the various social agencies worked together.

The Innately Rebellious

Teen years are a time for rebellion. The following quote is a reminder from the sages. "Our youth now love luxury, they have bad manners, contempt for authority; they show disrespect for elders, and love to chatter in place of exercise. Children are now tyrants, not the servants of their households. They no longer rise when elders enter the room. They contradict their parents, chatter before company, gobble up their food and tyrannize their teachers."[49] According to Plato, it was attributed to Socrates who died in 399 BC. Some things never change.

Parents try to blend their child's need for independence with clear consequences for their actions. Wanting to make decisions on their own, teens measure success in terms of independence while their parents evaluate it by rightful actions. The Amish know this tumultuous time well, which is why they let their youth participate in Rumspringa, a period of "running around."[50] Adolescents, especially boys, are allowed to test the waters of freedom before joining the church. Though parents do not encourage their children to be wild, they do turn their eyes from the behaviors they view as unacceptable, believing that their youth will outgrow their rebelliousness.

During Rumspringa, the adventurous may drink and party late into the night, joy ride in cars, wear the latest "worldly" clothing, and attend movies. The more rebellious may even go bar hopping, smoke, dance in nightclubs and engage in premarital sex. Their parents (and minister) may have a thing or two to say about their behavior but they are not shunned by the church. The Amish believe that by getting rebellion out of their system, the teen's period of deviant activity will pass, helping them freely choose to stay within the faith rather than leave permanently for the outside world of the "English." Most, but not all, do end up returning to their religion and the Amish lifestyle. Having been grounded in the community's values since birth, they have absorbed an ethos that is difficult to abandon.

Though the transition from childhood to adulthood may be turbulent for all teens, it is especially difficult for those without adequate adult supervision. In a "caring family," behavioral guidelines are introduced and practiced throughout childhood. Over the teen years, most parents increase their youth's opportunities to problem solve and make decisions. In the early stages of a child's independence, they are monitored, encouraged and discouraged as their behavior dictates, with loving parents available to pickup the pieces should their child fall. Attentive parents try to lead their adolescents toward responsibility and autonomy. Understanding that rebellion is a part of growing up, they learn to work around it.[51]

According to the late American sociologist Joy Dryfoos,[52] youths need to achieve the following skills to move toward responsible adulthood:

- Finding self-definition

- Developing a personal set of values

- Acquiring competencies necessary for adult roles, such as problem- solving, and decision-making

- Acquiring competencies necessary for social interaction with parents, peers, and others.

- Achieving emotional independence from parents

- Becoming able to negotiate between the pressure to achieve and the acceptance of peers

- Experimenting with a wide array of behaviors, attitudes and activities

At-risk children have the same needs but must deal with additional difficulties resulting from living in a climate of uncertainty and fear. If they grow up and remain functionally illiterate (the new untouchables), they risk never becoming responsible adults.

Neglected children lack parental guidance and older family friends willing to intervene when necessary to help them find their way. Left alone, without good role models, they have neither the training nor experience with which to base sound decision-making. Many react instead by joining gangs, engaging in criminal behavior, or getting involved in drugs or prostitution, thereby setting them on a course of self-destruction. If severely depressed, their actions can tragically can lead to dangerous, and even fatal, consequences.

It took five years for Zach to become a contributing member of society with enough life and work skills to make us believe that he could forge ahead on his own. He had to learn table manners, proper English, how to communicate his needs, and to manage money. Numerous times he had social and financial problems that required adult intervention. In other instances, we became involved because of a bad decision he made that affected his ability to remain in his training program. Though it was his life, we were there to help him evaluate the consequences of his actions and nudge him toward sound decisions. His issues were emotional, due in part to not understanding the causes and effects of his behavior. When the slightest thing went wrong, he became excessively upset and instantly depressed. He had to learn to relax before he could deal with his problems.

Just as many parents temper the unsavory idiosyncrasies of their children, those counseling troubled youths develop individualized treatment plans for each child in their care. Patience and understanding are important attributes for a caregiver to have because progress does not happen in a straight line. Two steps forward and one step back is the norm. Since it takes years for a youth to find the courage to leave home, an equal amount of time may be needed to overcome a childhood filled with trauma."

SECTION III
HELPING HANDS

Stories of Helping Hands

T HOUGH MUCH CAN BE DONE to solve the problem of disenfranchised youth and many people are engaged in doing so, progress is slow. According to a 2017 PEW research study, the number of youth—teens and young adults— living on the street appears to be growing. There is no one reason. It's drugs, the economy, housing and lack of jobs. And though there are successful, well-analyzed treatments, funding is inadequate to make a dent in the problem.

The following interviews are of youth leaders who, after overcoming traumatic childhoods, pursued careers with homeless services. Their stories are related as they were told to me. As you read, ask yourself why these men and women were able to surmount their problems. Note how often neighbors stepped forward to help. Do you know people who have stepped forward to intervene on behalf of a needy child? Whose responsibility is it—government, family, or neighbors— to right these terrible wrongs?

Passion: Dewey Taylor
Job Corps

"As one of five children, I was born into a middle-class family in a black Northeast Portland's neighborhood. To the outside world, I appeared to have it all—a big home, lots of love, family, friends, two committed parents and celebrity contacts. Though my father hadn't completed high school, he was a strong and talented black man who buzzed with determination and energy. Yes, he sure did. Dad was only fourteen years old when the Great Depression began, causing him to go into survival mode. After years of being poor and trying to make ends meet, he became a stickler for education and hard work. He was a role model that was hard to keep up with.

"Dad initially worked by day as a Kirby vacuum cleaner salesman but got a job with the Portland school district. At night he was transformed into his real self as a professional drummer. He excelled at the mouth harp as well and became known as one of our country's most exceptional jazz musicians. Performers visiting from out of town were always showing up on our doorstep, stopping by to talk and play a few bars. Our house was filled with music and celebrities such as Mel Brown, Count Basie and Duke Ellington. Lots of times, Dad was asked to accompany visiting bands when they played in Portland. He was eventually inducted into the American Jazz Hall of Fame in Kansas City. I was real proud to be his son.

"Dad inspired me to follow in his footsteps as a professional drummer. I started playing at an early age and though it is not a full-time thing with me, drumming gives me a wide group of friends. Several nights each week I join one band or another in local bars and have a lot of fun with the fans. Music is the perfect antidote for the long hours I work as a painter and instructor. Though I come home tired, it's easy to lose myself in the music.

"Mama also motivated us kids to want to be successful. She had left school at the end of seventh grade. After getting married, she got busy bringing us up. But despite being a wife and mother, she returned to school to get an RN degree. Mama was a real determined woman and left a mark on me and my sisters. She showed me how hard work can be turned into a successful career. Nothing, and I mean nothing, got in her way when she went after it. Mama considered education to be the most important way forward and tried to instill this value in us kids, though in my case her lessons were slow to be absorbed.

"My friends thought I was wealthy because I lived in a five-bedroom, two-bathroom house that my family purchased for $1,100. It was considered expensive at the time. I just found out that in 2014 the house sold for over $900,000. Amazing, huh? By neighborhood standards, I was certainly well off. Surrounded by four pushy sisters, I learned early to compete for the one bathroom we children shared since our parents appropriated the second one to themselves. My sisters primped as beauty queens before a date which caused lots of shouting fights. I always moved quickly to be the first one to slide through the door each morning.

"Living in what, back then, was a safe black neighborhood, I spent a lot of time with friends, playing and roaming the streets and speeding 'round from place to place on bicycles. We were basically good kids and on weekends and vacations were given hours of freedom to travel country roads that were nearby. Leaving home early in the morning, we played basketball, baseball, built clubhouses and forts. Our big risky excitement was climbing over farmers' fences to steal a few apples or cherries without being caught. At the end of the day, we always returned home starving and ready for a good cooked meal.

"When school busing started, I was sent out of my neighborhood to Woodstock Elementary. I remember my first day as though it was yesterday. I had just got off the bus when a white girl came over, rubbed my cheek and said, 'I just wanted to see if that came off.' I pushed her hand away causing her older brother to come rushing over, shouting that he was going to "beat my black ass" after school. The day ended with my first black/white cultural encounter — a fight that led to both of us being expelled.

That fight was the beginning of racial turmoil for Dewey. In 1962 the NAACP charged Portland with having racially segregated schools. In 1965, the literacy tests used when registering people to vote finally were banned. That same year in Portland ushered in school busing of black-American students in order to "improve racial balance,'" a practice which continued until 1980.

"In my neighborhood," continued Dewey, "James Brown's 'say

it loud — I'm Black and I'm proud,' was shouted everywhere. It was the late sixties and black pride and race riots were a big part of our lives. It sure affected me and my friends. Portland had its own 'revolution' in '67 that began on the same day as the Detroit riots. For two nights, two- to three-hundred people threw bottles and rocks at automobiles in the Albina (black) neighborhood. I was a kid, so I wasn't completely sure of what was going on but years later I read the Oregon History Project which said that the riot worked and communication between the city and Albina residents did improve a bit.[53] But I remember that those living in our part of town were uneasy and the feeling continued for several decades.

"Remember the 1977 TV series *Roots?* It started just as I reached high school. When it was first shown, tempers were so high that my parents wanted me to stay home. White kids started calling me names from the movie. They shouted 'Hey *Chicken George*"' or sometimes *'Kunta Kinte'* when I walked down the hall. In response to white bigotry, our community paid more and more attention to men like Malcolm X and Martin Luther King Jr. My parents, though, kept hammering their education and go-slow messages. They were nervous and kept repeating, 'elevate yourself and become someone and then you can make a difference.' Another phrase they liked was, "get it in your head and then throw it from your heart." Unfortunately, my head was somewhere else and their messages were not exciting enough for me. I responded better to black leaders telling me to, "walk proud," and I looked for every excuse I could not go to school. The 70's were tough, but I was often reminded by my parents that race relations were not as bad as those they had faced in their early years when the Ku Klux Klan was on the march."

———⟨⟨⟨•••••••⟩⟩⟩———

Note: The Oregon History Project, mentioned above, gives a full accounting of the black community in the early 1900s. During the 1920's the KKK flourished in Oregon claiming 14,000-20,000 members. It wasn't until 1926 that the state repealed its Exclusion Law which had previously barred blacks from living in the

90

state. It was only in 1927 that black citizens were they given the right to vote. WWII was a period of substantial growth for the African-American population due to employment opportunities in Portland's shipyard. The unions balked at letting them join, however, and insisted that jobs only be opened for them for the duration of the war. Though black workers were required to pay dues, they were denied benefits. Most lived in a new town called Kaiserville (later Vanport) built near the shipyards north of the city. Signs erected in other parts of Portland notified residents that "we cater to white trade only." In 1947, the Urban League went after the Housing Authority for supporting discrimination, but it was not until 1957 that integrated housing was allowed. In 1948, a massive Memorial Day flood in low-lying Vanport left 39 people dead and displaced all residents of what was, by then, the second-largest city in Oregon. Most of the town's African-American residents moved back to the Albina area in Portland's northeast and remained there until they were again pushed out due to gentrification.

During the late 40s, Oregon real estate agents followed the National Association of Realtors Code of Ethics, saying that "a realtor shall never introduce into a neighborhood a member of any race or nationality whose presence will be detrimental to property values." Finally, in 1949, the Fair Employment Act empowered the Labor Bureau to prevent employment discrimination. The following years saw laws prohibiting interracial marriages overturned and discrimination in vocational schools banned. In 1957, the Oregon Fair Housing Act finally banned discrimination against African-Americans when buying or renting places to live.[54]

Dewey's story continues. "As a youth leaving the confines of Northeast Portland I thought of white boys as crazy. When trying to earn money by selling candy for a club I was in, I was chased and told, 'get out of here nigger.' I fought back. In those days fighting was frequent even among my friends. It didn't mean anything and wasn't done with meanness. With my buddies, as soon as the fight was over, we continued what we were doing together. Fighting was done with hands. Weapons were never an issue and teens were rarely approached by police and put in jail. 'Boys will be boys,' was the general rule of the day. It wasn't until the late '60's that racial tensions got so bad that they became riots causing attitudes to change."

⸺⸺⸻⸻⸻⸺⸺

With poverty continuing due to economic inequalities, drugs and gangs have escalated. African-Americans remain on edge due to the arming of police with discarded weapons from the Middle East wars and the ease civilians have in obtaining guns. Racism continues in Oregon. In 2008, four George Fox University students hung an effigy of Barack Obama from a tree with a sign saying "Act Six reject." They wanted to eliminate a scholarship and leadership program for Portland students, many of whom were in the minority. In 2014, protests broke out in the city as a result of disproportionate police brutality. Area youths took up the cry for use of police body cameras, an independent police review board, reduction of the excessive jailing of young adolescents of color, the elimination of police brutality, and canceling the use of lethal shotguns for crowd control. They reminded the public that Black Lives Matter. The day after Donald Trump's presidential election in November 2016, a black University of Oregon student was confronted by three taunting white boys in blackface and the KKK announced a victory party to take place in North Carolina. Oregon and the nation as a whole have not seen the end of racial discrimination.[55]

⸺⸺⸻⸻⸻⸺⸺

Dewey added, "My nervous energy was epic and Mama decided that rather than use my hands strictly for fighting, I needed another outlet, so she taught me how to crochet. I can see you smile at that, but that year everyone in my family received sweaters and scarfs for Christmas, the result of my handiwork."

"When I look back to my youth, I think of myself as a social idiot. I got into fights every day and my grades suffered due to cutting school. Occasionally, when I did find out that there would be a test, I would have a burst of energy, take the exam, and ace it. I wasn't stupid, you know. There was no problem with my mind and I wasn't drugged out. Marijuana and wine were the drugs of choice among my friends, but because I was an athlete concerned with performance, I mostly stayed away from foreign substances.

"It's just that learning did not rank as high a value on my personal list as it did on my parents', and when I reached middle school, girls were a much more interesting pastime. I was tall, not bad looking and was greatly attracted to flirtatious young women. Due to daily workouts, I was in great physical shape. Today most of my fitness comes from working long hours as a painter but back then I spent a lot of time at the gym. I was interested in boxing and trained regularly, building upper body strength. Working out also helped me become self-confident in dealing with the ladies. When I put on my gloves I could beat most anyone — or so I thought until one day Dad showed me otherwise.

"Skipping school became routine, even though my Dad got furious about my poor attendance when the vice-principal, a Masonic Lodge brother of my father's, ratted on me. However, no amount of talking, strappings or punishment had an effect and I continued to play hooky. Even though I did not attend school regularly, I never did get out of daily chores. We Taylor children mopped, vacuumed, dusted or got a 'whoopin' if tasks weren't completed. Mama was tough, and though my parents tried to run a disciplined household, they were not always home and couldn't keep tabs on me. I was independent-minded and determined to have my way.

"At the age of fourteen, fun time came to an abrupt end when much to my dread I found out I was going to become a father. With the birth of my daughter, playtime turned into responsibility time. Pampers had just hit the market and they were expensive. My parents insisted I earn money to support my child, so early morning and late afternoon newspaper routes were added to my schedule. And though I was not forced to marry my high school sweetheart, I always stayed in touch with her and my daughter. Years later, I fathered a second child with the same woman. Though I later got married and divorced, for some unknown reason, I never married the mothers of any of my four children, yet I am close to them all.

"By sixteen, I realized that my life was going nowhere and wondered what to do with myself. One evening, I was watching television when a news clip about Job Corps came on. I immediately became glued to the program. The narrator said it was a place that used hands-on learning to help kids complete high school while learning a trade. The possibility of going to Job Corps energized me enough to contact the local center and to my surprise, I discovered that my aunt worked in their office. She helped smooth the way for my admittance.

"Since girls were my downfall, I thought it better that I go to an all-male school some distance from home."

Fort Simcoe, based on an Indian reservation in central Washington fit Dewey's situation, and as he later told me, "I fell in love with it and adapted well to the discipline and the kindness shown by teachers who understood boys like me. Job Corps was more of a military-oriented program than it is today. Students were given uniforms and made responsible for their actions. Under their strict rules, it took only two warnings before you were kicked out." Dewey disapprovingly told me that, "today, enrollees are often given several chances, and even when suspended they are often taken in at another training site."

Job Corps note: Fort Simcoe, located in White Swan, WA is an arm of Job Corps, a free educational and vocational training program administered by the U.S. Department of Labor that helps young people ages 16 through 24 improve the quality

of their lives through hands-on career technical and academic training.[56]

Job Corps was created in 1964 as part of President Lyndon B. Johnson's War on Poverty and Great Society initiative. The administration's plan was to expand economic and social opportunities for minorities and the poor. Over two million youths have been trained since its inception. Eligibility requirements are that a youth be living in a high-poverty area or participated in the school lunch program. An intake officer informed me that, today, homeless youth are given priority. Most adolescents accepted into Job Corps are deficient in basic sills such as reading, writing or computing and are unable to solve problems at a level necessary to function on the job. Youths, without a high school diploma, are enrolled in GED classes in addition to vocational training tracks. Recreational activities, physical rehabilitation, personal financial management, driver's education and counseling also are offered. One of the key reasons for Job Corps' success is attributable to the strict discipline and behavior standards administered in a caring atmosphere.

Across the nation, 125 centers are currently in operation. After a youth graduates from the program, Job Corps provides transition support and workplace counseling, though due to budget constraints, the follow up program is not as good as it once was. Despite its altruistic mission and the good it accomplishes, funding for Job Corps is an ongoing source of debate between liberals and conservatives in Congress.[57]

It's not easy for a homeless youth to get accepted into Job Corps. It takes perseverance, including emailing on a weekly basis. Zach had to do this for over six months. Once in, to be successful, the youth has to be ready to make behavioral changes. Many participants come from rock bottom — without hope before they were willing to give the program a try. Zach was enticed to enter Job Corp because it provided a place to live and food for his belly for a couple of years. It was better than going to jail. Of

those who do graduate, 87 percent are placed in jobs, enrolled in school full time, or enlisted in the military.

Dewey continued, "When I entered the program at the age of sixteen, I thought that my physique lent itself to becoming a bricklayer. Before long I realized that this was not a good choice because the lime used in the mortar ate away at my hands. Painting was my second choice and it became a passion of mine in short order. I applied myself to the trade with lots of vigor.

For a recreational outlet, Dewey continued to box. He recalled one incident with a smile. "While sparring with my painting instructor, I went head-to-head in a match and won. The victory went to my head and I decided that I no longer had to follow instructions in class. The instructor, DK Watson, was a no-nonsense man I will never forget. During one rebellious moment, he grabbed my shirt, and roughly pushed me right to the wall, reminding me immediately of the time my father flipped me when I did not follow directions at home. 'Don't get your Dewey's confused,' my father had said. 'I am Dewey Senior.' Now the instructor was quick to reinforce the difference between 'man-sense and boy-strength,' a lesson I try to impart to my own students."

DK made a lasting impression on Dewey, remaining a lifelong mentor and friend. Dewey speaks of the time he was taken aside by DK and told, "you have potential, but you have to learn how to get out of your own way. You have the ability to paint or even teach and I can show you the way, but you need to want it. I was fortunate to have several Job Corps guides who were patient, and years later I never forgot them. I looked D.K. up a number of years ago through an online search and called to thank him again for his understanding. This man was the main reason I was able to go where I was meant to be.

"After graduation, I was offered many industrial and commercial jobs. Taking a break from painting, I spent three years in the military before returning to the trade to find that blacks were more welcome in the union when I returned. As a member, I became assured of a good income, a pension, vacations and life insurance. Ultimately, I was able to buy my own house and provide support for my family. I remain close to my four children and many grandchildren. You should see our family reunions. They are boisterous, raucous events where I can be found tending the barbecue."

As a musician, Dewey regularly plays his drums in local bars and during church services. Zach, Cory and I were invited to attend one Sunday morning service and found it quite a cultural event. I was impressed with the sense of community and caring exhibited by everyone. One young man was obviously in trouble with the law, facing a court date. He was asked to come forward to be surrounded by family and friends who placed their hands on his back, showing support for his ordeal, and praying for a fair outcome. It was an emotional moment with tears filling most everyone's eyes. When the Reverend asked Cory and me to introduce ourselves, we did so, saying how proud they should be of Dewey because he had inspired Zach to learn a trade and become a fully functioning member of society.

Dewey later told me, "As I aged, I decided that I wanted to give back to the community and influence the lives of young people by working in Job Corps. I thought myself to be in a good position to communicate values I had growing up. With the kids, I emphasize how important it is to stay focused on their education and on learning a trade. I tell them to take advantage of Job Corps and work as a team. I also pass on my father's wisdom to, "be the best you can, drive hard, stay determined, push and work hard."

As a result of his passion, Dewey's program graduated the greatest number of students. Unorthodox methods based on his own early experiences tended to make other instructors a bit nervous, but they appreciated his success. He was hard on the kids and would not tolerate any slacking off. They had to paint correctly, learn how to use the material or see required to do fifty pushups.

Dewey continues to deal with racial issues. The Job Corps

site he worked at, for example, does not have a racially mixed staff in proportion to the students served. He eventually left his teaching position to continue as a trainer at the IUPAT local 10, the painter's union in Portland. Dewey also claims that there is still a good old boy network of white workers who do not want people of color taking their jobs. However, Dewey is not worried about employment. He has developed a lot of contacts who have appreciated his work over the years, so finding his next job has never been a problem. His 2016 marriage was a large affair with approximately 300 people in attendance representing all races and from various socioeconomic spheres. They were there to show their love and respect for this caring man.

Dewey stays determined, believing in himself and knowing what is best for his students. He still has a temper and occasionally will, as he says, "fly off the handle," which is not a welcome trait in a teacher. But with the kids in his heart and his accumulated national network of trades workers, he is able to find his students jobs after they complete their program. Dewey stays in touch with his graduates, often mentoring them for years. He is proud of young adults like Zach who commented, "I used to sleep under bridges, and now I am working on top of them." That statement brings a smile to Dewey's face and makes everything worthwhile.

Dewey agrees that public schools are not able to deal with the many social and personal problems of their students. Though Job Corps does a good job for a great many, he says that the program does not go far enough to ensure a positive longterm outcome for graduates. Though graduates are helped to find their first job, they may not understand how to manage their free time or invest their earnings. Knowing how to shop, prepare food, socialize safely or even how to clean and set a table may not have been taught to them as children. Young workers also find themselves with inadequate resources to lease an apartment requiring a security deposit and last month's rent in advance.

Most employers depend on their employees owning a car to travel to constantly changing job sites.

Dewey and his friend, Dale Robertson, started a nonprofit corporation with a dream of responding to many of these needs. Their goal is to establish a long-term mentoring program. They received a grant to start such an enterprise in local schools but their ambitions go beyond the educational system. They want to obtain a multi-bedroom house where youth can live for a year after graduation. During that time they will be encouraged to establish a bank account and learn to budget and manage their paychecks. They will be driven to work on time which will enable them to save money for an vehicle and future rent deposits. It takes a long time for children raised in poverty who have lived on the streets to learn socially acceptable ways of interacting. Emotional and psychological problems related to independent living may require several years of attention by caring adults. Overcoming childhood neglect does not happen with the wave of a magic wand nor is it a straight-line proposition. A few steps forward often are followed by a backwards slide. Five years is not an unreasonable time to turn a life around.

COMMITMENT: KEVIN DONEGAN JANUS YOUTH PROGRAMS

My first interview with Kevin Donegan took place in his small office in Northeast Portland a few months before he retired. Arriving in a panic, I entered the lobby of Janus Youth Programs quite late for my appointment. I had been a victim of every type of traffic impediment possible—a long slow freight train, a car accident, rush-hour traffic, and a missing cell phone.

As I pushed through the glass door I was greeted by a man, casually dressed, at the receptionist's desk busily concentrating on his task at hand. He seemed aware of who I was and not at all concerned about my tardiness while I anxiously waited to be shown to my appointment. It was some time before I realized that the unassuming fifty-four-year-old typist was the man whom I was there to meet. As he completed what he was doing, I waited, wondering what type of person could work with homeless kids year after year without getting depressed. I imagined that heart-wrenching stories were a daily event and could not understand how he managed to keep his sanity. In my earlier years, I worked in a mental health clinic and found it upsetting to listen to one traumatic tale after another.

Kevin was a short, stocky man with a relaxed down-to-earth attitude. He did not seem like the type of person who could raise money or manage a multi-million dollar budget but rather a man focused on how best to eliminate suffering.

Once invited into the close quarters of his office, I was directed to one of the two easy chairs pushed against the wall away from the clutter of files piled everywhere. As soon as we started to talk, it was as though a switch turned on, for he put daily concerns out of his mind and gave me his full attention. His personal story was of overcoming one barrier after another and I immediately became immersed in it.

"When I was a college graduate I made an appointment with a counselor just to see what counseling was all about. I was considering going into the field as a career and never imagined that I might need help. During my first session, the counselor expressed surprise that I had never seen a psychologist to address issues in my upbringing. I was a survivor I guess, with the odds stacked against me throughout my childhood, though I never knew it. After a few visits, I realized that Socrates was correct when he said *the unexamined life is not worth living*. To become a fully functioning human being I had to learn how to transcend instinct, and I became determined to do so."

Kevin's story is a brittle one, not only of survival but of transformation. Somehow he was able to maintain his compassion while overcoming adversity. "My early experiences allow me to empathize with street kids," he said.

"I was born into a two-parent household with a brother and

two sisters. My father was in the military, and the first two years I spent living in Japan, though I do not remember anything from that time. Both of my parents were active alcoholics. Dad was a binge drinker and Mom self-medicated herself with regular intoxicants. I don't remember her ever being sober. My earliest memory is of wandering down a street following Mom until she noticed my presence. When she realized I was there, she turned and gave me a swift smack, telling me that I was not wanted, and shoved me back toward home. I realized then, at the age of four, that I was unloved by my mother."

"I don't remember my older half-brother but know that when I was two years old, he and his girlfriend died from carbon monoxide poisoning. The two lovers had just eloped, were stranded in their car on a cold winter night and unwisely closed the windows. The trauma of their deaths marked the start of an increasingly painful time for my parents and older siblings.

"After Dad's military service ended our family moved back to the U.S. I was still a baby and not conscious of the friction that existed between my parents. Their fights were bad enough to cause them to separate when I was four. Mother wound up with the girls and Dad took my brother and me to live in Montana where he ran a small business—a bar. Our house was attached to the bar and I spent much of my youth stocking shelves and occasionally operating the entire place when my father went on month-long binges. I was the youngest, yet more responsible than my brother, a person I tried to avoid. He was well-known in the juvenile justice system for committing a series of petty crimes.

"With such poor role models, and without family members or friends who had graduated from high school, it's surprising that I made it all the way through university studies. Even today I can hardly believe I obtained a master's degree. One thing that may have helped me is that despite the trauma of living with an alcoholic father, I did know that I was loved. I never doubted that fact for a minute. Dad was very proud of me, and when he was sober, he was very supportive. I clung to that knowledge throughout my school years.

"It was by luck that I happened to be in the corridor one day when a high school counselor walked out of her office, spotted me and said that due to a last-minute cancellation there was room for another student to join a field trip to Montana State University. Did I want to go? Not having anything better to do, I agreed and had a most amazing few days that changed the course of my life. I loved staying overnight in the dormitory and realized that college would be the fastest way to get away from home. It was my ticket out and with my good grades, it was easy to get accepted with a scholarship.

"College was a lot of fun and four years passed quickly. After graduating with a business degree, I joined the Peace Corps, working in Belize with disadvantaged children. My first assignment was at an orphanage where I taught child development skills to the staff. I was later asked to meet with adolescents who were incarcerated in the country's brutal prison system. Another time I was stationed in Belize City with the responsibility of investigating child abuse/neglect cases. The incredible experiences I had while in the Peace Corps inspired me upon my return to the U.S. to enroll at Bozeman for a master's degree in counseling."

"It was not long after I was settled in at school that Dad died. His passing meant that there was no reason to stay in Montana, so I left as soon as I could for a more adventuresome life in Portland where I immediately got a job as a caseworker for Janus Youth Programs. So you see, this place is where I started and it will also be where I end my career."

"Originally my goal was to work with residential students at a university rather than the homeless. When a job opened up at Reed College, I was happy to move on and willingly left Janus. For the next ten years, I went from one position to another, eventually becoming director of residential life. I was quite satisfied and felt fulfilled, but, as my career blossomed, the rest of my family were on a downward spiral. Their lives never stopped impacting mine."

"My brother and I were never close. In fact, I would describe us as having a violent relationship. When he lived in Montana, he was constantly thieving and not surprisingly wound up in prison.

I visited him from time to time, though not frequently. After all, he was my brother. Finally, he was placed in a drug rehab program in Portland, a great distance from our home in Montana, so I didn't see him again until my father's funeral, though periodically I would get a phone call when he was high or wanted money. Finally, in an angry moment, I put an end to the relationship, telling him that I only wanted to hear that he was dead.

"Two months later the Sheriff of Oregon City called to say that my brother had jumped in front of a vehicle and was dead. The only identification on his body was a paper found in his pocket bearing my name and phone number. Without that he would have been listed as an unknown street person. I continue to feel guilt to this day because of how I cast him off. I am a counselor and supposed to know better.

"With his death, it was my responsibility to find my mother and tell her what had happened. Still drunk much of the time, she and my schizophrenic sister lived in Portland under a different last name. They continued to support each other's alcohol and drug habits. This was not a family I wanted to stay in touch with but as a dutiful son, I did help from time to time with such tasks as arranging for my mother's cataract surgery. As Mom aged, I tried to convince her to go into an assisted living center and leave her drug-infested neighborhood. She rebelled at the suggestion, not wanting to give up her freedom and addictions. Once more I decided that I had had it, and would have nothing more to do with my mother or sister. The next thing I heard was the following year when my sister died from cirrhosis of the liver.

"Eventually, senior services came into play and, though Mom did not like it, she was taken to a lock-down senior center. She called once to ask me to spring her but I absolutely, with no uncertain words, refused. She was in the best place she could be and remained there until her death. I now had only one sibling still alive. My sister, Charlcie Ann, was about eighteen years older and we never had had much contact with each other.

"So I was surprised when, a few years ago, my nieces called to tell me that their mother was close to death and in a coma.

Did I want to come visit? Walking into her hospital room, instead of facing the 250-pound woman I had known, I saw one who weighed barely eighty pounds looking exactly like my petite mother. While sitting by her bed her eyes opened to stare at me and she murmured a few final words before turning into herself and dying."

"With my last sibling gone I believed family worries were over. But fate has a strange way of unfolding. One afternoon I received an email from a niece who said that she had just been contacted by a woman named Veronica who claimed to be my schizophrenic sister's daughter. I could not imagine how that could possibly be.

"Do you want to meet her?' my niece asked. My response, an absolute no, changed to yes, shortly before the meeting was to take place. Curiosity got the better of me, though I suspected the worst — that she too would be mentally ill and possibly addicted."

With moist eyes, Kevin faltered a few seconds before continuing. "You might imagine my surprise when the restaurant door opened and through it walked Christine, a poised, attractively dressed woman, along with her young daughter, Bella. Christine looked so much like my sister that there could be no denying the relationship. She carried a letter from the child welfare office that said that she had been abandoned by a mentally ill woman named Veronica at the age of one year. The baby was adopted as the second daughter of a well-to-do family in Portland's West Hills, where the baby flourished. Having completed a degree at Oregon State University, I discovered that Christine lived in Portland with her family, only a few blocks from my house.

"I was excited and overwhelmed by our meeting. We talked and talked and established a wonderful, close relationship immediately. For the first time in my life, I was embraced into a normal family and started to realize that not everyone is crazy or on drugs. Until that moment, my childhood experiences as well as those of numerous youth center clients, reinforced the notion that most families are dysfunctional. Suddenly, I was introduced to what so many Americans are fortunate to have been born into — a stable, loving household."

With these words, Kevin heaved a big sigh and wiped his eyes. He told me that he planned to retire shortly because he was exhausted and burned out. He mentioned that he had always been internally motivated and was never bored. "When I was at Reed, I bought property and saved money for retirement and now I can get by without working."

Kevin was comfortable sharing his story because, as he said, "every family has a hidden problem with one or another relative." His openness is part of the reason he was a successful counselor. His father's love helped him become a compassionate person. Kevin was able to identify with teens and make them feel comfortable sharing personal information. As a single man, he now lives half the year on property he owns in an expat community in Mexico. He enjoys maintaining a large circle of friends and is sure that he will continue to volunteer his expertise where needed.

Janus Youth Programs was started in 1972 as a demonstration project providing residential care for adolescents.[58] It operates one of the largest nonprofits in the Northwest with more than 40 programs spanning Oregon and Washington. As a collaborative organization, it works with other Portland agencies to screen more than 1000 youth between the ages of 14 and 26. Other providers include Outside In, New Avenues for Youth and Native American Youth and Family Association (NAYA). At the time of this interview, Kevin was program director for homeless services where he oversaw a large operation providing for homeless and runaway kids.

In addition to intake screening, Janus provides a sixty-bed short-term shelter and makes arrangements for many more. Athena House is a seven-bed facility for those needing longer care. Staff is actively involved in a program called the Yellow Brick Road which was established for those who have no viable safe place to go. Each evening staff and volunteers spread out through the city and surf the streets to locate those in need. Their goal is to bring the kids into the system by providing information and referrals. Each evening approximately 287 young people are given a place to sleep. During the year Janus Youth Programs provides more than 43,000 meals to homeless youth.

Janus serves about 300 youths directly with case management services. Much effort is put into family reunification counseling and mediation, school re-enrollment, and vocational programs. The first priority, however, is to offer youth basic crisis response needs involving shelter, food, hygiene and recreation. A 24-hour, seven-days-a-week crisis response advocacy team offers both mental health and physical support.

Staff members work with the police who can drop off adolescents they have picked up for committing a misdemeanor or who are suspected of sexual abuse. Their extensive list of programs focuses on teen parents, community gardens in low-income and crime-ridden areas, scholarships for continuing education and residential treatment programs aimed at transitioning children to independent living.

"I've heard every depraved story possible and it does get very depressing," Kevin said sadly as he continued on. "There are mothers who pimp their own daughters, selling them off to become prostitutes as they themselves are. They introduce them to men who, in order to gain control, turn them into addicts. The young women I speak to all claim to love their pimp and say they would do anything for them.

"Every teen I see is either heroin-addicted or has mental and emotional problems. It is a difficult population to work with and unfortunately there are not many successful outcomes. When successes occur, I grab on and celebrate. Of the 1000 children we serve, fewer than 50 percent succeed. Yet, there are good reasons these adolescents are on the streets. I respect their instincts. For many, it's a matter of surviving a violent home life.

"Very few kids come from healthy, vibrant families. Financial insecurity, violence, drugs and alcohol are the major causes for leaving home. Unfortunately, parents often start their own kids smoking or taking methamphetamines. Since they don't know how to problem-solve or save for bad times, they live from one week to the next. The future is so far from their thoughts that when they do have money it's gone in a flash."

"Street kids don't understand that actions have consequences. For instance, one girl I worked with didn't transfer the title of an automobile she purchased from her sister, and later was tied to a felony that had been committed by her sibling. When mistakenly taken to jail, it reinforced the notion for her that the world was out to fuck her, rather than understanding the role that her own actions played.

"When a teen drops out of school it's downhill from there," Kevin said. "As runaways get a taste of homelessness, sometimes they actually start to enjoy it. Why would they want to go to school when life on the street is an adventure? They quickly learn how to get three meals a day and shelter without having to do homework or listen to boring lectures. Even violence is fascinating, exciting and addictive—better than watching TV.

"I spoke to one young prostitute who told me that she had moved in to live with an emergency-room doctor. You can read in *The Oregonian* about a former mayor caught kissing a boy in a bathroom in City Hall, or of writer at a local newspaper who had a heart attack in bed with a prostitute. Politicians and businessmen turn prostitution into quite an interesting job, sometimes enjoyed by poor young women. In most cases the girls have never been treated as well as they are when taken out by a man with money. Fancy clothes and good food are otherwise hard to come by. Situations involving well-heeled men are, of course, hushed up," he added.

"Weapons, money and drugs are the lessons of the street. When no one is at home to set boundaries and limits, friends become the biggest influence. Lamentably, these acquaintances do not usually have the teen's best interest in mind. It's a parent's job to take responsibility for their children and keep them from hanging out with whomever they want," Kevin said. "Once on the street, it is not likely you'll be introduced to a better heeled set of friends. Dropouts feel uncomfortable with college and vocational bound teens, preferring to be with those who have similar, more familiar experiences."

Zach is a good example to use when explaining the difficulty poor kids have in transitioning to a middle-class lifestyle. In the early years of boarding with Cory and me, he often talked about his initial discomfort and the many months it took for him to adjust. He still says that there is a disconnect between his past and present circumstances, though he quickly got used to living in relative luxury. The manners and language of everyday parlance are different in wealthier neighborhoods. There is a lot more cursing among the laborers he works with, many of whom share his background. Zach has become somewhat bi-lingual in his use of the English language.

Kevin continued, "Kids want to belong to a group, whether street family or gang, that shares the same values. Think back to your high school days where there were different cliques for the jocks, geeks and sorority girls and you'll understand that need to be with others who are similar.

"Our goal at Janus is to break through negative scenarios and help youth understand the consequences of their actions. It's a difficult task because our services must focus on immediate crises more than long-term mindset rebuilding. I don't know of any organization teaching kids about responsibilities and consequences. The foster care system is broken with horrendous stories coming to light about negative situations.

"In general, kids really want a connection back to their biological family. I believe we need to strengthen those ties as much as possible and teach parents how to interact with their children more appropriately. By the time these adolescents are in their thirties they warm up to the idea of family. Everyone wants to go to their childhood home at Christmas. But the seeds have to be sown while young."

Kevin and I spent quite a bit of time brainstorming about what could be done to improve youth homelessness. He mentioned Friends of the Children founded by Duncan Campbell, a non-profit organization engaged in preventive work which pays counselors to intervene at an early age and ask them to stay involved with their clients through high school. Staff performs the services of an attentive parent, checking on homework, school attendance, and emotional well-being.

<hr/>

Friends of the Children works to change the way the world views vulnerable children by providing them with a sustained relationship with a professional mentor.[59] A "Friend" is assigned to each child, starting in kindergarten, who guides them through school until graduation. Friends spend an average of 16 hours per month with the child, engaging him or her in both academic and enrichment activities. According to their website found at www. friendspdx.org, mentors work "to build basic life skills, self-confidence, academic success and resiliency." They operate a series of camps, offer outdoor expeditions, and provide teens with spaces for relaxation, a computer lab and study clubs.

One person can make a difference. Its founder, Duncan Campbell, was raised in poverty in a dysfunctional family. When he achieved success as a businessman he decided to help other children avoid the type of stress he lived through when young. The research he conducted as an adult led him to conclude that a close, sustained relationship with a caring adult who brings positive expectations was the most important factor in developing a healthy productive child. *Friends of the Children* was established in Portland in 1993 and has since spread to Boston, New York, Seattle, Klamath Falls, Tampa Bay and Cornwall (UK). Consistent intervention aimed at skill development and perspective helps children change the story of their life.

Another program Kevin has high regard for is CASA, or Court Appointed Special Advocates for Children.[60] This is a national association that works with state and local members to support and promote advocacy for abused children and those in conflict with the law. They gather information that is then passed on to inform judges. The biggest difficulty CASA volunteers have is that their service to each child is of limited duration, usually about one-and-a-half years. Kevin believes that "long-term intervention is needed in order to be effective. It may take four to five years to overcome a lifetime of neglect."

CASA is a national program started in 1977 by a Seattle juvenile court judge who had concerns about the decisions he was making about children's lives based on insufficient information. His pilot program grew to encompass more than 946 community groups across the nation, promoting volunteer advocacy for abused and neglected children. CASA trains volunteers, offering technical assistance and quality assurance. It recruits and works to make the public aware of its advocacy. It has one of the best volunteer training programs and supervision arrangements of any group I studied. After thirty hours of training, volunteers are assigned a client and work under the direction of a supervisor. Ongoing training is given on a monthly basis. Volunteers often form a tight social network around their supervisor. There is a need for more volunteers to step forward, particularly in rural areas, and for more men to get involve. CASA helps judges and care workers determine the best permanent home for a youth under age 18 brought before the courts. To do so, they interview everyone who is in contact with the child including parents, relatives, foster parents, teachers, medical professionals, attorneys, social workers and neighbors in the community. Then they write a thorough report with recommendations that go to the judge. CASA volunteers are occasionally assigned one or more children from the same household. If a child is assigned to temporary or permanent housing, CASA follows up to make sure that the situation is working out. If there are issues at school, the volunteer might advocate on the child's behalf. In the Portland area there are approximately 4,000 children who could benefit from a CASA volunteer. Due to funding limitations, only one-third of them are served.

For more information, see CASA's website, casaforchildren.org, which includes heartfelt testimonials telling of the great good they do.

Kevin mentioned a TV program he had watched that discussed the astronomical costs of foster care. He agreed with the newscaster's comments about foster care being a broken system and that many foster care placements are worse for the children than keeping them in their homes. Kevin' s solution? "Instead of foster care, give money to the family along with direct financial supervision from an advocate who will teach them how to manage. Let's provide adults with incentives and while doing so, teach them parenting skills. The cycle of drugs and poverty will just continue to operate as it presently does if we do not intervene in a different way."

With a long sigh, Kevin continued, "HUD (the U.S. Department of Housing and Urban Development) is a major source of funding for youth services, but most of the money goes for housing, not support services like counseling. All too often, a newly housed youth will invite their street buddies to their apartment, allowing them to sleep on the couch or floor. The evening turns into a late night party complete with alcohol, drugs and loud music. As the noise increases it annoys neighbors, who complain to the landlord. It doesn't take long before the newly housed youth is evicted. Street adolescents need coaching in behavioral mores that will help them succeed in a middle-class environment. Basic knowledge of how to shop, cook, clean and stay safe is foreign to the way they have been brought up. They need to learn manners, life and job skills, and embrace basic principles of society."

Kevin's comments remind me that street teens want access

to excitement just as do most kids living in comfortable homes. They look for activities that provide an adrenaline rush. Wealthier youths are sent on excursions such as Outward Bound, wilderness hiking, skiing and rock climbing. They participate in team sports that test their fortitude and get to travel to distant locations for games. In tribal societies, rites of passage were a test of adulthood that welcomed youth as members. Some Native American tribes sent teens on quests to get a vision of a future guardian spirit while surviving in the wilderness with skills they learned as children. College fraternities and sororities still give daring challenges to initiates before they are accepted as members. Not all of them are commendable. I remember one sorority that required pledges to steal a meat item from a local supermarket. Gangs similarly require initiates to get involved in a criminal activity in order to gain control over their new member. If the youth wants to leave, for instance, the gang leader can threaten to go to the police and turn him in.

Homeless teens need alternative ways of increasing adrenaline than trolling the streets and getting into trouble. Participation in legal physical and mental challenges can help break through antisocial barriers. Challenges that test endurance, provide focus and require problem-solving can help youth improve self-esteem, develop a sense of belonging and establish better relationships with adults.

Joining the military used to be an acceptable option for poor children, providing adventure, occasional adrenaline spikes and instilling discipline. Surviving basic training is a rite-of-passage of sorts. "Join the Navy and see the world," the slogan goes. There was a time when teens could enter the military without a high school degree. Not today, making that route unavailable for most homeless youth.

Zach chose a different path to excitement, finding a profession that provides a rush from painting on high bridges and hanging off the side of water towers — the higher the better. I think it is time to develop rites for all teens — ones that fit into the needs of contemporary society. Mandatory national service at the age of eighteen might be a way for youths to be challenged, to learn work ethics, and to practice being responsibility to others. Some might select military service and others community work. There are wonderful models that have been developed by organizations such as the Youth Conservation Corps, AmeriCorps, and the Peace Corps.

CENTER OF THE CYCLONE - KATHY OLIVER OUTSIDE IN

The first agency that took Zach in was Outside In so that is where I began my investigations. Kathy Oliver, the director, is a strong believer in social justice. Her reputation as an aggressive, yet strategic leader, is well known throughout the community. Her compassion, determination, yet practical optimism comes through when she talks. She told her story in her matter-of-fact style.

"I was born in a small town outside of Seattle into a family holding strong fundamentalist Christian beliefs. In some ways I grew up outside mainstream culture, as not only were movies forbidden, we were not allowed to have a TV. However, as a result, I read voraciously–every book in the town's small library, fiction and nonfiction.

"In my family, the man was the head of the household and women were expected to be subservient. I had four siblings, two sisters and two brothers. Education was not valued for girls and careers not expected. When I told my parents I wanted to go to the university and study philosophy, the answer was no."

"But eventually I married a young engineer and we moved to Oregon. I applied to the managerial training program of a large retail store but was told I wouldn't be accepted as I was female, married and of childbearing age. They offered me a job in the mailroom instead.

"I did work in that mailroom, but I was still determined to get a college education. I started attending Portland State University and continued on in school until I finally graduated with a Ph.D.

in Urban and Public Affairs. My family declined to show up at my graduation. But while I may have lacked their support, all along the way there were people who believed in me: the librarian in my home town who let me know when a new book arrived, various teachers who encouraged and supported me, and others. I realized the importance of these mentors in my ability to believe in myself and achieve success.

"I became passionate about issues of social justice: gender, race, poverty and animal rights. There was so much that was dire in the world and seemingly so little I could do about it. I decided to start with the injustice around me. I became the first director of the Portland Women's Crisis Hotline where I stayed for seven years, helping women who were survivors of rape, incest and abuse and helping educate my community."

"I also came out as a lesbian, left my husband and moved in with a woman. I remained friends with my former husband (and credit him for our continued relationship) and we have had lunch weekly for the past thirty years."

"In the 1980's I accepted the position of development officer for *Outside In*. The organization was in a bit of disarray and lacked leadership. To fill this void, a few years later I was asked and accepted the position of executive director, and today I manage a $12 million budget," Kathy told me proudly. By the date of my interview she had been running the organization for over thirty years.

"One reason I chose to work at Outside In and one of the reasons I stayed is that in the 1980's it was one of the few places in Oregon one could be 'out' at work as a lesbian. That was important to me.

"I quickly noticed that a high percentage of the young homeless people we saw identified as 'queer' and that this was a major reason they were rejected by their families. We started support groups for LGBTQ homeless youth in the 1980s, which, at the time, was very controversial, and we also started the first Resource Center for transgender people in Oregon.

"While I saw the importance of providing basic needs for homeless youth, I was most interested in starting programs that helped end homelessness — housing, health care, a school, an employment program and treatment programs ,along with caring adults who would believe in them. I wanted every homeless youth who wanted to go to college to be able to do so. We now help forty-eighty homeless youth each year enter college.

"I was interested in providing innovative services and programs that weren't necessarily what society said our clients needed but what our clients said they needed and wanted. These included a syringe exchange, Project Erase (a tattoo removal program that removed hate-based and gang-related symbols) and the Virginia Woof Dog Daycare/Job Training Program.

"Syringe exchange was particularly controversial when I opened it in 1989. It was the first publicly funded program of its kind in Oregon and the third syringe exchange program in the nation. It provides many benefits, including protection against HIV and Hep C, a bridge to treatment, and removal of 1 million syringes per year which otherwise might end up in public spaces. But it also gives drug injectors a clear and important message — '"we think your life is worth saving."

Thirty years is a long time to be dealing with troubled youth and I wondered about burnout. She responded in her clipped direct style, "I stay working because of the strong belief that I can make a difference."

Kathy sat comfortably in her desk chair in her small office piled with papers while her companion dog lay silently by her feet. Zed (Z the Executive Dog) is the third border collie she has brought to work over the years. *Outside In* is a dog-friendly workplace and as many as eight dogs can be seen at the agency at any one time. Kathy understands that homeless youths often travel with dogs and, rather than banning them, she accommodates them. Roomy, covered dog kennels are available in the courtyard so clients can park their dogs while getting services. It is the one place she named after herself — the Kathy Oliver Dog Waiting Area.

Kathy was quite willing to discuss her agency but not comfortable when the focus turned to herself. She certainly was not a publicity hound, though she has a reputation for not letting people step on her toes. Very early in her career, Kathy noticed that youths of diverse sexual orientations had problems fitting into society and had few resources to help them succeed. From then on, the LGBTQ community became a focus of operations. She became politically active and in 1992 organized neighbors and businesses to take a stand against Measure 9, an anti-gay rights, pedophilia, sadism, masochism and public education bill that drew national attention to the state ballot. Kathy wrapped their entire block with yellow ribbon, declaring it a hate-free zone. Outside In was successful in overcoming the conservative Oregon Citizens Alliance. When the measure failed, the gay rights movement in Oregon was born.[61] In 2015, Oregon was rated the second friendliest state in the country by the Movement Advancement Project due to landmark legislation ensuring LGBTQ rights.

***

Outside In's vision has expanded greatly since its inception.[62] It is a remarkable, diverse and effective organization that now serves adults as well as youths with healthcare needs. The breadth and scope of the operation is a monument to Kathy who fulfilled many of her initial goals.

Founded in 1968, Outside In is a nonprofit organization that provides housing and counseling for homeless youth between the ages of 17 and 24, and medical services for all in need of care. "Our mission is to help homeless youth and other marginalized people move towards improved health and self-sufficiency," according to its website, www.outsidein.org.

It started in the basement of the First Unitarian Church, an ally in the fight for social justice. At its inception, it was a coffee house and an evening health clinic, one of the first free clinics in the United States to provide health care for Portland's "alienated youth" population. It was not long before staff realized a great many clients coming through the door were teens with a variety of longer-term problems including mental health issues and substance abuse problems. A large proportion were gay and lesbian adolescents having been pushed out of their childhood homes by conservative parents. In the late 60s gay youths between the ages of 14 and 25 were still a hidden population to most agencies. Outside In recognized that the number of homeless adolescents entering the clinic was growing and expanded its focus to include job training, drug and alcohol treatment and housing.

Teens run away for a variety of reasons—poverty, abuse, an unsafe environment, drug addiction, sexual orientation, gang membership, mental health or criminal activity leading to expulsion from school. Moving to the streets is often a survival tactic for abused kids. Outside In staff receive specialized training in order to serve these traumatized youths.

Kathy manages a creative, expansive operation that receives funding from both private and government sources. About 146 employees bustle around several buildings providing services. The largest part of their operation is a federally qualified medical center engaged in allopathic medicine, alternative medical approaches, dentistry, and primary care. Referrals come from the police and other area agencies for drug and alcohol treatment that for some is offered in-house, while for others by sister agencies. Zach was referred to a sister program for treatment for drug addiction.

The mental health facility engages in innovative therapies that serve nearly 4,000 youths annually. Services for gays and lesbians began in 1980, propelling Outside In into the forefront of national leadership in providing for the entire range of LGBTQ youths. In 1998, the organization became one of the nation's first to offer needle exchanges (approximately 800,000 a year).

While browsing the lobby bulletin board I saw announcements for alcoholics and heroin-addicted anonymous treatment groups, gatherings for a trans-women support group, and invitations to

117

domestic abuse meetings. There were opportunities for tattoo removal (over 3,000 removed each year), healthy relationship classes and information about contraceptives. Notices of shelters for single women, cancer screenings, and services for veterans were posted alongside recreational opportunities offering yoga classes and participation in a street soccer team. Removing tattoos is especially important for those seeking jobs. If you have gang colors, hate symbols or maybe a name visibly tattooed, it can be life-changing to remove them.

Outside In has 100 housing units for transitional and permanent supported housing for up to two years. The lucky few to qualify start out in supervised, five-person dorm rooms, but as they progress they graduate to private studio apartments. For those with children, one-bedroom suites are available along with pregnancy and parenting programs.

An additional 720 youths are served in day programs. Case workers identify and offer intensive counseling to those who come for help, serving approximately 300 annually. They guide their clients toward returning to school to obtain a high school diploma, permanent housing and employment.

"Involvement in sports and wholesome activities aid the recovery process," Kathy continued. "Meditation, mindfulness and yoga can seem insignificant, but I've seen them help youths make changes. We offer Street Yoga and Living Yoga, and those who are drug-affected quickly realize during class that they can't hold a tree pose.

"Adequate housing lies at the core for getting kids off the streets. Youth who are invited to join our housing program are well screened and have to demonstrate that they are serious about changing their life. They agree to our requirement of spending a minimum of thirty hours a week in some type of fruitful pursuit like working toward their GED or getting job skills.

The housing program boasts a 90 percent success rate. I was mesmerized by the passion in Kathy's voice as she continued.

"We partner with Portland Public Schools to operate an urban education program focused on both academic learning and employment and serving another 300 homeless teens. Our ultimate goal is to get students to enroll in community colleges where they can continue their education and develop friendships with other kids who are not living on the streets. There are vocational and professional tracks to choose from. Quite a few go on to study at Portland State University, just down the street, where they are encouraged to participate in a social activity. Everything we do is aimed at keeping them from sliding back. We have quite a bit of success. A few students even go on to obtain doctorate degrees. Two of them are even serving on our board of directors," Kathy said with pride.

"Almost all of the young people we come in contact with arrive with limited or no job skills. To give them a chance at getting experience we started several commercial businesses. Have you heard of Virginia Woof?" she asked me. "It is a doggie daycare center, completely run by homeless youth, grossing over $400,000 a year. It also provides a paid, on-the-job training for 20-25 homeless youth per year. Though they hire professional staff they also promote youths from the job training program into regular permanent positions."

Kathy's entrepreneurial streak is strong so she was not ready to stop at one successful venture.

"We started a summer bicycle business called Bespoke Smoothies. We hire kids to use their pedal power to ride around the neighborhoods and make smoothies in electric blenders attached to their bicycles. By being employed they learn work habits and what it means to be an entrepreneur. They have to keep records of their sales and make sure they have the right ingredients with them before they go out each day."

When I asked Kathy what her next dream was for the agency, she responded, "Short-term I would like to be able to serve 1,000 youth each night. The need is so great. Long-term I would like to help end youth homelessness."

———

Each agency I studied has a slightly different clientele. What type of teen does Outside In serve? I learned that 30 percent of those evicted from their homes are from the LGBTQ community. Over 86 percent come from families that live below the poverty line with most others near poverty. Males outnumber females 2 to 1. Approximately 63 percent of the population is Caucasian.

Thankfully, there are thousands of compassionate people working, not only in Portland, but in every city in the country to help homeless youths. I am continuously impressed with the care and commitment given to making life better for these distressed adolescents. People like Kathy and the volunteers who help *Outside In* make me feel hopeful. By working together to deliver consistent ongoing care and by applying resources strategically, they prove that it is possible to make a difference.

———

"It would be great if there was a simple easy solution that worked for everyone. But when children receive poor or no parenting, are abused and perhaps simply thrown away, it's difficult to effectively turn that around. Jobs, education and housing are core." Kathy left with these words spinning round in my head. After 38 years at the helm, Kathy retired in 2018. She left knowing she made an impact on the lives of homeless youth and others at the margins.

Dynamo for Change - Sean Suib
New Avenues for Youth

"Our foster system is broken," said Sean Suib, director of New Avenues for Youth, an organization dedicated to the prevention and intervention of youth homelessness. "The only way we're going to fix it is to get it out of the hands of the government. There are smart people in the system but they can't change anything. The system, like the children they serve, is traumatized. There is not enough money to operate successfully, but that's only part of the problem. Because the system operates out of a place of crisis, it cannot think strategically or even beyond its most basic function — survival.

"Evidence of this can be seen in the many recent highly publicized examples of the system failing to act to keep children safe, despite clear information about danger. I don't want you to think the people running the system are bad. To the contrary, many are caring, hard working and well-intentioned. They just cannot get beyond their systemic crisis to prevent its perpetuation.

"To understand the intersection between foster care and homelessness, it is helpful to think about the Department of Human Services (DHS) as an impoverished single parent responsible for rearing 10 children at the same time. With too little money to meet every child's specialized needs, DHS can only focus on keeping the most vulnerable children as safe as possible. Older children are less vulnerable when compared to those who are younger with higher needs. By the time they get to be an adolescent, a system like DHS is not designed for, resourced for, or able to focus on or meet a teen's needs. As a result, a large percentage of the kids who leave the foster care system at the age of 18 find themselves homeless within three years. The private sector needs to take over."

I was sitting across the table speaking to this tall man whose every pore seemed energized as a change agent. As director of New Avenues for Youth, he moves purposefully among the many challenges he has to confront each day. Though busy overseeing the center's diverse programs, he had invited me into his small office and graced me with his rapt attention as though I were the only thing in the world that mattered. In my effort to understand the basis of youth homelessness, I had not considered the foster care system and wondered what should be done. Sean shared his thoughts.

"There are critical intervention points that have to be addressed before transitioning a child out of state supervision. Children need social capital, people not paid to be in their lives, who can be called at 2 in the morning if needed. They need to learn life skills, accountability and be given leadership opportunities and ways to connect with their community to practice the skills of being an adult. Programs like ours try to sprinkle as many of these proactive experiences into the young person's life as possible."

I quickly discovered that New Avenues was quite innovative in its approaches and that its work with youth had come a long way from the juvenile detention policies practiced in the past by social service agencies in conjunction with the judicial system.

"We're beginning to understand the unique circumstances that face foster children," he continued with intensity, making sure that I followed his words. "Many of them have spent years being shuffled from one home to another, often falling through the cracks educationally and emotionally. We already are making a difference with an array of programs and targeted interventions. One of the interventions we're most excited about is a partnership with a nonprofit called Bridge Meadows."[63]

With a bit of digging I discovered that Bridge Meadows is a multi-generation housing community where low-income seniors live in community with families that have adopted young foster children.[64] In this model, the entire community works together to help heal and raise these kids. The impact the community is having on the lives of both children and seniors is impressive. Statistics for Bridge Meadows who 100 percent of youths attend school regularly with 85 percent doing better academically; 97 percent of residents have maintained stable housing; and 90 percent of the adoptive parents have accessed the available supportive services; and 85 percent of the elders report that they have found greater purpose through interaction with children, parents and other elders. It appears to be a win-win situation.

"Building on the strength of Bridge Meadows' model, our

organizations recently combined resources to build a second housing facility (a 15-unit apartment complex) dedicated to teens aging out of foster care. Named New Meadows, when complete, the facility will sit on land adjacent to the Bridge Meadows campus and leverage relationships and social capital to foster youths as they move into adulthood. New Avenues will wrap a comprehensive program around housing residents by providing mental health counseling, case management, life skills classes, education and college support and job training."

As I listened to Sean talk I couldn't help but imagine that he could have been a successful businessman, spending his working hours amassing a small fortune. He is engaging, has people and organizational skills, and is a strong spokesman for his cause. Sean knows how to work with teams of people in the community from low income to wealthy donors who make up his board. He also is a tradesman with years of construction experience. It would have been logical for him to run his own company, yet he chose to work with the disenfranchised. I wondered why Sean selected a nonprofit route. Why was he so ferociously passionate about what he was doing? With little prodding he shared his story.

"I grew up in a large mixed family with four full and three half-siblings. My biological parents were Russian Jews who met in the Bronx, married while in their teens and got divorced when I was only four. It was a bad split, with lots of fights. After they separated I became increasingly distant from my father, who was not financially supportive of me or my siblings. At first, I saw him on weekends, but after the age of 16, we did not get together again for twenty years. We eventually did reconnect but our relationship remains cool. Over the years my father was involved in a variety of businesses that ranged from insurance adjuster to newspaper writer."

"After their divorce, Mom was left to care for four kids. She did not have a job or education but had enough drive to return to school in an effort to keep the lights on. She had little time for us so we kids had to learn to fend for ourselves at an early age. Seeking security she remarried. Her new husband was a good man but wrestled with demons like violence and alcoholism. My home was very tumultuous, things being thrown, yelling, some physical abuse. It was not a happy, healthy home, not something I wanted to return to after school, so I roamed the streets and connected with other marginalized or alienated kids.

"My stepfather was a full-time fireman who supplemented his income by working in the trades. He knew carpentry, plumbing and wiring—skills that were passed on to me. There were times when I accompanied him to the firehouse. The men were all intoxicated in those days. During the 6190s and '70s, Coke machines were even set up as dispensers for beer. Drinking was part of the fireman culture, and it was not unusual for firemen to drink on duty. The South Bronx had a reputation as a borough that was always burning, so there was lots to do. My ste-p dad's station was very busy, and in the relaxed environment of the times, I was allowed to go on calls—an exciting adventure for a young boy. I thought it was spectacular, though it was extremely loud. I did sleep at the firehouse a few times. I was likely ten at the time.

"Most of my childhood was troublesome. I was a delinquent, always one step away from trouble and, at times, just skirting danger leading to jail. I remember experimenting with fire and just being fascinated by the potential for destruction. In one incident, I nearly lit my school on fire. I still don't really understand how that blaze did not go up. But it did scare the heck out of me, and I think I realized even as young as I was, that I had dodged a bullet that could have changed my and other lives forever. This may have been where I first began thinking about the concept of trajectory and the realization that many people find themselves on a path. Whether going in a good or bad direction, the powerful thing is, it doesn't take all that much to change that trajectory. It really is a hopeful way to view the world." Sean paused a moment as he reflected on what he said.

"Since my parents were not home, I was left on my own and easily slipped into bad activities like drug use and at times selling. By the time I reached high school ,I was a person to go to for anything and everything that was popular in those days."

"But drugs were not in my blood. While I did dabble, I was primarily interested in making money, and to that end, I held every kind of job you could imagine. I carried groceries, worked at a fast-food chain, an amusement park and on construction sites. I caterered, sold carpet cleaning services and office paintings. At one point I even worked in a rat lab, handling rats that were being used for experiments. Since home life was disruptive, working was another way to be away from Dodge City. Regarding school, I can't say I had much success in my early years. I was pretty withdrawn, had a low opinion of my ability and since there was no parent at home, I never received reinforcement of any kind for developing study skills. I went through most of my childhood believing I was not very smart or capable.

"In tenth grade, two events coincided to save my life. The first was a class I took in biology. Up until then, I was a failing student. For some reason, I became completely enthralled by biology. I had always liked critters and was often seen in childhood photos carrying a net or a jar filled with bugs or frogs. To this day I still remember the pages in a textbook that I practically memorized. Not only did I pass the tests, for the first time ever, I actually was excelling in something. I even scored 95 on the New York State Regents test."

"Was the biology teacher special in some way?" I probed.

"No, it wasn't the teacher that enticed me but rather the subject matter. There was a person who did have an influence, though, and that was Miss O'Connell, my English teacher. Along with my siblings, I had a bad reputation as a trouble-maker but somehow she saw something in me. She acknowledged me. Until then I had always been invisible, probably doing as many disruptive activities as I did in order to get attention. But Miss O'Connell spoke to me outside the classroom, demonstrating that she cared. I became a real person. I transferred to her classroom, but even there I was a marginally successful student. It was just that I had been seen and that made all the difference to my psyche.

"By eleventh grade, I was getting As and considering college as a way out of the neighborhood. After attending several state colleges, changing majors as I went, I graduated magna cum laude with a degree in psychology. My psych professor impacted the way I studied. He told me that his class was tough, and if I wanted to pass, I would have to learn the material so that I could visualize each page to see where the questions came from. I used this technique to get through school and still practice it today."

"How did you get interested in social work? I asked.

"In my last year of college, I filled in my curriculum with a few credits in social work and interned with kids in foster care. The experience crystallized the concept of trajectory for me. I could see directly that for many of these vulnerable kids, small things could have a huge impact on their lives. However, I did not think about graduate school at that time. I needed to get a job.

"Getting through college was a financial burden. I had to supplement my college stipends by working. Sometimes I was employed as a dorm monitor, while other times I worked in the trades. When I finally graduated I learned quickly that it was tough getting a job with a bachelor's degree in psychology so I continued to work in construction. My job was in eastern New York, in the 80s, in an area where the crack epidemic had taken over the neighborhood.

"On my way to work I would step on empty crack vials and other discarded drug paraphernalia thrown on the streets. It was a dangerous district of dilapidated brownstones. I saw African-American families with matriarchs who worked long hours to hold their families together only to be rewarded by watching their children become diseased by addiction. It was depressing and seemed hopeless. Families put bars on their windows and doors because no home was sacred.

"My truck kept getting broken into and my tools were stolen. When I arrived at work I needed to make several trips to bring them inside. By the time I returned to retrieve more supplies they were gone. Ultimately I said to myself, "surely there has to be something better." So I saved my pay for a month and picked up and left. Traveling with my dog I saw the country, starting with Washington, D.C. where once more my truck was vandalized.

126

This time all of my possessions were taken. D.C. still leaves a bad taste in my mouth."

"I traveled on, working at temporary jobs from time to time. When all of the money I had was gone there was no place to go but back home, a depressing thought. As I approached the city I knew that I couldn't stay there. I said once more to myself, 'No way. I can't go back.'"After three months of saving, I left. By then I had a girlfriend who was on an archeological dig in Nevada who invited me to visit. When her program ended, the two of us took off for the West Coast.

"By the time we arrived in Portland we were broke ,but determined to stay. Because of my experience in the trades, I immediately got a job working for a small company even though I did not have a plumber's license. It is funny looking back for I had to go into hiding every time inspectors came on site. My girlfriend got a job in a fair-trade retail shop.

"For months we lived in the back of my truck. While some might have seen it as homelessness, I don't relate to it that way. While we didn't have a lot of money, we did have friends and skills and I could always have picked up and gone back to New York. It did give me a taste though of what it is like to have to scrape to get by. After a while, the pumping company began putting pressure on me to join the four-year apprenticeship program and become licensed. But the more I thought about it ,the more I wanted to get a job working with adolescents. At the time Janus Youth Programs was hiring so I accepted work there. It took only one night of working at Streetlight, their homeless street shelter, beforeI knew that this was what I was going to do for the rest of my life. I was struck by the kids I met and their resiliency. Over the course of several years, I worked in a variety of capacities at Janus, yet I was more ambitious. I wanted to take on a bigger role and was attracted to Outside In because they were really innovative and cutting edge.

"Getting hired by Outside In was harder than I thought it would be. Though I had applied many times, I kept getting rejected. Persistence paid off. Finally, with the help of a friend who worked there, I was offered a job. It was and remains a great place to work with innovative practices and committed staff. I learned quickly, though, that it too had its own internal politics."

As Sean spoke, he appeared relaxed with his past and quite candid in his remarks. One of the insights from his childhood particularly interested me. He tells staff that you never know what person or event will provide that critical impetus for change. You can believe you're not making a difference and then discover years later that something you said buried itself deep in an adolescent's mind. Many young adults return to thank us years after receiving our services.

I was curious to know about the origins of New Avenues for Youth. "We originally were an outgrowth of the Salvation Army. Several businessmen and women who served on their board, under the leadership of Joyce Furman, wanted to put more resources in the Army's youth services program. They were willing to raise funds to do so but were turned down by the national organization. Deciding that youth homelessness was a growing need, they split from the Army in 1996 and started New Avenues for Youth," Sean said.

"When the idea of opening a new agency in Portland first surfaced, existing service providers were not very happy. The New Avenues founding board espoused a new philosophy of 'outcome-based' services. During the planning phase the founders went around the country and studied various successful homeless youth agencies. They focused on a program in San Francisco called Larkin Street (which is still around today), and modeled New Avenues after it. The model was not rocket science, but it did have some discerning elements. For example, key aspects of its success with youths included creating a continuum of services that met basic needs for engaged youth while also focusing on skills and steps away from street life.

"Larkin taught us about the value message communicated by the condition of the spaces you make available for youths. Hence, if you create nice, well-kept spaces, youths will feel respected and honored and are more likely to live up to high expectations. We copied their hiring practices which centered on master's level and highly qualified staff, and importantly, we adopted a core belief in outcome-based services and accountability. New Avenues programs were built around tracking service delivery, evaluating impact and making changes based on data. We practiced modern day QA (quality assurance), which did not really exist in the nonprofit culture at the time.

"While I admired what Outside In was doing, I felt like New Avenue's approach might have an even greater impact on kids. I started working there one month before their doors opened as one of a staff of just three. I've been here for the past eighteen years, having served in every capacity imaginable. I've been running operations here for the better part of 16 years, first as the associate director and for the past 4five years as the executive director."

<hr/>

According to Sean, New Avenues played an important role in the establishment of the Multnomah County's homeless youth system. As the newest provider in town, New Avenues was a vocal advocate for improvement in the community's response to youth homelessness. Through this drive, the New Avenues Board reached out to the Citizen's Crime Commission, an influential community interest group that took on local livability issues. The commission became interested in the effectiveness of the county's public investment (about $800,000 which was spent to address youth homelessness). They funded a report that turned the community on its head. The findings revealed that though there were many effective services, there was little cross-agency coordination, no shared outcomes, and sparse communication between the various entities working with homeless youths. With that report the Multnomah County Homeless Youth System was born when the four agencies came together to approach the board of commissioners to request and receive additional funding to create a system for homeless youths. The four agencies at the time included Janus, the Salvation Army, Outside In and New Avenues for Youth. After several years the

Salvation Army dropped out and the Native American Youth and Family Center (NAYA) took its place.

⊶∘∘∘∘∘∘∘∘∘∘⊷

"We all have slightly different roles and different but supportive approaches," Sean explained. "Janus Youth Programs is one of the largest nonprofits in the Pacific Northwest. It is a huge national organization with youth services as one part. They work through partnerships and collaboration with a great many agencies. Most of their funding comes from public grants and that has an impact on their approach and culture.

"NAYA serves a variety of family needs for Native and other minority populations, including education, housing, elder services and homeownership. Their program devoted to homeless youths embraces about 90 kids, most of whom are from communities of color. Outside In and New Avenues have the most in common with similar-sized youth programs. Outside In has a very robust community health services operation that is focused on low-income adults and youths. They receive significant public funds as a federally qualified health center.

"New Avenues strives for a balance of public, foundation and private revenue. Too much public money can be very restrictive, inflexible and often dictates the quality or approach to services. Hence New Avenues puts a lot of organizational resources into mobilizing community support and utilizing flexible funding to push outcomes and innovate."

"Do you have hope that we can come to grips with this expanding homeless youth crisis?" I asked.

A smile crossed Sean's face as he responded, "I was just on the phone with a past client who is getting ready to take the bar exam," he said. "I remember when he first arrived, addicted to heroin and close to death's door. Do I have hope you ask? Absolutely. My day is filled with possibilities. We're learning all the time how to do a better job. Hope comes from providing a positive experience. The

130

more of them that are sprinkled into a child's life the more likely he or she is to survive.

"Some youths come to us bearing psychological and, at times, physical scars, while for others the manifestations of abuse and neglect are less apparent. Each young person is unique and their path different. Counselors try to grasp what factors will lead to a positive trajectory. The youth's life experiences influence how we work with them. We start with their strengths."

"We know that to succeed as adults, children need to feel validated. One individual who takes the time to 'see' a child and relate in a meaningful way can spark change. Often children who act out destructively are just looking to be noticed. They want someone to say *you exist* and that you are inherently good and capable.

"Kids crave a safe environment with boundaries. Without one, children often react opposite to what you might expect. They wind up pushing people away by how they act or dress, make racist comments and engage in aggressive movements. These are all defensive safety measures to keep people from hurting them again. On a good day, we can be a neutral, safe place for young people to learn new ways of being in a relationship with adults. Despite their efforts to push us away, we remain constant and non judging and our door never closes on them. This is how young people heal.

"The most important variable in our success is the staff we hire. As the front line, are everyday heroes. They all work incredibly hard, and they give their time, energy and soul every day. Though we try to take care of them, our society does not value their work the way it should. The secondary trauma our direct services folks endure is tragic, yet they show up and they serve as anchors for these kids in what can be terrible storms. I continue to work on and struggle with how to better support and care for these folks."

Sean ended by summarizing these difficult issues. "Eradicating youth homelessness is an incredibly complicated endeavor. It involves addressing male white privilege and institutional oppression and racism. It means unwinding hundreds of years of economic policies that enslave and impoverish masses, and it includes addressing education policy, criminal justice policy, drug policy, food access, and affordable housing access. We will not solve youth homelessness by pulling one kid at a time out of the river. That said, real youths are floating by and what we can do today, right now, is to change the direction that these young lives are flowing.

New Avenues for Youth operates a drop-in day service Center that offers meals six days a week, showers, clothing, laundry, computer access, and legal counseling. Pets are welcome and a monthly veterinary clinic is on board. Drug, alcohol and mental health counseling help youth develop healthy decision-making skills. Special attention is given to LGBTQ youth in the Sexual and Gender Minority Youth Resource Center.

The organization operates a fully accredited Alternative School that works with foster, at-risk and homeless youths. They are engaged in GED preparation, college prep and experiential learning.

A career-focused training program prepares youths for employment through job training and employment-related real-life opportunities. To do this they operate a variety of enterprises. Most recently they initiated New Avenues Through Soup, a street cart program that develops work skills such as teamwork, management of goods and inventory, customer service, finance and accounting and sales. The workers offer a variety of nutritious soups to hungry customers. They own two *Ben & Jerrys PartnerShop* franchises and a screen-printing business called New Avenues INK.

One of their more unusual offerings is an artist mentorship program that uses music and art to help build confidence and channel creativity. They give kids access to recording equipment, rehearsal space, music, art and computer lessons.

132

Sean is particularly interested in the foster care system and, after our discussion, I could understand why. Today more than 400,000 children and youth spend an average of 20.4 months in foster care.[65] 51 percent do reunify with their family and 22 percent (11,820 children and youths) are waiting to be adopted. They come from varying backgrounds that are similar to those taking to the streets. Some have been through trauma, abuse and/or neglect. All are in need of a safe, loving home.

Though there are many problems with the foster care system, I mention six here.[66]

1) Thousands of children are placed in group homes or institutions with meager support rather than with caring families.

2) Teens who age out of the system have inadequate support and approximately 30 percent contribute to the homeless population.

3) Foster parents need more support to achieve success. For example, many families cannot deal with kids who identify as LGBTQ.

4) There is not enough focus on reunification. Children from the same family often are separated, wondering if they will ever see their siblings again.

5) The child's needs often go unheard. Many foster parents are not good listeners, others are abusive, and without adequate communication back to the court, the foster care solution may be as bad as the original home.

6) The system has too many rules that slow down adoptions, reunification with parents, and placements with family members rather than through the courts.

AN ADVOCATE - KANOE EGLESTON
NATIVE AMERICAN YOUTH
AND FAMILY SERVICES

Born on the outskirts of Oahu, Hawaii, Kanoe Egleston grew up surrounded by the love and attention that all children deserve. "My father was employed by the Bishop Estate, a non-profit land trust donated by Bernice Pauahi Bishop, the great-granddaughter of King Kamehameha I, who united the Hawaiian Islands during the 18th century. Mom worked her way up as a customer service representative at the local telephone company," Kanoe said. "Dad loved his job, since it was a culturally responsible agency that gave him an opportunity to bring his values into their service delivery system."

His ethical beliefs played an important role in developing the young woman who sat across from me in NAYA's offices. Her flashing brown eyes sparkled when discussing the work she was doing. She leaned forward as she spoke, peering directly at me to capture my complete attention. The island Kanoe grew up on was replete with relatives who entertained and shared their heritage with the youngsters born into their extended family. There was always an aunt or uncle nearby to babysit or provide a different perspective than the one given by her parents. Kanoe's multiracial background—she says she is part Scottish, Puerto Rican, Chinese, German, Portuguese, Japanese and Hawaiian—helped her grasp the nuances of being a member of a population that deviated from the majority.

"My grandmother taught me a lot," Kanoe said. "Grandma met my grandfather during the second world war when he was stationed in Japan. They married and had two children who they brought to the island to raise. At the time Pearl Harbor was still on the minds of most people, and a Japanese wife was not welcome. Grandma Americanized her name, stopped speaking her native language and buried her background. As a result, her children grew up ignorant of part of their heritage.

134

"It wasn't until we grandchildren came along that she decided we were missing a great deal by not knowing where we came from. Grandma set her mind to teaching us to speak Japanese, learn some of the traditions and do crafts such as flower arranging. In college, I continued to study Japanese."

At the age of eighteen Kanoe decided to expand her horizons by attending college on the mainland. "Leaving home was traumatic, for until that time I lived a pretty charmed life attending private Montessori and Waldorf schools. Mornings were filled with academic subjects and afternoons were for the arts, music, and crafts. There were no grades but the staff gave total attention to developing each child's strengths. There were only seventeen kids in my graduating class."

Kanoe mentioned with nostalgia, "It wasn't until I went to the University of Oregon that I realized how different my upbringing was. It was not only that I had gone to a small private school, but my Hawaiian skin was darker than that of most students and it isolated me. Even the way I spoke English was different. Common words I used in conversation weren't understood by my classmates and vice versa. If it wasn't for the university's peer mentorship and diversity program I don't think I would have lasted."

What made you decide to work with disadvantaged youth?

"Being thrust as I had been, into a racial and cultural divide, made me interested in working with homeless teens. I decided to get my undergraduate degree in psychology and sociology. Part of the program included working with disadvantaged youth. It made me realize what happens when children do not grow up in a loving circle. I realized that my community was how I stayed alive and had hope. These kids felt hopeless. "

A few years later, Kanoe continued her education at Portland State University to pursue a Master's degree in Social Work. "When I graduated, I decided to work for NAYA in part because I could help children get reconnected to the community."

NAYA operates from a philosophy developed in the 1980's by Terry Cross and the National Indian Child Welfare Association (NICWA).[67] Known as the Relational Worldview Model Cross conceived a way of integrating Native thought processes with the concept of balance. Rather than just documenting disadvantaged children and providing a linear, European, cause-effect way of looking at problems, Cross suggested that life has harmonious relationships, a balance of context (culture, community), mind (cognitive and emotional processes) body (genetic, gender, condition, health) and spirit (learned teachings, metaphysical and innate, both negative and positive). When speaking of world view he includes the collective thought processes of the people or culture he is working with.

NICWA views the linear view as narrow for you don't see the whole person. The *worldview model,* on the other hand, is rooted in tribal cultures. It is intuitive and not oriented around time. Healers working with their clients look for balance in the four parts that affect the person's life. The concept is fluid, directed by the individual's interests and strengths. And it celebrates small steps that lead to successfully meeting goals. They see the quadrants as being in a constant state of change throughout each hour of the day and with every experience.

An example comes from NICWA writings.

"Death is an example of an event that threatens harmony. When we lose a loved one, we feel grief emotionally; physically, we may cry, lose our appetite, or not sleep well. However, spiritually, we have a learned positive response, a ritual, called a funeral. Usually, such events are community events, so the context is changed. We bring in relatives, friends and supporters. In that context, we intellectualize about the dead person. We may recall and tell stories about him or her. We may intellectualize about death or be reminded of our cultural view of that experience. Physically, we touch others, get hugs and handshakes; we eat, and we shed tears.

136

These experiences are interdependent and play off one another in multi-relational interactions that, if successful, allow us to resolve the grief by maintaining the balance. If we cannot, then, in a Western sense, we are said to have unresolved grief or, in some tribal cultures, to have a ghost sickness or to be bothered by a spirit. Different world views often use different conceptual language to describe the same phenomenon."

Once the event that caused an imbalance is understood, the helper's goal becomes one of assisting the individual to return to a state of balance. NAYA's services wrap around the various imbalances and problems that their clients face. Kanoe explained, "someone may come here for a particular reason, but they probably need other help as well. For instance, finding housing may be the immediate concern of the person walking through the door, but obtaining a GED, health services, a transportation voucher, or getting off of drugs may be equally important."

One of the most difficult problems Native Americans face is that of intergenerational trauma. It is embedded into the psyche of their youth. Kanoe explained the concept by asking me to put myself in the place of a young person growing up without roots.

"Imagine being from a Native American family and having your ancestral land and livelihood taken from you. You are moved from one location to another, eventually confined to a reservation with few opportunities for jobs. The new reservation was set aside to accommodate Native people from many tribes including those who were never friendly. Once they were settled, a decision was made by white authorities to remove children from their parents and put them into boarding schools where they were forbidden to speak their native language or practice familiar rituals. The overwhelming feeling of hopelessness that overtook most who lived on the reservation gave rise to alcoholism and truancy. Drugs and genetically poor tolerance for alcohol played havoc with what little self-esteem was left. Boredom, fighting and abusive relationships became a familiar way of life.

"Poor treatment by white America contributes to Native people having a high rate of suicide. Healthcare is minimal, and education continues to be below standard with large numbers of dropouts. Youths have little grounding in who they are and are confused. Feeling inferior, they don't know where they came from or where they are going. They lack pride, knowing that they belong to a conquered and downtrodden race. Yet even though the situation appears dire, there has been a lot of progress made in learning how to work with this population."

Kanoe explained what is being done to help youths overcome the handicaps and hurdles placed in their way. "We try to get kids reconnected to their culture. Belonging to a community is how I stayed alive as a child and as an adult it made me realize how important it is to provide communal grounding. Every Wednesday evening intergenerational families join together in a meal. Between fifty and seventy show up at any one time. After dinner, there is a host of options to connect youth to Native crafts and culture. There is a group involved in making moccasins and another weaving baskets. One group of teens made a canoe and now go on paddling trips in the Willamette and Columbia Rivers. A drumming circle is a very popular activity. It goes on for hours providing an opportunity for everyone to dance. It's a lot of fun.

"Peer mentorship is a big part of our program. Mentors pave the path to modeling a more successful lifestyle. Rather than just zoning out on drugs or booze, mentors introduce sober ways of having fun such as bowling or sports.

"Some of the people who walk through our doors are hungry." Kanoe said. "They can't think straight because they are filled with fear."

***

NAYA is a large organization with many arms.[68] I only focused on its activities targeting adolescents. Four counselors work with about ninety to one-hundred homeless youths who come from Native-American or black communities. A parent advocate was recently hired to work with those who arrive pregnant or are already a mother. Quite a few (15 percent) of the women they serve already have multiple children they struggle to support. Having not learned parenting skills from their own families they pass on poor habits to their offspring.

There aren't many youth programs in the community focused on homeless parenting. Most of the overnight facilities run by Janus Youth Programs ask clients to leave each day. They either go to NAYA, Janus's day shelter or to Outside In. Though Outside In and New Avenues have transitional and longer-term housing, they can only accommodate a small number of people each. The lucky few are highly motivated and willing to work towards what the agency considers to be a productive goal. Housing is one of the biggest issues all homeless people face. It tends to be the defining crisis that brings them into shelters in the first place.

Similar to the other organizations in Portland's youth network, NAYA pays attention to those between the ages of fourteen and twenty-five. When they get older they are transitioned into adult services. While under NAYA's tutelage, the main goal is to provide them with life skills in order to survive independently. The staff teaches youths how to cope and where to find help when needed. Babysitting is a big problem for young mothers. It is difficult to go to school or work when there is no transportation and you have to take care of a child.

NAYA's building, previously was a Portland Public Schoos facility. It is located in an industrial zone, distant from local neighborhoods. Those who come to the agency have to find a way to get there using public transportation. This is not always easy to do. Most come from the north and northeast sections of town. Many of the kids are afraid to go too he downtown shelters which are unfamiliar and seen as dangerous. They are

much more comfortable taking the No. 75 bus to the NAYA center rather than negotiating city streets.

"We also help the two-spirit kids," Kanoe told me.[69] "These youth identify sexually as being non-binary, of having no connection to one sex or another. We unite them with others so they can be part of a comfortable community.

"Native communities have a long history of admiring two-spirit people as special. They are held in high regard because of their spiritual gifts. Transgender nonbinary people are considered to be doubly blessed because they have both the spirit of a man and the spirit of a woman."

I was fascinated by her explanation that was so different from my upbringing. We continued on with the conversation turning toward gangs.

"Gang affiliation among Native-American youths is another area of increasing concern. Young kids from poor neighborhood are regularly trapped into joining a gang for their own survival. Once they join, many wish they had not and though they feel unsafe and want to get away, they don't know how. We've trained outreach workers who spend time on the streets and in parks speaking to gang members in 'change-talk' conversation.

"A lot of effort goes into preventing eleven to fifteen-year-olds from joining gangs in the first place. To do this, workers reach out to get help from the entire family. Parents want their kids to be safe and healthy and in general are not supportive of gangs. Mentorships, peer, and home relationships all come into play in trying to keep these kids safely in school. Without a high school degree, there is a 90 percent chance they will stay homeless for the rest of their lives."

Native American Homeless Youth Services (NAYA) is the fourth organization receiving funds from Multnomah County Homeless

Youth Services. Their approach is embedded in culturally appropriate services that involve the local Native community. They pull in resources from community mentors and a variety of other organizations to address their specialized needs.

As advocates for the homeless, NAYA takes in youths when they are in crises, helps them develop a plan, then feeds them into appropriate programs that are offered either within their organization or somewhere else in the community. They developed a great variety of programs to engage youths in a more sustainable way. Early College Academy provides a culturally relevant, hands-on, student-centered learning environment for ninth-through twelfth-graders. Classes are small and the curriculum integrates Native culture, family and community outreach, and partnerships with Portland Community College. Its goal is to get more Native-American youths to attend college or trade school. Counseling is provided for career exploration and help is given in order to obtain funds for scholarships. When I was president of the Oregon Museum of Science and Industry (OMSI) we worked with the Native American Engineering Club at Portland State University to provide a culturally relevant camp experience. Salmon Camp exemplifies of how community groups can join together to provide programs that address societal differences. The Confederated tribes of Warm Springs partnered with OMSI to bring Salmon Camp to their reservation. Participants learned about their Native culture as well as how salmon make their journey downstream to the ocean. Campers followed their trail by traveling the salmon route, counting numbers, tagging fish and observing behavior. They eventually wound up at the Pacific Ocean where they learned that fish live in the ocean for several years before returning to spawn. At the completion of summer camp, Native-American Engineering Club members continued working with the kids the following school year.

My partner comes from mixed Native-European origins. He is a totem pole and mask carver, a skill he acquired in his youth from his father. For many years he and I would don his masks and give story telling presentation about the origin of the "people.- We performed at schools, clubs galleries, and senior centers. Invariably a child or two in the audience with Native heritage would approach him shyly, often standing glued by his side with pride before the other children. It was one of the few times these children were recognized as being part of an important culture.

The Portland area has the ninth-largest Native-American Population in the United States, representing 380 different tribes.[70] According to 2000 U.S. Census Bureau statistics, 19,209 are Native people associated with one tribe and 38,926 are from a mixture of affiliations. Some are tribally enrolled and entitled to benefits under treaties while others are not.

The metropolitan area traditionally was occupied by Multnomah, Kathlamet, Clackamas, Chinook, Tualatin Kalapuya and Molalla tribes. Others arrived along the Columbia River for summer encampments. The population declined after European contact as a result of illness combined with territorial and federal policy designed to eliminate Native peoples. Diseases in the 18th and 19th centuries brought disaster that killed nine out of ten people.

From the mid-1800s through 1960, boarding schools were part of a campaign to integrate indigenous people into Western culture. In the 1950s, the Federal Relocation Policy forced one-third of the Native population to relocate to seven major cities including Portland. In 1954, the federal government stopped recognizing many tribes that had previously been recognized. These discarded tribes were stripped of their rights. Their lands were taken and social services revoked. It wasn't until 1977 that the Confederated Tribes of the Siletz Indians became the first group to regain federal recognition. The Grand Ronde and Klamath also fought successfully to have their terminations repealed. Many tribes still struggling for recognition are bitter.

Their people come to Portland for jobs, a place to live and to find community and were thwarted at every turn.

Native-Americans are disproportionately poor. They have the highest rates of homelessness and unemployment of all ethnic groups. Depression, addiction, and diabetes are not uncommon. And 24 percent of children are in foster care while only 37 percent of high school students graduate. (2006)

Resources are limited due to chronic undercounting and the false perception that Native people no longer exist. The public inaccurately believes that education, healthcare, and social services are fully paid for by government or gaming/casinos. As a result of misinformation, access to services is limited.an Despite overwhelming problems, many who do make it become successful tax-paying members of the community. Their success often is a result of the many agencies and mentors focused on their needs. The last census claims that 40 percent of Native people are under the age of twenty-five. In Portland there are over twenty organizations, staffed with Native Americans hoping to inspire young people to become future leaders of the city, their tribes, and community.

Youth Homeless Service focuses on personal and social development through cultural identity and mental health and alcohol/drug abuse services. They provide intensive case management, on-site clothing closet, food pantry, and on-site and mobile screening for shelter and other safety services. The staff works to create healthy relationships and a sense of community.

A Youth Leadership Council meets bi-weekly and is composed of youth from several NAYA programs including Early College Academy, Academic/Life Skills Program, Gang Prevention Program and recreation programs. The council develops service learning projects, outreach materials and engages in leadership education. High school credit is given for participation. Field trips, an important part of the program, are provided to engage interest and expand their horizon.

One of the organization's more interesting approaches to drug and alcohol treatment prevention incorporates music, art and a variety of healthy, fun and sober recreational activities. Since each youth comes with a different set of problems, specific support services are provided for individual needs. Mentors are key to the program and work with kids on an individual basis.

Sunrise East offers education and career focus for up to three years covering everything from one-on-one coaching, career readiness training, work experience and more. Youths get help developing a personalized pathway to a future career. Incentives such as paid internships and being provided with credentials and certificates are seen as valuable to the participating youths. The program trains kids in job and interview skills and provides financial support.

NAYA also works in a preventative way with foster children, gangs, the disabled, high school dropouts, pregnant teens, runaways and juveniles who have experienced difficulty with the law. The problems they deal with are complex and take time and the effort of a committed staff.

NAYA is an example of one of many programs operating throughout the United States. The Bureau of Indian Affairs is the place to go to find information about regional offices. Go to www.bia.gov for more information.

SOCIAL JUSTICE - KATE LORE
THE ROLE OF CHURCHES

"Life has a way of repeating itself, transferring experiences through time from one generation to the next," said Kate Lore, who at the time was Social Justice Minister at the Unitarian Universalist

Church in Portland, Oregon. "As an adult, I've worked hard to break the conditions and mindset of poverty experienced by my ancestors, but doing so has not been easy. This is due not only to the lack of resources, but to a culture of shame and secrecy. It's as if part of my destiny is being controlled by unnamed family ghosts.

"The story of my father's side of the family dates back to Monticello, Virginia where my Irish forebears served as indentured servants of Thomas Jefferson in return for passage to America. These farmers eventually paid off their debt and slowly migrated westward, first to Minnesota and then to California. Generation after generation lived hardscrabble lives, never owning the land they farmed, never getting a good education, but always working, working, working. Many of these relatives could be characterized as bad apples. Unspoken shame still permeates the family relating to the fact that my father was the product of a forced incestuous relationship between his teenage mother and her cousin. Also, my paternal grandfather never met his son nor me because his entire life was spent locked up in prison. Though I know he eventually died of cancer, I've never found anyone who would tell me what he had done to land behind bars.

"Knowledge of my mother's family begins with the Dust Bowl. Though I tried, I never found a relative willing to talk about the past. What I do know is that my mother's family shared many similarities with my father's. They were poor, hardworking tenant farmers who migrated west in order to feed their family. They, too, ended up in California, seeking a better life. But like characters out a John Steinbeck novel, Mom's side of the family migrated to Monterey's Cannery Row to work the anchovy canneries. I still carry memories of Cannery Row. It was the era before it became a tourist destination — the smell of fish and stale booze, the site of rusted boat hulls and passed-out winos and the sounds of seagulls screeching over the next incoming fish haul are captured in my mind. Industrial Cannery Row faded over time and eventually the cannery jobs did, too. My grandparents never escaped the poverty and alcoholism that has plagued and continues to plague my mother's family.

"My parents' lives came together in the mid-50s. They met as young adults in church, both eager to break free from their families of origin and have good lives. Married in 1957, their first child came along three years later. Tragically for my sister and me, their love did not last long. By the time of my birth, Dad was having an affair with another woman.

"Born in 1960, I was unaware that my parents were not doing well as a couple. I was only six months when Mom moved us, children to join Dad in Tanzania where he had accepted a teaching job. She hoped by doing so that his affair would end. My sister, who was then three and I spent the next several years speaking Swahili and living among people native to that land. I found out later that during the entire three years we lived abroad, my father had continued corresponding with the woman with whom he'd been seeing before we left. But the final shock didn' t set in until we arrived back home at the San Francisco airport. My mother still had luggage and children in hand when my father turned to her and said; "This is where we part ways. I'm leaving you. You're on your own." With that announcement he took a few of his personal belongings and left the airport to live with his lover. I would not see him for, many years to come.

"We found ourselves stranded, possessing nothing. We didn't know where to go, nor did Mom have any idea of how she was going to find our next meal. In this emergency situation she wound up moving back to her childhood home with alcoholic parents, not a safe place for kids of any age, and bad for little ones who had just lost their father. It was worse for my sister than me, though, because she was always Daddy's little girl, the one who had my father's heart—or so she thought. Once abandoned, my sister started acting out. She became the 'evil one' in the family, and I reacted by becoming super sweet. My behavior was an effective survival technique. By being a loving, cuddly kid I could get what I needed. I may have been plain but I was smart. Looking back I wondered if my lifelong 'good girl' behavior was largely a reaction to the way my sister acted. I'm not sure. But I have come to believe that my compulsion to be good and the compassion I have for others comes from someplace deep within.

"Without a college degree, the only work my mother could find was minimum-wage employment. When she worked, we were left in the care of our grandparents. Two lively little girls living with inebriated adults was a dangerous situation. That became especially apparent when one day my grandfather had had enough of the noise my sister was making. He drunkenly grabbed a fork and lunged to stab her in the hand. Thankfully she moved in time or she would have been maimed. Mom realized at that moment she had to move on, but again was lost about what to do and where to go.

"She sought advice from a previous mentor, a woman who had been her second-grade teacher in elementary school. Connie Sellars had taken a liking to her as a youngster coming to school from an alcoholic family. Connie got her involved in church and encouraged her to sing in the children's choir. She and my mother remained friends, writing to each other throughout her trials. Being a good Samaritan, Connie offered us a place to live in a nearby house that she recently had inherited, asking only $75 a month in rent, an amount that was never raised over the years. If it were not for the kindness of this one individual, I'm not sure what we would have done. Housing is a prerequisite to so many things: security, status and stability.

"Still, I felt shame living in our house. Paint was peeling off the walls and the grass was never cut because we couldn't afford a mower. We never owned a car, which meant that for ten hours a day my sister and I were left at home to raise ourselves while mom rode buses long distances to work as a clerk typist in a distant school district.

"Neighbors felt sorry for us, two little urchins abandoned by fate, and they treated us kindly even though our presence "brought the neighborhood down." They helped fill the house with cast -ff furniture, responding to our needs compassionately. I attribute their help to the fact that homeless families were a rare phenomenon back then. Neighbors were less inclined to judge us and more inclined to help out. The was before the 1980s when America suddenly began demonizing the poor. Americans still had compassion for the destitute and had not yet been exposed to President Ronald Reagan's portrayal of single moms as being lazy, unproductive 'welfare queens.'

"Our family had $60 to spend each week for all our needs including food, transportation, rent, utilities, clothes, glasses etc. My sister and I had three sets of clothing to wear in rotation throughout the year. I was always embarrassed when people came to visit. Though there were a few poor, black kids in the neighborhood, we were the only white ones.

"We were better off than my uncles, however. We had Connie, our fairy godmother, and they had no one. One uncle eventually died as a homeless man from alcohol-related issues. The other is still alive but he too is an alcoholic and lives with my mother for free about six months each year. When not staying at my mother's house, he goes to Thailand to reside with his third wife — a relationship based on economic hardship more than love. His children, my cousins, have always struggled and are carrying forward the family's cycle of alcoholism and poverty. One of them served time in prison for embezzlement.

"My sister and I used to talk often about our future. 'We will not remain poor all of our lives,' we proclaimed. And so we worked extremely hard in school and fought with all our might to succeed. Today my sister lives in Santa Cruz, California with a practice as a psychologist, and I am a minister in a large Unitarian Universalist Church.

"My spiritual mission started when as a child at the age of ten I took myself to the local Methodist church. At the time the Methodists didn't believe in divorce which made my mother stop attending. The members loved and embraced me for I was friendly and outgoing. After a few years, I became a sexton, worked in the preschool and was given a key to the church with instructions to go there whenever I wanted. Congregants had recognized a child in need, and their welcoming actions made all of the difference to my survival.

"But I did more than just attend church. As early as fifth grade I became involved in the civil rights protests and joined environmental rallies. Greenpeace had an office nearby, which intensified my concern for social justice.

"Connie, my godmother, continued to be a source of compassion and support. She was a wonderful mentor who saw my sister's and my potential. Both of us went to her house weekly to be taught to play the piano followed by snacks and talks that inspired children hungry for adult direction. Playing the piano was exhilarating because it was something I could feel good about. It became a passion that lasted well beyond my college years. Connie also took the two of us on nature trips where we were introduced to the healing aspects of the outdoors.

"Our school was a wonderful escape, a place I loved that allowed me to blossom. Always hungry for knowledge, I was put in a gifted program, given extra classroom responsibilities and was well regarded by my teachers. They showered me with special privileges, knowing I was from a 'broken home' as it was called back then. They could see that I was bright and hard-working, and they responded with compassion instead of pity. Even so — though I went to an affluent high school and people were nice to me, I felt ashamed of being poor.

"Good grades eventually led to grants and scholarships at the University of California in Santa Cruz. It's there that I met my first husband. We were both political activist and fell in love. He, too, lived simply, wore Goodwill clothing, and seemed to relate to my background. I believed that we shared similar childhoods. It was not until the night before my wedding that I discovered that he was actually from a very wealthy family. He had rejected his privileged life and left his parents to forge on his own. His father was an oil man, and by marrying a poor girl it was his way of "'ticking it to his parents.'

"As is typical in very wealthy families, my sisters-in-law were raised by nannies, went to finishing schools and were debutantes presented to society when they were sixteen years old. What a contrast to my upbringing! Furthermore, my husband's family lived on a private island with special social mores that had to be observed. People dressed, moved about, spoke to each other, and entertained in prescribed ways that were foreign to me. I felt more in common with the servants. I had never been treated as poorly as I was by my in-laws. Although it caused me pain and humiliation at the time, I've had years of introspection to process it all. I realize now that the twenty-five years spent with my husband's family was a gift of sorts. Learning to survive in that entitled environment later helped me feel 'fluent' in a wide array of social settings and with people from all sectors of society. It also is what generated a vow that I would eventually make to never allow my own—or anybody else's—dignity be compromised for lack of money or privilege.

"Over time my in-laws also benefited from introspection. They came to appreciate the fact that I had brought their wayward son back into the family fold. By the time their son and I divorced in 2007, we had come to a kind of peace that was tolerable on both sides. Love and warmth were not handed out easily in that family. My love of children and affectionate nature ended up being deeply appreciated by my niece and nephews. It pleases me greatly that these close bonds continue to be strong.

"My penchant for spirituality and introspection helped me grow and deepened as a result of my experiences with hardship. Although I later left the Methodist Church, I grew up believing that there was a man named Jesus who was always walking at my side—a man who loved poor people and kids. Although I would eventually move on, I owe the Methodists a great debt for the resiliency and self-esteem that I first acquired in Sunday School classes. It was no small accident that I ended up taking my own children to United Methodist Sunday School when they were small. With time and maturity, they appreciated the fact that I eventually switched them over to First Unitarian Church.

"My kids were ten and fourteen years old when I got the call to go to seminary. Up until that time, my primary focus had been domestic. Unfortunately, I did not realize how threatened my husband would become when I began pursuing my own career. Having been raised by nannies, he was ill-equipped to handle childcare responsibilities. He found children to be burdensome. As I was excitedly studying for the ministry and still working for First Unitarian Church in Portland, our marriage began showing signs of strain. 'Nothing a little marriage counseling can't sort out,' I foolishly assured myself.

"Three days before I was ordained into the ministry, I received the shock of my life. Upon returning home one day, I found our children outside, apparently locked out of the house. They informed me that their keys wouldn't work. I checked my key next, with the same distressing results. Roger had changed the locks and blocked every entry. To add insult to injury, he also closed our joint bank accounts and went to live with his mistress. Roger, liked my own father, walked out of his wife's and children's lives that day. Luckily, I still had a job. Just as with my mother before me, though, I was penniless and had two kids to feed and house. It was déjà vu — the past repeated. I felt like the Earth fell out from under my feet.

"This wasn't supposed to happen! I had done everything I could to make sure that my kids would never experience this type of vulnerability. My guilt and shame were rampant. I was furious with myself and with my husband. What was I to do?

"Our homeless situation was traumatic but temporary, though it took a great many years to get over the emotional turmoil caused by the abrupt end of a 24-year marriage. For the second time in my life, though, I was saved by the kindness and generosity of friends and family ,and life has returned to normal. I'm remarried now and my sons live nearby but on their own. I still find myself wondering, though, about the thin wall between my life inside a house and the many people living on the streets. For instance, how were my sister and I able to do what generations of family members had not been able to — not succumb to alcoholism and prolonged homelessness? I attribute our success to four things:

1. extra help and support from family, friends and neighbors when we were vulnerable.

2. a strong sense of purpose.

3. access to grants and scholarships that allowed us to go to college for free.

4. a willingness to look at our lives and our families honestly and with courage.

"The help I received from neighbors is not as easily available today. In my ministerial work, I noticed that citizens are jaded to the plight of homeless families. They are frightened by them and are therefore less apt to help out. Housing prices have escalated so high that homeless families are hard pressed to ever find affordable rentals, even from friends or relatives, such as the $75/month rent extended to my mother. College tuition also has escalated, narrowing the educational opportunities that lead away from poverty. Pell Grants that used to pave the way for poor, motivated kids to go to college dried up years ago.

"The other two attributes that impacted my life will still make an important difference to a distressed child. One is to develop a strong sense of purpose and the second is to have a willingness to look at your life and family situation honestly and with courage. These are easy words to say, but not easy to do without counseling. Families facing the type of crises and family history that shaped my life need a great deal of support that is not readily available.

"I am where I am today because of a combination of hard work and extraordinary good luck. I came of age at an exceptional time in history when homelessness among families was rare and our country was united in wanting to improve the lives of the poor. I believe that I owe a huge debt to society, which is why I initiated the opening of two shelters for homeless families, both of which rely on the goodness of people who support them with money and volunteer service.

"This situation needs to change if we want to stem the rising tide of youth homelessness. Few of us are immune from the possibility of someday becoming homeless as I discovered when it had happened to me as an adult.

"Surviving poverty has had many ongoing consequences. I have an ongoing need to give back to others. So many people helped me that I wonder if I will ever be able to do enough for the thousands of needy individuals I work with each day. When others suffer, I too suffer. Deep down I keep thinking that I have enough and don't deserve anything else. I can live very simply and feel guilty not doing so. My money and soul are spread thin, yet a part of me realizes that I must take care of myself as well if I am going to maintain a degree of sanity and solvency.

"In the past, I rarely traveled, and only took my first trip in midlife to Israel and Palestine. Now I am curious about how the rest of the world lives and thinks. It would be wonderful to visit Tanzania, to find my African roots.I am remarried to a wonderful man and look forward to evenings at home. Being close to the Earth provides me with a great deal of joy. Hours spent gardening provides an inner peace that makes me feel whole.

"I believe that I owe a huge debt to society, which is why I initiated the opening of two shelters for homeless families, both of which rely on the goodness of people who support them with money and volunteer service. We are in this life on Earth to help one another, and I implore others to stand with me in this mightiest of tasks.

"It may sound strange, but I am concerned about what is happening within wealthy families. I've seen the bad side of what money will do. Many kids I have known who have everything handed to them don't want to follow rules. They take drugs, want to get away from any responsibility to their families, and cherish their own freedom. above that of others.

"Those growing up in poverty often become better people because they understand what it is like to have nothing. They have to learn what they were made of and have the opportunity to become stronger because of it. It is our job as a society to provide assistance so they can overcome the handicap of their poor beginnings.

"In 2016 I left my position at First Unitarian Church to take over management of a five-county program operated by Volunteers of America for abused women. With a $5 million budget, I was closer to the trenches and was able to make a difference in the lives of women and children who lose their homes due to abusive situations. From this job I moved again to answered a call to return to the ministry at Quimper Unitarian Universalist Fellowship in Port Townsend, Washington."

<hr/>

"Homelessness in America is a revolving-door crisis. Though many people exit homelessness quickly, many more individuals become homeless every day.[71] On any given day at least 800,000 people are homeless in the United States, including about 200,000 children in homeless families. These children are physically and emotionally vulnerable and likely to have problems as adults. The homeless services system started with federal funding through the Stewart B. McKinney Homeless Assistance Act has helped this population with emergency services, transitional and permanent housing, and supportive services for the disabled.

The National Coalition for the Homeless unites nonprofit organizations and churches in the fight to end homelessness.[72] They have a directory of local homeless service organizations, many of which are church groups. They have taken on a variety of projects that include programs to make communities aware of the problems of homelessness. The coalition members promote a universal living wage, are advocates against hate crimes and violence, and encourage the homeless to vote so their voice counts.

Churches play an important role in intervention by providing soup kitchens and in some cases overnight shelters. Typically, they feed people in parks, or house the homeless in overnight shelters where they may require the homeless to attend services and read the Bible. Sometimes church programs are more harmful than beneficial according to Invisible PEOPLE, an organization dedicated to changing the way we think about people experiencing homelessness. By not giving the homeless life skills they just return to their old ways. Focus needs to be on housing, jobs and health services if we are to make a dent in the problem. There are churches that are known to work together to help the destitute find employment and housing. For example, in Macomb County near Detroit there is an Emergency program involving a group of churches that commit to providing shelter on a rotating basis for a week at a time.[73] Ninety churches have joined together to pool resources to help over sixty people get back on their feet in their first year.

In Portland, First Unitarian Church provides a family shelter by day. It coordinates with the Goose Hollow Family Shelter at the First United Methodist Church to provide overnight lodging between 7:30 p.m. and 7:30 a.m. The Unitarian church started Outside In which is now an independent Youth Services agency. The Church of Jesus Christ of Latter-day Saints in Salt Lake City provides breakfasts for homeless youths. The list goes on and on. However, these interventions are mostly emergency solutions and not designed to end the crisis facing the nation. Churches are influenced by what Scriptures say about responsibility to the poorest and most vulnerable among us.

We are to be generous to those in need because this honors our Maker. Proverbs 14:31

We are to show respect to the poor. James 2

A generous man will himself be blessed, for he shares his food with the poor." Proverbs 22:9

We are to offer hospitality, clothing, shelter and food. Matthew 25:31-46

Quran 17:26-27

155

Most of all, we are to love. This means being patient, being kind, not putting ourselves over the other person, but bearing other's burdens and enduring with them. I Corinthians 13

These Scriptural sentiments need to be translated into practical realities. It would help if more churches participated in one or more of the following ways:

Offer hospitality. Open a shelter or drop-in center in your house of worship. If this isn't possible offer weekly game nights, field trips, or arts-based programs.

Take a moral stand. Create a speaker's bureau, write Letters to the Editor, meet with elected officials to advocate for homeless services.

Feed the hungry. Provide a food box or feeding program that maintains the dignity of those in need of food. Allow them to select the food they want.

Raise money and hope. Open up a thrift store that benefits homeless people. Take it a step further and convert it into a job-training site.

Build affordable housing. Nothing helps stabilize lives like access to affordable housing. There are now tax breaks that make this a win-win proposition.

Ask. Don't presume to know what homeless people need. Take some time to develop relationships with some homeless people and ask for their ideas about what your church, synagogue or mosque can do to be of help.

An aside: Just as there are compassionate clergy benefiting their congregants, there are also those who commit unsavory acts. The sex scandal coverups that have come to light throughout the Catholic hierarchy are a case in point. The story of Jimmy James is included as an example of what can happen to a child who is molested by a priest. In addition to religious organizations, pedophiles are found in community centers, clubs, schools, daycare centers and among family members. Parents who encourage their children to talk freely about any topic, including sexual ones, are better able to eliminate unsavory situations when they occur. It is important to take a child's comments seriously, especially when showing fear of a previously trusted acquaintance. A lifetime of grief and emotional problems is the likely outcome for a youth subjected to sexual abuse.

Drop Out to Dean - Rene Zingarelli Community College

"My life came to a jolt when I discovered I was pregnant before the age of sixteen. Taught by nuns, my conservative Catholic high school had no place for unwed mothers, and since abortion was not an option, I dropped out to marry and have my baby. It did not make any difference that I was a straight A student—my shame was immense, and I was scared. Suddenly, instead of being taken cared of, I had became the caregiver and took responsibility quickly with assistance from unhappy but ,supportive parents and in-laws. Mom particularly helped by letting me know that eventually, I would be fine. She told me that though this was not the plan, if I built a good life for my family, I would have three to four years on those who waited to marry and have a family. Her words still bring tears to my eyes for they were a strongbox after affirmation that spoke to the power of believing that good can come out of a challenging situation.

"My young husband and I were lucky to have help from both sets of parents. We lived first at his family house before we struck out on our own. My husband continued in school, eventually getting a doctorate as a marine biologist and environmental consultant. Not one to be left behind, I completed my high school diploma while earning college credits at a local community college. I transferred to Portland State University, a four-year institution, eventually receiving a teaching degree, though that was not enough to get a job in many school districts. A master's degree of arts in teaching was needed which I eventually achieved from Lewis & Clark College by going part time.

"Life was not easy for my growing family, but it was busy and challenging, leaving little time for boredom. My second daughter was born when I was nineteen, my next son at twenty-four. But after a thirty-two year, mostly happy marriage, it did end in divorce. Now I am blessed with nine grandchildren, three great-grandchildren, and have a large close family and look forward to noisy wonderful gatherings.

"It was difficult to land a full-time teaching job after graduation but one evening at a friend's barbecue my life took a surprisingly different direction. I met a man from Clackamas Community College (CCC) who told me that they had received a grant to start a college program for high school dropouts. He suggested I apply for a position if other work was not forthcoming by September.

I was offered the job on the basis of my experience subbing in special-needs classrooms. They decided I would fit in well as a member of a group of four instructors. I grabbed the opportunity and began a lifelong journey into the minds and souls of teenagers who needed special attention.

"What an amazing learning experience it has been to work with these youths. Our staff was informal with instructors addressed on a first name basis. Stuffiness and traditional labels did not work with these students.

"The first kid that I interviewed for our Tri-City Alternative Program started the conversation by calling me 'sweetheart.' I put a stop to that immediately and stated in no uncertain terms that I was not his sweetheart and would not be spoken to that way. It turned out that the youth had been bounced out of school for placing a bomb in the bathroom in order to scare a fellow student. It exploded but thankfully no one was hurt. He currently was on probation. When I asked him why he wanted to get into the program, the teen's responded, "because according to the terms of my probation I have to be in school." That was not good enough for me, so I retorted, 'that may be so, but according to the terms of *our* program, no one will be admitted who doesn't want to be here.' I sent him home to think about it and amazingly enough, he later returned to become a committed student. He eventually passed his GED and found a job.

"Kids came to us because they wanted another shot at school. Many had no real choice. They grew up in poverty, often with parents who did not believe in education. They lived on the fringe of society and were headed for failure. Without direction or mentors they didn't fit into a large high school and needed individualized attention.

"Though our program did not deal with homeless kids directly, our students had a variety of problems that could not be solved in their homes. Some youths were addicts, others had learning disabilities and a few were even gifted. All needed a different setting to be able to complete school successfully. By the time they spoke to us the system had never worked for them. What they learned in school was not to trust adults or society, so it was no wonder they were failing.

"Twelve high schools in the county fed us students and I say with pride that 85 percent of them succeeded. How did I know we were successful? Success was measured by students completing their GED or obtaining a high school diploma and then going on to attend a community college or employment.

"Over the twelve years I taught at CCC, our team came to realize that some of the issues these children had were so difficult that it would take more than one organization to tackle their problems. A triangle of agencies that eventually emerged consisted of three parts — one that that tackled drugs, another created jobs, and one that focused on education. We developed close communication with Clackamas County Mental Health Drug and Alcohol Division and a joint partnership for job training with ETBS (Employment Training and Business Services, formally known as CETA)

"The program flourished and I wrote a grant for a "Young Parent Opportunity Program" to start a similar curriculum for teen parents and young mothers on welfare. I understood their problems well and was a strong role model who could speak to their issues. Moms need childcare, a place to live, and adequate transportation. Most of all they need to develop self-confidence, to have a small voice in their head constantly drumming the kind of encouragement my mother's and grandmother gave me. The program was funded for fifteen years, and even after I left the program I would return to speak to the new students and share my story.

"After many years, I became a dean of the Division of Extended Learning Service at CCC, overseeing a host of human services programs. As an organizer with grant-writing abilities, I devoted twelve more years to this leadership role before retiring in 2003. In my early years as a teacher I was involved in counseling, advising, creative problem-solving and basic skills. As an administrator, I was responsible for many departments including Basic Skills, ESL, Alternative Programs, Library, Instructional Media, Distance Learning, Human Services, and Criminal Justice. It was quite challenging. These programs kept many young people from living out their lives on the streets. I am most proud that by believing that they had a future and giving them tools and a path for success, many turned their lives around.

"Time does march on, however, and nothing stays the same. A new administration was hired and the direction the college chose to take swerved. School districts started their own alternative programs, preferring to keep state money in their district's pockets. Vocational options increased as a sprinkling of high schools started to address the needs of less academically minded youths. I am pleased to see that many of these alternative programs are quite effective at what they do.

"Once retired, I made a change in my own life. In addition to working with disadvantaged youths for so many years, my heart lay elsewhere. Our family suffered a terrible loss to cancer when my five-year-old grandchild, Alexandra, died after a two-and-a-half year battle. "From those bleak days, my daughter and her husband decided to do something to help others who had to face life-threatening illness by starting the Children's Cancer Association. I served as an early board member and volunteer. Today over

1,200 volunteers work with seriously ill children in an effort to create joy for them and their families. As our literature states, 'we search for rainbows in every moment by helping them to listen to the sounds of life — laughter, music, grief, compassion — and foster hope and healing.' For over twenty years the organization, now headed by my daughter Regina, and her husband, Cliff Ellis, has been assisting families who face the biggest battle of their lives. I remain involved, helping to raise millions of dollars in aid. Our last fundraiser brought in over $1 million in contributions — quite an accomplishment.

"To keep my own sanity I enjoy playing in a marimba band known as Chicamarimba. We are a group of eight women who fell in love with the instrument and wanted to learn something new. For the past 16 years, we have been performing in the Pacific Northwest at festivals and community events."

Rene ended her interview with a big smile and a friendly, "Come see us play sometime."

GOOD SAMARITAN - CATHI HOWELL
INDUSTRIALIZATION CENTER

Over the course of the past year, I interviewed people who devoted a great deal of their time helping disenfranchised youths. A great many became involved because they had overcome their own dysfunctional childhoods and as adults wanted to give back to the community. They act out of a sense of *noblesse oblige*, the responsibility of privileged people to act with generosity and nobility toward those less privileged. Some were parents who had learned, through trial and error, how to raise their own socially conscious children and now wanted to apply what the knew to other youths. These good Samaritans are disturbed to see less fortunate children falling through the cracks and concerned about the growing number of dropouts, the homeless and runaway youth. I was interested in exploring why a financially comfortable person would take the time to explore the causes of poverty and work to make a difference in the lives of disadvantaged children. It seemed to me that if I better understood their motivation, I might be able to rally others to volunteer their time.

There are many good souls helping children overcome the terrible scars of child abuse. Cathi Howell, an, experienced businesswoman is one of them. The work she and many volunteers do gives me hope that our community can come together and find solutions. Perhaps, you too will be inspired to volunteer

"I grew up in a privileged family boasting a heritage as a fifth-generation Oregonian," said Cathi Howell, an energetic, fit woman who worked out on a regular basis at an upper-class sports club. "Both sides of my family can claim a lineage that goes back to the start of Oregon's statehood. Mother was a bookkeeper with a variety of clients and was able to work out of the house so she was always there to nurture me. Dad was a professional musician, who wrote commercials, played in the symphony, at weddings, and for fashion shows. I was lucky to live in such an active and creative household. Our family was embraced by friends with similar spirits. We lived on the east side of town where everyone we knew was employed so I had a comfortable and secure upbringing. Portland had a population of only 200,000 during my childhood. Grant High School, my alma mater, was excellent, as were most of Portland's schools. Summers were idyllic, spent at relatives' farms and ranches where I could roam and play freely in both Washington and Oregon. Life could not have been much better, for I was secure in knowing that my extended family was there for me. College was the expected path to take and I followed it, studying commercial art and developing it into a career.

"I got married and later divorced with one daughter to raise. But it wasn't long before I remarried an East Coast man who brought with him two children and the stability that comes from being marketing director for a major accounting firm. He, too, was creatively evolved and developed a hobby as a portrait artist and ukulele player.

"As my workdays unfolded, an entrepreneurial streak that I didn't know I had led me to open and manage a successful retail business at four Oregon locations. Common Threads grew from being a one-of-a-kind art fabric store into a gallery operation with a variety of arts and crafts artifacts for sale. It was an ambitious undertaking that I enjoyed until my age caught up with me. Over many years of operation, I burnt out from the responsibility of managing personnel. So I sold the business and decided not to take on any more work than I could handle by myself. For a while, I devoted myself exclusively to designing and making fabric art and supplying my creations to a large number of local stores.

"The time came to recreate myself, and I decided to leave the commercial business word to embrace other activities. A chance meeting with an old friend at my high school reunion suggested I get involved with disenfranchised youths. And so began an adventure that changed me as much as I hoped I influenced the teens I came in contact with. Until that time I had never really known what it was like to be on the brink of despair.

"My first introduction to the organization was at a fundraiser for Portland Opportunities Industrialization Center (POIC), a program with roots that go back to the Roosevelt era. It was intriguing but also shocking to see the other side of the economic spectrum — an eye-opening experience to say the least. Teens in the program came from both white and African-American families though the majority were black. All were poor with little interest in learning or bettering themselves. As children, they had lived through so many harsh realities it boggled my mind.

"When first involved, I noticed that attendance was terrible. Our faculty spent a lot of time trying to help kids overcome their problems but the kids had to do their part, too. Consequences were put in place to ensure that those enrolled had a reason for staying. Today, if they miss ten days in a row, they are kicked out of the program — no exceptions.

"Without a degree or job experience, there is little hope for disenfranchised teens to have a good future. POIC's goals are many, beginning with helping youths graduate with either a diploma or GED.[74] We arrange for apprenticeship programs, develop life skills, locate places to live, and eventually help them find employment. Our youths have to learn the most basic of skills, such as how to wash and dress. They require instruction in how to have a polite conversation and to make a nutritious meal. They need to be taught ways of getting along with other people at work and at home. Many of the children we assist with are homeless, so additional arrangements have to be made for their housing. Quite a few attendees are in the foster care system which creates its own set of problems.

"Similar to Job Corps, staff uses every trick known to youth educators to influence attendance. They hand out coupons just for showing up and give cash for good performance. Tough love and consistency are the best ways to work with children from abused backgrounds where no one cared or paid attention to them. In their homes, there were few controls on their behavior ,with no training or role models showing them the way to participate in society."

Cathi's intense caring came through with every word she spoke.

"Serving this population is expensive. Classes are small in order to give special attention to each child. The ratio of adults to students is high with volunteer mentors playing an important role. In order to ensure our students' success, we stay involved with them until they are twenty-five. We recognize that there are a great many problems to be faced once they graduate from high school and are living on their own. Being thrown into an environment that is foreign to the way they were raised is not an easy transition. They face difficulties if they decide to go to a community college, a place that feels strange and cold. Once employed, they struggle to stay in the job.

"In the early days of my involvement, sixteen people ran the program and I offered to help coordinate the volunteers who assisted as teachers and mentors. Noticing a need for an art teacher, I took on that task, bringing in my own supplies in order to teach several times each week. I was very fearful at first. Many of the kids were much bigger than me, their language was coarse, and they talked back.

"'You can't make me,' or 'Who do you think your are?' were commonly heard," Cathi said. "Most of the kids were distrustful of a white woman from the other side of the tracks, and in the beginning they weren't willing to share their lives.

"I had no classroom skills for working with this population so I just had to wing it.

"Since I was not a psychiatrist, I put my effort into developing a curriculum that would be appealing. Over time their work became an outlet for their troubles and a way to express their perception of the environment they occupied. They spoke to me through their projects, teaching me about the difficulties of poverty.

"At times when I would notice something disturbing I would bring my concern to a social worker, but I never tried to pretend I was more than an art teacher. In other instances, my students would discuss subjects that I knew nothing about, such as what life was like in jail, or how to survive by breaking and entering in order to steal. They sounded so confident in pursuing illegal activities that it surprised me. I just listened and tried to bring them back to the art at hand.

Rosemary Anderson High partners with POIC.[75] It was started in 1983 in Portland as an alternative opportunity for academic studies. Along with their second school, Rosemary Anderson East, academics were integrated with POIC curriculum in order to offer career training. Transition staff puts in a lot of effort to keep graduates on track by taking on the role of a caring parent concerned about their future.

A new school recently opened at a location on the outskirts of the city where, due to gentrification, poor families are moving in increasing numbers. Though poor, most of these children are still sheltered by their families, so they are not as bad off as their inner-city cousins. An active mentorship program composed of volunteers is a model of what a community of concerned citizens can do for dispirited youths.

Over the past 35 years, POIC started seeing many other problems not being addressed by the community, so it applied for grants to meet these needs. A teen pregnancy program was initiated to keep young mothers in school. These young girls are taught how to care for their children with the goal of breaking the cycle of poor child-rearing practices that they experienced in their own families.

The Community Healing Initiative started with a grant to address gang-related issues that have blossomed in many parts of the city. The program brings the entire family into sessions aimed at helping their children move on from the deadly path their kids have taken.

"Drugs are always a problem, not only for their direct use but as a lucrative sales commodity," Cathi said.

"We get money from the per-student allocation of Portland Public Schools as well as from a variety of grant sources. The problem with grants is that beneficial programs may last a number of years but then could be eliminated due to budget cuts or the changing whims of granting agencies. Despite the difficulties, however, our program continues to grow."

Cathi said, "Today POIC has three locations and works with 560 students. We take pride in having a 90 percent graduation rate for high school students who either get their diploma or a GED. In 2012, 56 graduates earned over $50,000 in college scholarships to further their education. I am hopeful and feel good being a part of building a more opportunistic community for these teens."

CREATING READERS - GINNIE COOPER PUBLIC LIBRARIES

I got to know Ginnie Cooper when she served as executive director of the Multnomah County Public Library system in

Portland. Unfortunately for Oregon, after implementing needed program changes and raising renovation funds for the Central Library, in 2003 this dynamo was hired away by the Brooklyn Public Library System where she served for four years. Once her Brooklyn mission was complete, she moved on to tackle an even greater challenge as Chief Librarian of the decayed Washington, D.C., library system. Ginnie gained national prominence with her transformative plans that tripled circulation, added a thousand computers, to the sprinkling of 100 that were currently owned, increased attendance dramatically, and left a legacy that included seventeen new or renovated libraries. Ginnie returned to Portland when she retired, but continues to serve as an advocate promoting literacy. One day over lunch, we discussed the research I was doing into youth homelessness. Ginnie made a casual remark about the support libraries gave to mentally ill, poor and homeless populations. I didn't know that poor people visited libraries in search of help with personal problems. As Ginnie said, "Public libraries serve whomever walks into the library without regard to whether or not they live in a fixed residence." She also reminded me that "this has always been the case. In the early 1900s, immigrants came to learn English and to peruse newspapers to look for employment."

I was intrigued and made an appointment with the current director of the county's library system, Vailey Oehlke and with David Ratliff who manages the Central Library. It was an informative introduction to library management by dedicated people doing all they can to improve the lot of those they serve. I was impressed at the wide variety of services they offer. They certainly have their hands full attending to the needs of the educated and uneducated alike. They, too, reminded me that libraries always have been this way.

Why would anyone want to be a librarian? My initial assumption was that most people become one because they are bookworms, enjoying the solitude of sitting in an easy chair ,alone in a quiet room, not because they have a burning desire to serve the mentally ill or those living in poverty. I asked Ginnie to tell me what led her to become a librarian. I also was curious to know what instigated her concern for disenfranchised patrons.

"I grew up in a small town of about 10,000 in Worthington, Minnesota. As a child, I was an voracious reader. Mother said that reading was great but why spend money on books when you can use the library. It was easy to get on my bike, speed two blocks away, and return with books before the television program changed. It was during these trips that I met people with expectations that differed from mine. The library was visited by people of different races and religions, which as a young girl I found intriguing. It was one of the reasons I became a librarian.

"Since their inception, public libraries have helped the homeless, the poor, immigrants, and the mentally challenged, not just wealthy, educated patrons. Library members are different today than those who joined in the past. We now see a higher number of laid off, middle-age men and women who can't find a job. Many are heads of households who, because of circumstances beyond their control, have lost their homes and have to sleep in their cars. They send their children to school without the benefit of a shower, clean clothes, a good night's sleep or adequate food.

"During the day, libraries are a service center for those who would otherwise spend hours wandering. When the weather turns cold over one-hundred people wait outside to come into the warm Central Library Building. Though many need library services, others come simply looking for a safe place to spend the day. Overnight shelters provide early morning breakfast but by 7 a.m., they usually release their guests to wander the streets. A few reopen for lunch and dinner, after which their dining areas again close with recipients asked to leave. Beds are rarely available before 7 p.m., making the hours feel long on cold and rainy days. A few shelters do have small day rooms, but they're crowded with limited materials available to fight boredom. Users report that while drop-in centers make them feel homeless, they never feel that way in a public library.

"Homeless parents arrive with their children seeking warmth, shelter, social contacts, story time, parent-education programs and help reaching social service agencies. Unfortunately, there is usually a wait, sometimes a year or more, before they can get shelter, for family centers have long lists of people hoping to gain access. Many shelters only accommodate one parent with their children, so the spouse is forced to go elsewhere. Partnered adults may use the library as a place to meet the following day.

"Since so many use the library as a safe haven, staff is challenged to keep bathrooms clean and ensure that other members are not disturbed by body odors and noise. It's not fun to have to ask an odiferous patron to leave until he or she showers. Homeless youth are primarily there to search for jobs, check their email, and get out of the rain."

Zach, a frequent user of the library, was a poor reader, like many of his friends. His main goal was to use the library's free wifi connection which often meant an hour's wait for a computer. During the interval, he would look at graphic novels and magazines. Once on the computer he did look for community services and at potential job opportunities.

A chair provides a welcome rest for weary bodies, yet due to crowds, many visitors have to sit on the floor until one is available. Sleeping is not allowed, so those who do doze off are awakened by staff and asked to leave.

Library patrons often complain that homeless and poor visitors discourage more affluent people from visiting. Quite a few wealthier members let staff know, in no uncertain terms, that they do not want to rub elbows with those who are destitute. Rather than accept the library as a resource for all, they see it becoming another homeless shelter. They also fear adolescent members who act belligerently. Their foul language is distasteful to those who enjoy good literature. Problems with teens, however, are rarely caused by homeless youths who are happy to be in a secure location. Troublemakers are more likely to be those who are mentally ill or drug addicted.

Special training in how to serve less fortunate patrons, has been slow in coming. Only recently have courses on special-needs populations been added to library graduate school curriculums.

Most older staff are left to learn on the job. To help this specialized population, many libraries have started collaborating with outside service organizations that provide social workers, hospital and health care, education, churches services and day care.

Libraries establish behavioral rules to prevent illegal activities from taking place within their walls. Disruptive visitors can be asked to leave for sexual misconduct, intoxication, unruly behavior, smoking or not following staff instructions. Loud noises, skating, and consuming food are never allowed inside. Body odor or garbage that disturbs other library users, and animals (except for service dogs) also are not welcome. Restrooms are off limits to shaving, bathing, hair washing or changing clothes. Most often there is a limitation on how many possessions can be taken into the building since most facilities cannot accommodate shopping carts, large bags or bicycles.

Center-city libraries with adequate budgets offer a rich variety of programs with wide appeal. Whether homeless or housed, young or old, members join computer classes, enjoy book talks, and attend lectures on a wide variety of topics. The computer shy are taught how to establish an e-mail or open a Facebook account. Educational workshops abound that promote writing abilities, parenting skills, job search know-how, and where to look for housing. Health issues and searches for government assistance are among the questions reference librarians are most commonly asked.

Ginnie played an important role in setting up Portland's reading readiness programs for young children. Storytimes for preschoolers and parenting classes for adults are part of offerings taking place at numerous branch libraries. To motivate adults to pay more attention to their children's early reading habits, adult learners are given information on brain development and the lasting effects of neglect and trauma in early childhood.

Though outreach services abound, it's still difficult to reach all who need services. According to a PBS report, about 15 percent of the 5000 visitors who visit the San Francisco Public Library every day are homeless.[76] In 2009, that library became the nation's first to address the problem by hiring a social worker. The Huffington Post reports that there are twenty-four public libraries that currently provide support systems for homeless patrons. Multnomah County followed San Francisco's lead in 2015.[77] Social workers play a key role in de-escalating difficult encounters and in providing information about where to go for shelter, food, a shower, medical care, and counseling. The Martin Luther King Jr. Library in San Jose, California has gone a step further by establishing a virtual "Lawyers in the Library" program.[78] Visitors can make an appointment for a 20-minute free consultation that takes place over the internet in an assigned room.

Ginny mentioned a library that added showers inside the building. Though, that is rare, there are mobile units that roam inner city streets, often parking outside of libraries and other public spaces. A few large city libraries want to provide space for special services, such as barbering, eating and counseling.

Librarians continue to look for ways to build trust and convince young people that the library is a worthwhile place to visit. In addition to dispensing free information, entertainment, computers, gaming and music, it also is used as a meet and greet location. Youths can safely hang out with friends, away from the stress of wandering the streets, and without fear of being hounded by the police.

Examples of Model Library Programs can be found in Tips and Tools from the American Library Association's Social Responsibilities Round Table and Office for Literacy and Outreach Services.[79]

MODEL LIBRARY PROGRAMS[80]

Baltimore County (Mary.) Public Library Street Card-Resources for Help was Created by the Baltimore County Public Library in cooperation with the Baltimore County Communities for the

Homeless, www.bcpl.info/community/street-card. The Street Card provides information on employment, food and emergency assistance, health, financial support, legal issues and shelter. Information is available in print and online.

Denver (Colo.) Public Library Community Technology Center, http://denverlibrary.org/ctc. Denver Public Library's (DPL) Community Technology Center team provides regular visits to the area day shelter for homeless and low-income women. Women receive instruction on job interviewing techniques and technology skills. Once the class is over, participants receive bus tokens to go to the main library for a tour and to get library cards.

San Francisco (Calif.) Public Library, www.sfpl.org/. San Francisco Public Library formed a homeless and poverty outreach library team in partnership with the city's Department of Public Health and the SFFirst unit (San Francisco Full-Integrated Recovery Services Team). The full-time, in-house social worker and the SFFirst director, a psychiatrist, provide staff training to better serve the community. Their team includes formerly homeless people who go through a 12-week vocational program. These "health and safety associates" reach out to homeless patrons in the library and distribute information on where to find shelter, showers, and hot meals.

San Jose (Calif.) Public Library Homelessness — A Panel Discussion, http://sjpl.org/tags/homeless. In an effort to improve library services to those experiencing homelessness, the San Jose Public Library initiated a panel discussion to help library professionals learn about the issue. The event brought together library professionals, students and social workers. The resulting web page compiled resources, statistics, and information.

Traverse Area Library District, www.tadl.org/. The Traverse Area District Library partners with a faith-based winter shelter to offer on-site book club meetings. This partnership fosters outreach and promotes community through open dialogue and shared experiences.

Pima County (Ariz.) Public Library Homeless Service Agencies, www.library.pima.gov. Pima County Public Library's Homeless Service Agencies guide provides information (phone number, address, description) for local services. Information is organized into categories (veterans, domestic violence, youth) that can help individuals find the specific assistance they need.

Queens (N.Y.) Library, www.queenslibrary.org New York's Queens Library provides outreach service to homeless shelters. The library coordinates these services with the city's Department of Education family shelter liaison. The outreach service promotes the library's programs, events, and services. The library also highlights family offerings, children's programs and job search help. Baltimore County public Library.

SECTION IV
INTERVENTIONS

T O UNDERSTAND WHY SOME PEOPLE manage childhood traumas successfully and others do not, I explored many relevant studies. The following section shares my voyage into academic investigations and counseling offices as I tried to make sense of the complex way the human mind develops. Coming to grips with the idea that adolescents are immature people who need the help and support of their communities is an essential first step towards developing plans for a way forward.

THE ADOLESCENT BRAIN

Modern imaging technologies provide information about teen brains that challenge long-held assumptions about the nature of maturity. Scientists can even pinpoint differences between adolescent brains and those of mature adults.[81] Though youths tend to be physically healthy, relatively strong, and boast excellent mental capacity, they still face perils due to having an immature brain. Parents and car insurance companies are not strangers to this observation for there is data that shows that teens have more auto accidents than adults. Are the accidents due to insufficient experience behind the wheel or the brain's immaturity?

Pictures of the brain in action show that adolescent brains are guided more by the emotional and reactive amygdala than by the more logical frontal cortex. This means they are more likely to act impulsively, get into accidents, become involved in fights, misread social and emotional cues, and engage in high-risk behaviors. They act before thinking, rarely consider the consequences of their actions and don't want to change their inappropriate behaviors.

Having lived through the teen years with five children, I can certainly attest to having witnessed a range of erratic behaviors.

For a great many years, Dr. Jay Giedd has been investigating the teen brain.[82] Using MRI screens, he and his colleagues have been able to observe various parts of the brain light up when their subjects complete specific tasks. After studying 145 youths at two-year intervals, the scientists noticed a difference in gray matter in the prefrontal cortex between mature and teen brains. They believe that during the teen years the cortex slowly gains reasoning skills and develops more control over impulses as it matures. What surprised them was that changes in the prefrontal cortex occurred at a much later age than previously thought.

As adolescents age, it appears that the gray matter in their brain decreases, becoming pruned of connections that are not regularly used. This pruning is not a smooth slow decline but rather takes place on a bumpy road. Giedd calls this winnowing down period the "use it or lose it principle." He says, "if a teen is doing music, sports or academics, those are the cells and connections that will be hardwired. If they are lying on the couch, playing video games or watching MTV, then those are the cells and connections that are going to survive." Brains of poor youths are handicapped because they lack opportunity and encouragement to get involved in new activities.

Neural connections in the brain also tend to increase during adolescence. According to the National Institute of Mental Health, "the extent of connectivity is related to growth in intellectual capacities such as memory and reading ability."[83] This is why those who cannot read by the time they are teens have lifelong difficulties with literacy.

The path to maturity has to be looked at on the psychological front as well, because it is a time of heightened emotional responses. Brain centers and signaling molecules can form a system that produces urgent, intense emotional reactions that the youth may not be able to control, triggering him to act impetuously. When I was thirteen, I remember coming home from school and going to my bedroom to find my bureau askew and my grandfather hidden behind it. Not realizing that he was trying to fix an electrical outlet, I became hysterical and started shouting. I did not stop to think, for as my adrenaline escalated I became out of control. Once I settled down, I was tremendously embarrassed.

Paul Thompson at UCLA identified that a fiber system relaying information between both hemispheres of the brain shows that different parts of the cortex mature at different rates.[84] First to develop is the part that deals with basic functions like processing information from the senses to control movement. Among the last to mature are the areas responsible for impulse control and long-term planning. Thompson's biggest surprise was discovering that the growing brain prunes itself by cutting off whole clusters of cells. "Of particular interest to educators was discovering that the fiber systems influencing language development and associative thinking grow more rapidly before and during puberty and diminish afterward. These findings reinforce studies on language acquisition that show that the ability to learn new languages declines after the age of 12."[85]

To fully understand adolescent behavior, biological changes need to be considered in addition to the neurological ones we have been discussing. For example, reproductive hormones play a major role in the developing brain for biochemistry not only shapes sexual growth but impacts behavior. And stress hormones, which also increase during puberty, intensify emotions to cause strange conduct that often leaves parents baffled.

When considering intellect, an adolescent's brain is similar to that of an adult's. In fact, many believe that its capacity to learn is greatest during the teen years. The differences lie in how adults and youth access different parts of their brains to solve problems, control impulses, and deal with emotional content. These deviations impact the way adults and youths react to particular situations.

Once scientists recognized that teen brains are not mature, they realized that immaturity impacts actions as much as do surrounding environment, genetics, social issues and child-rearing practices. Though it is not always easy, most parents help

179

their children navigate through the turmoil of school and social activities. Sadly, those raised in poor or dysfunctional households are more vulnerable since they don't have navigation guides readily available.

It is important to be cautious about research into the adolescent brain because, though it provides us with information about what the brain looks like, it does not tell us how it functions. Though scientists may share hypothesis about such things as the role of an immature frontal cortex plays in risk-taking by adolescents, they cannot definitively conclude what behavior is caused specifically by what part of the brain. Studies remain works in progress.

I found it fascinating to read research conclusions from Newcastle University in England saying that women's brains mature when they are in their early twenties while men's lag until their late twenties or even thirties.[86] The study gave a list of men's top maturity failings, such as driving too fast, playing loud music, finding rude words amusing, playing practical jokes, staying silent during an argument, and not being able to cook simple meals. Having raised two sons and three daughters, my observations informally confirm many of their findings, as would most of my friends who have raised both boys and girls. Slow maturing boys can test a parent's patience and make them wonder at times if their sons will ever grow up. Thankfully, most do.

Sleep also influences behavior for regulation is a brain function that is greatly affected by fatigue. Children in unfit homes and those who moved to the streets often have their rest interrupted by loud noises or having to squeeze into an overcrowded bed. Sleep deprivation can increase impulsive behavior, contribute to an inability to focus and, in extreme cases, can lead to depression.

Young people living in a digital environment also are vulnerable.[87] Christopher Bergland in Psychology Today comments that the human brain has not evolved fast enough to develop the neural networks needed to survive in a technological era. Children, especially boys are not designed to sit in chairs all day. They need to be physically active or they become "thrown into a constant state of cortisol-fueled fight-or-flight behavior.

Though his advice is a personal opinion, it is based on concrete evidence that boys are not doing as well as girls in school.

At every grade level girls exhibit superior social and behavioral skills than boys. They achieve better grades and are more likely to continue with advanced training after high school. A Pew Research Center report confirmed this claim showing 71 percent of young women enrolled in college immediately after high school as compared to 61 percent of men. The completion rate for entering male freshmen was 27 percent, while for women it was 36 percent.[88] Knowing that boys mature more slowly than girls, perhaps educators need to alter behavioral expectations and show more patience with their male students.

During adolescence, the quickly changing balance of emotional responses explains why youth look for novelty and act impulsively without regard for consequences. With brains in transition, teens test the water by exploring life in its many dimensions. The result of youthful experimentation, however, can have long-lasting consequences. For instance, intense drinking can permanently affect an adolescent's biological makeup and increase the risk of alcohol dependence in later life. Within a caring family that shares social and cultural mores, teen excursions are likely to be monitored and safe. Without adequate adult support, consequences can be drastic.

Despite all that is understood about adolescent brains, information still remains fuzzy. Scientists do not yet know if a particular behavior or ability is the result of inherited brain structure or change brought on by environmental factors. They question how the environment interacts with genetic predisposition and how much a traumatized brain can grow and be reshaped over a lifetime. They wonder if the brain plays a role in the high rate of illicit substance abuse. And researchers still do not have an answer as to why mental illness symptoms emerge during adolescent years. The hope is that further study will help adults create environments that allow for exploration and experimentation while avoiding destructive behavior.

REPATTERNING

Repatterning the brain to overcome physical or emotional trauma takes time and patience. As children, we crawled by coordinating muscles to move—first the right arm, then left leg, left arm followed by right leg. These learned neurological processes were developed on the floor before we stood up to walk. The hours spent practicing movement affected our brain. On-off switches were formed to help coordinate muscles that were later used for locomotion, posture and balance.

Our nerves are alive with energy, and each time we perform a new exercise or learn a new fact we make neurological connections. The more active we are, the stronger the network of nerves becomes, expanding over time to keep us functioning well. Sedentary individuals run the risk of losing their ability to move with ease.

Cross-crawl marching is a therapy used by people suffering from certain types of traumatic brain injury.[89] When a shock to a person's neurological system leaves them confused and uncoordinated, their muscles start to relax and they become disabled. Repatterning exercises have been proven to help. When I lived in Cambridge, Massachusetts, I had friends who volunteered to help a disabled veteran relearn how to walk. Each afternoon, five people arrived at the man's house to take a limb or his head in hand and move it in a cross-crawling rhythm until he could do it properly on his own. Similar to an infant's movements, once the pattern was mastered he moved on to crawling and eventually to walking.

Traumatic experiences precipitating emotional problems can be accompanied by a loss of security and trust in others. A newborn raised in a nurturing environment develops confidence that adults will be there to care for him. But when there is trauma caused by abuse, hunger, loss of home or drugs, the child's brain becomes shocked. Instead of growing in an orderly manner, newly scrambled neurological connections lead to confusion and stress.

Researches can actually see the impact of long-term physical and psychological abuse when studying brain scans. Two systems, the limbic and the cortex, are of special interest.[90] The limbic system, often called the *emotional brain,* controls emotions that drive survival. It is the center for a fight, flight or freeze response. It communicates with the more rational cerebral cortex which is slower to respond.

Most well-adjusted people rely on the cortex to navigate their way through life. It plays an important role in memory, attention, perception, awareness, thought, language, and consciousness. However, a child experiencing frequent abusive encounters develops an overactive limbic system, ready to fight at the slightest provocation. Instead of staying calm to problem-solve and deal with the situation at hand, a perceived threat may be misinterpreted and cause inappropriate reactions. The nervous system of victimized children are on constant alert because it anticipates further danger.

Interestingly, repatterning is used for minimizing dyslexia, ADD, handwriting and coordination problems, and other learning impairments that might be the result of childhood stress.[91] As a therapy for emotional disorders, there are a variety of remedies that come under its umbrella. They include eye movement desensitization, neuro-feedback, play therapy, holistic parenting, and energy psychology. Repatterning is considered a natural, healing approach relieving trauma caused by abuse, stress, anxiety and fear. It has been shown to improve concentration, memory and enhanced sports performance. Though it may take many years of therapy to counteract childhood trauma at least there are hopeful processes available for those willing to engage in the exercises.

Eye Movement Desensitization and Reprocessing (EMDR)[92] is a relatively new branch of behavior modification that was introduced in 1989 by Francine Shapiro. It uses the patient's own rhythmic eye movements to soften emotionally charged memories of past traumatic events. The practitioner moves fingers back and forth in front of your face asking that the hand gestures be followed by your eyes. Simultaneously, the therapist asks you to recall a disturbing event. Emotions and body sensations are explored as the therapist slowly shifts your thoughts to more pleasant ones. Some practitioners use music or foot tapping instead of eye movement. Those using this technique do so because it weakens the effect of negative emotions. According to the EMDR Institute, "in successful EMDR therapy, the meaning of painful events is transformed on an emotional level. For instance, a rape victim may shift from feeling horror and self-disgust to holding firm the belief that, 'I survived it and I am strong.'" Over time, clients begin to feel empowered.

At least 20,000 practitioners are trained to use EMDR since Shapiro developed the method. The American Psychiatric Association supports its effectiveness for acute and chronic PTSD and other trauma-related injuries, and it is in use by the office of Veterans Affairs. EMDR has helped traumatized teens overcome a variety of horrendous experiences.

Much of what we know about the brain comes from studies conducted with senior citizens. We now know that cells continue to develop and neurological paths are created throughout life. Educators are busy designing effective ways of continuing the learning process for elders. The following news is both good and bad.

The good news: You have the power to change your brain. The brain can reorganize itself when confronted with new challenges, even through adulthood. A consortium of researchers including Columbia University, Harvard, Blue Cross Blue Shield, and Abbott Labs have developed a program called Luminosity.[93] Basically, they put together a series of exercises aimed at increasing memory, attention, speed, flexibility and problem solving. It works for those willing to put in the time and effort. Unfortunately, the company went overboard in some of their claims.

Support for their program, however, continues. It comes from many, like Shelli Kesler, assistant professor of psychiatry and behavioral sciences at Stanford University. She ran a study to measure how well Luminosity's brain training transferred to the real world by sampling 41 breast cancer patients who underwent chemotherapy treatment. Years of studies showed that Luminosity participants were psychologically and mentally helped by its training. Results are promising, and though not conclusive, it certainly cannot hurt to engage in brain exercises. I believe homeless youths benefit from these types of challenges that are perceived as fun rather than work.

The youth-service agencies I toured filled their social rooms with puzzles and games designed to stimulate the thinking process. It is a common sight in big cities to see youths on the street playing chess, checkers and cards competitively. As these youngsters succeed in their games, self-esteem improves and learning becomes easier.

The bad news: Findings of the American Psychological Association show that young people who smoke cannabis run the risk of a significant and irreversible reduction in their IQ,. Even once a week use is not safe and can result in addiction and neurocognitive damage.[94]

A study of 1,000 people in New Zealand had similar results.[95] Those who started using cannabis below the age of 18, while their brains were still developing, suffered a drop in IQ. They had an average of 8 percent drop in their intelligence test results, putting them at a disadvantage throughout their lives. Drug treatment programs present these findings in an effort to reach youths before it is too late.

The great news: There are many changes in how scientists access the aging brain. They used to look at the brain in terms of neuron failure. They now say that if you don't have a specific disease that causes loss of nerve cells, then most neurons remain healthy until death. The rate of change appears to be affected by lifestyle factors rather than old age. For instance, a lower weight may keep people from getting diseases like Alzheimers and Diabetes.

Education and the brain are subjects of national interest. Those who use it don't lose it as quickly. Reading, doing puzzles, getting a good night's sleep, staying away from drugs, and exercising regularly increases mental capacity. Marion Diamond, a friend and past professor of neuroscience at the University of California-Berkeley, was the first to show that the brain can change with experience and improve with enrichment. She was a remarkable woman who stayed active and sharp thinking until she died at age 90. Marion advised older people to change jobs, hobbies and exercise routines in order to build new capacities for thinking. She also advised that seniors be sure to have fun, for stress is an inhibitor to a healthy brain.

Her advice works equally well for all ages, and can be applied to abused youthw. Knowing that the brain can grow new neural connections throughout life has shown that improvement for adolescents is possible. By changing their lifestyle to one that includes good food and sound sleep, healthy brain cells have a chance to grow. Though they may have been neglected as children, they are still prime candidates for improving neurological connections.

As the song by The Doors says, "I've been down so Goddam long, that it looks like up to me — Yeah, why don't one you people c'mon and set me free."[96] A step toward positive change can turn into an avalanche of brain cell development. With the acquisition of workplace and social skills, physical exercise, elimination of drugs, and employing mindfulness practices, synapses multiply and bring better conductivity to the right places.

RESILIENCY

Developmental psychologists study ways that adversity can be transformed into positive outcomes. They want to find the reasons some people function well while others, facing similar situations, do not. About thirty years ago some researchers started taking a broader approach that explored molecular, individual and family levels. Their explorations led to a therapy called resiliency. It is an interdisciplinary approach that combines medical, social service and educational resources.[97] First proposed in the 1980s, resiliency focuses on individual strengths and the flexibility needed to survive trauma. It rests on psychological research that differs from past studies that cataloged risks with a goal of finding ways to fix problems. Earlier investigators looked for the factors contributing to poor outcomes with the idea of identifying high-risk youths in order to intervene and fix their problems. Their purpose was to help troubled youths become adept at meeting societal norms. Behavior modification was a common form of therapy they used to change disruptive conduct.

An example from my own casework occurred when employed by a community mental health facility. My patient, a college student, was afraid to get out of his car, cross the street, and enter a grocery store. During our sessions, he was asked to sit comfortably in a dark room with his back to me. I talked quietly to direct his thoughts and asked him to raise a finger as soon as he felt tense. After leading him through a few relaxation exercises, I slowly asked him to imagine getting into his car, driving to the store, and parking across the street. Each time he raised his finger, I went back a step and repeated the process until he felt comfortable. I focused on things he did well, such as his confidence in driving, interest in going places, what he would purchase when he walked into the store, and how he would carry it back to his car. Eventually, he was able to imagine opening his car door and stepping outside without feeling panicked. As he became more confident he could envision crossing the street and entering the store. Over the course of several sessions, his imagination took him calmly through the steps he would need to take in order to shop. A year later, I saw him on the street and he effusively thanked me. His life was positively affected by this behavior modification technique.

A resiliency paradigm is designed to enhance strengths as a way to initiate change.[98] It is a more holistic approach, recognizing that each youth has positive attributes that should be acknowledged and built upon. Healthy behavior is reinforced by assets that already exist within the person. The therapist's role is to identify and use these strengths as a basis for developing personal competencies that lead to feelings of accomplishment. The *Relational World View Model* mentioned in the previous section about the Native American Youth Association, is similar in concept.

With a resiliency approach, counselors investigate family, community and cultural factors that either disrupted or were helpful to the youth's development. Only after completing in-depth research into background factors is an integrated treatment plan proposed. As counseling continues, client and therapist work together to set goals, anticipating in advance that the path will never be a straight one since problems are not one-dimensional. For example, a child can develop academic competency and receive good grades but still exhibit emotionally risky behaviors due to other factors.

Mentors play an important role in resiliency therapies. Volunteer or paid staff, taught to appreciate the youth's strengths, encourage targeted education goals and skill development. Often this is the first time that someone has paid attention to the teen, offering praise as progress is made. Over time, budding feelings of self-worth have a snowball effect building toward healing and growth.

Cultural inhibitors also play an important role in resiliency. For example, a youth from a minority community who experienced or perceived racism has a harder time than one who has not been treated similarly. The story of Dewey Taylor's first day of being bused to an all-white school, demonstrates the shock of experiencing racism for the first time. It wasn't until the Black Panthers and James Brown shouted, "I'm black and I'm proud!" that Dewey mustered the strength to pull his life together.

Though a youth eventually may acquire job skills, negative cultural experiences can interfere with work and cause anti-social behavior, depression, anxiety and feelings of inadequacy. Promoting full resiliency requires understanding. Changing the cultural and social environment is commonly part of the treatment plan.

The counselor's goal is to help the youth lower risk factors that produce negativity. Eliminating drugs and alcohol often is a first step. By focusing on growth and adaptation, promoting self-actualization, altruism and harmony, youths are empowered to think more positively. Programs designed to promote self-care may include nutrition, use of condoms, drivers-ed, and outdoor survival challenges. Small steps are rewarded over and over again, raining down positive feelings of accomplishment.

Leland Leonard, director Tsehootsooi Medical Center in Arizona writes about Navajo adolescents and resiliency;

> *"Resilience is the natural, human capacity to navigate life well. It is something every human being has — wisdom, common sense. It means coming to know how you think, who you are spiritually, where you come from, and where you are going. The key is learning how to utilize innate resilience, which is the birthright of every human being. It involves understanding our inner spirit and finding a sense of direction."*[99]

Resiliency strategies are influenced by bioneurology which examines changes to cell structure that occur to those raised with poor nutrition, stress and drugs.[100] With better understanding of toxic stress, scientists documented its effect on the brain's ability to learn. Epigenetic researchers recently concluded that unhealthy environments can even change DNA so that it is carried on to the next generation. For instance, a pregnant mother living in poverty with poor nutrition can permanently affect the genetic makeup of her child.

Sean Suib from New Avenues for Youth introduced me to yet another way of thinking about the brain. He told me there were two types, and his comments were intriguing enough that I investigated further. Simply stated, one brain type is overstimulated while at rest and the other is understimulated. I believe mine is overstimulated. My brain does not like going on roller-coaster rides or being exposed to extreme circumstances. We who are overstimulated are hypersensitive since our brains are continuously at an "all systems go" level.[101] Our brains often cause us to have social anxiety and exhibit fear-based responses.

When it comes to taking physical risks I am cautious even though I like to get up on the roof and sweep off leaves. I am smart enough to attach a rope if I have to go to a particularly dangerous spot where the ground is 40 feet below.

Those of us with overstimulated brains have a difficult time becoming independent unless we learn to calm our minds. It takes courage to acquire self control and strike out on your own. In my twenties, I was held back by anxiety and fear. I turned down a wonderful position offered by the Boston Children's Museum when first graduating from college. I had to learn how to overcome my disability and eventually did so through the practice of Transcendental Meditation. Over time, I learned to relax and enjoy the chaos of a stimulating work environment. I started thriving under the pressures of decision-making that were required in a challenging job as president of the Oregon Museum of Science and Industry. Though I now consider myself more of a risk-taker, when it comes to financial and business activities, I am rarely impulsive. Moves are well analyzed and calculated.

The second brain type is understimulated.[102] Those with this type of brain have constant feelings of boredom. They are the thrill seekers who love roller-coaster rides and high-speed car chases. These individuals are in danger of depression and acquiring compulsive behaviors like drinking, smoking, and gambling. They seek extreme activities to overcome boredom and have a propensity for poor impulse control. Understimulated brains tend to feel and move through life without thinking of the future. Understimulation often is paired with a psychological condition known as a motivational syndrome, defined as a low desire to participate in social situations. Those with understimulated brains often are apathetic to what goes on in the world outside of themselves.

Zach, as do many homeless teens, had an understimulated brain. When he first came to live with us he constantly complained of boredom. I asked him what he wanted to do for a career and he answered, "I'm bored after doing any activity for a week or two." He appeared unmotivated since nothing was of interest long enough to move him off the couch. He lay there staring into space for hours, not responding to suggestions to go out and enjoy the world.

"Visit a friend," I would say or, "If you're bored, why not join a bowling team, volunteer or get a hobby." The answer was always, "I'm not interested." However, when it came to physical risks his response was different. Zach was ready to jump into danger as long as it was physical and someone else initiated it. He spoke longingly of bungee jumping, skydiving, speed racing and skateboarding while he lay on the sofa with little energy or money to pursue these dreams. Cory and I were challenged to recommend a career that would appeal to his understimulated brain. It had to be one that put him on the edge requiring him to pay close attention to what he was doing.

It was my husband who noticed how much Zach enjoyed standing on the roof and peering over the edge without being tied on by a rope. The higher the roofline, the happier he was. His attraction to physical danger led us to suggest that he become an industrial painter. This career calls for painting and sandblasting water towers that are 75 to 100 foot and where he can hang over the side. It requires walking along narrow platforms and climbing cables on bridges that span large distances over turbulent water. Once enrolled, Zach embraced his training and apprenticeship program with gusto. He was even willing to read technical pamphlets relating to painting. With experience and maturity he learned to solve problems in a more analytic, less stressful way.

As he experienced success, his brain adapted and his personality changed. He became more energetic, waking up at 5:30 each morning in order to be the first one at work. Zach was full of stories when he sat down for dinner and was more outgoing with fellow workers. Though he put in 10-12 hour workdays, often seven days a week, he never complained of boredom. When home, he developed a hobby of repairing old skateboards and enjoyed the speed of go-cart racing. No one had to tell him to do these activities, for his successes at work taught him that self-motivation can bring rewards.

It is a challenge for case workers to find the right amount of stimulation that propels an adolescent towards self-motivation. Vocational training, rites of passage, and challenging sports offer opportunities for excitement that address this need. Unfortunately, these pathways are not always available to poor youths.

MINDFULNESS

Mindfulness is a new name for an old concept known more commonly as meditation. They both require the practitioner to "be here now." Dr. Jon Kabat-Zin[103] developed the practice of mindfulness for use as a therapy while at the University of Massachusetts Medical Center. He called it Mindfulness Based Stress Reduction (MBSR), which avoided some of the concerns of those who saw it as a religious practice. Now along with yoga, it is widely used as an alternative medicine and has proven to be a helpful aid for those suffering from psychological trauma.[104] The goal of mindfulness training is to cultivate greater awareness of the body and to learn how unconscious thoughts, feelings and behaviors cause stress. A mindful person is aware of emotional, physical and spiritual problems that result from unhealthy experiences. Mindfulness is shown to lower blood pressure and over-reaction to emotional situations. An offshoot therapy called Mindfulness-Based Cognitive Therapy (MBCT) is used to treat depression by providing exercises that connect thinking with its impact on feelings. Students learn how to work with thoughts and emotions when depression becomes overwhelming, producing feelings of negativity.

I am an outspoken advocate for mindfulness training and meditation exercises, in part because it helped me overcome stress. In the early 1970s when Transcendental Meditation was the rage, I wholeheartedly embraced its practice, turning a shy, scared woman into one with enough confidence to preside over two major science museums and a $10 million business. A more scientifically minded person would say that the practice taught me how to control my involuntary nervous system. Instead of adrenaline spiking inappropriately, I learned to remain calm in the face of perceived danger, making me able to analyze the situation. With stress under control, blood pressure and heart rate were lowed. Meditation was especially helpful when medical issues led to several operations. I went through the procedures by being in the moment and not worrying about things beyond my control. The reason I managed as well as I did was because I practiced every day for many years.

Every youth agency I investigated offers mindfulness or meditation classes. Six to eight-week courses are found in centers from New York to California, each claiming that it improves the physical and mental well-being of those enrolled. Benefits include enhanced neuromuscular coordination and strength, kinesthetic awareness, better sleep and reduced fatigue, improved respiratory function, management of stress, higher cognitive efficiency, lower anxiety, improved ability to function under pressure, and better student grades. Emotional advantages show a reduction in depression, more positive feelings toward self, strengthened resilience, balanced moods, improved sense of calm and an increased capacity to cope.

The growing public interest in mindfulness as a therapy influenced granting agencies to be more open to funding studies of its effectiveness. Grantors are interested in documenting the benefits, pitfalls and cultural implications of its use as a therapy. Results, so far have been promising.

Mindfulness practice lessens the likelihood of reactive, aggressive, negative behavior. Symptoms of general distress are likely to decrease, which is beneficial to street youths who are at high risk of suicide. Relationships improve when the youth becomes self-aware and understands how to self-regulate. Many documented studies indicate enhanced social skills after training.

Learning to be mindful is a lifelong process. Training may begin in a counseling center but it takes commitment on the part of the client to reap significant results. It is interesting to note a recent trend in public schools where mindfulness is introduced as early as the second or third grade. Educators believe starting the practice at a young age will positively impact their students' lives over time.

Related to mindfulness are exercise programs like yoga, Pilates, and martial arts that focus the mind while toning the body. Their goal is to achieve harmony by practicing mindfulness in movement. Practitioners document lower levels of stress, depression, and anxiety. Flexibility improves as tendons and joints become lubricated through increased blood flow. Sleep is more sound and back and joint pains decrease as ligaments and tendons become better aligned. Overall posture and muscle tone make the student healthy, focused and ready to engage in the task at hand. Exercises provide an energy boost that lasts throughout the day. With improved mental focus, the brain is better prepared to tackle tasks and unexpected events. Future planning, clear reasoning clearly and enjoyment of mental challenges are the benefits of tapping into focused brain power. For despondent youth, mindfulness and yoga exercises can positively affect self-esteem.

Hands-on Learning

Smart, intelligent, intuitive, creative, and brainy? Absolutely. Every parent knows that what Garrison Keillor said is true — we all live where "the kids are above average." Each one of our children belongs in a TAG program for the gifted and talented. But what about children who have no parent behind them, no one to push them to achieve and let them know how special they are?

Those attending poor schools don't participate in TAG offerings where classes are small, kids are taken on field trips, and open-ended challenges are part of the teaching curriculum. Zach often would complain to me about school. He hated going and was bored because he couldn't follow what was going on. Part of the problem was that he was a poor reader and became a lost soul the education system couldn't help. An interactive approach with individual attention early on would have made a world of difference to his willingness to participate in academic learning. Even in wealthier schools, TAG is an option offered to few.

When my son was in second grade, his teacher decided that he was not gifted and therefore should not take the test for getting into TAG. She came to that conclusion because he was ADHD and was one of those children who found it difficult to stay put. My husband and I insisted that he be given the opportunity, and his test results came back as we predicted. He had a very high IQ and was invited to join the program, which he greatly enjoyed.

All children are not created equal. Some appear to have an easy time with life while others struggle with hidden demons in a less than tolerant society. Teachers are challenged by attention deficit disorder (ADD), or ADHD (hyperactive) children. Unfortunately, public class sizes are large, and overworked educators find it easier teaching attentive students who focus and don't cause disturbances. Energetic kids have other ideas. They want to move about. Some create trouble because it's the only way to get attention. They are the class clowns who divert attention away from their poor academic performance. Since these troublemakers are bored and disruptive, words of praise are seldom sent in their direction. Interestingly, TAG classes tend to be small and full of action. Students are free to roam because they are working on projects that require physical engagement along with creative thinking.

If we are to prevent youngsters from becoming school dropouts, it is imperative to change the way we work with sprightly children. They will blossom with attention that rewards their achievements rather than punish them by focusing on poor performance. In an effective classroom, the educator recognizes each child's passions and encourages interests that lead to competency and pride. Sadly, teachers are pushed to teach to the norm (or to the test) and are overwhelmed by the number of students they supervise. Though they work hard and are dedicated, most often they are not given adequate administrative help to assist disturbed children.

It takes time to pay attention to the variety of ways people learn. The word "smart" was redefined by Howard Gardner,

Hobbs Professor of Cognition and Education at Harvard Graduate School of Education.[105] In 2011, his epic book "Frames of Mind" was rereleased after a 30-year run.

Based on observational evidence, Gardner says that individuals approach learning in different ways. People have one or more ways of seeking knowledge, starting with their primary intelligence mode. Gardener's eight learning paths include: *Linguistics* – the effective use of language and words. *Logical-mathematical* – the ability to calculate, experiment and solve problems. *Visual-spatial* – awareness of the surrounding environment. *Musical/auditory* – thinking that demonstrates a sensitivity to rhythm and sound. *Bodily – kinesthetic* use of the body to solve problems or make things. *Intra-personal* – understanding of other individuals. *Interpersonal* – understanding of the self. *Naturalistic* intelligence was added later to include those ecologically sensitive to the world and its environment.

Why are Gardner's ideas important to disaffected youths? They present a way for the educator (parent, counselor and teacher) to assess the learning style of each child in order to teach in a way that reinforces strengths. In other words, an educator, knowing what needs to be taught, should take advantage of different intelligence styles rather than squashing them if they do not fit into the curriculum.

Many of the homeless youths I met have stronger auditory and tactile senses than linguistic ones. When this is the case, hands-on activities are a way to break through barriers that stand in the way of academic learning. Trade and art programs help those with kinesthetic intelligence while music reaches auditory learners. This does not mean that these children do not need to read. What it suggests is that reading matter is best introduced through the use of their strongest intelligence path as a way of getting to the written word.

As a past president of science centers, I took Gardner's writings to heart. Interactive devices were designed to appeal to different types of learners. We used auditory, tactile, visual, olfactory and interpersonal approaches to reach the diverse intelligence styles of our audience.

Zach is an example of a child who did not, would not read. He was a tactile/kinesthetic and visual learner but not linguistically talented. I discovered that he liked skateboarding, so I used his kinesthetic interest to get him to read books about his skateboarding hero. Though he was 20 years old at the time I provided seventh-grade reading material to start him off. He knew the award-winning skateboarders and devoured the books. Later I discovered that he did not know why the Foourth of July was celebrated so I probed further and found out that he knew little American history. Since helping him learn to read comfortably was my goal, I gave him a comic book written by Harvard grad, Larry Gonick. *The Cartoon History of the United States* provides graphics as well as words. The book was enticing enough to keep Zach engaged. He is now a much better reader, and though he still prefers videos and interacting with tactile objects, he regularly looks up information on his iPhone and reads trade journals with ease. His choice to become an industrial painter was wise since tactile and kinesthetic intelligence are needed to be successful in that career.

As previously noted, kids who do not graduate from high school have a 90 percent chance of spending their lives on the streets. We need to do everything we can to engage children in learning from the time they are born.

LITERACY

A few years ago *National Geographic* had an article about Australian aborigines. One man was quoted as saying, "Why read? When you are hungry, can you eat a book?"[106]

My answer is yes. If you can read you have a better chance of getting a job, earning money and putting food on your plate. Many street youths do not subscribe to this viewpoint. Zach used to argue with me, saying there is no need to read. He insisted that he can get all the information he needs off YouTube. He would listen uncritically to videos with jazzed up messages. He never looked into the truth of their message. Over time reading became easier and his interest in the greater world grew. The time he said, "please, do you mind not talking for a few minutes? I want to finish this article," I knew our efforts were successful. At dinner when my partner and I got into a disagreement over the news, he immediately went to his cell phone to an internet fact finder.

<hr />

There are a staggering 32 million illiterate people in the United States.[107] About 19 percent of high school graduates cannot read with prisons having a 70 percent illiteracy rate. I fear to be at the mercy of uneducated voters who, without facts, make decisions that affect my life. They do not have the critical reasoning skills needed to wade through reams of misinformation. They listen to hate mongers, rabble-rousers and advertisers who manipulate emotions. Even those who are marginally literate, are unwilling to dig deeply for information, for reading does not come easy.[108]

- **44 million adults can not read a simple story to their children**

- **Those who don't read proficiently by thirdrd or fourth-grade are four times more likely to drop out of school.**

- **85 percent of juveniles facing court trials are functionally illiterate.**

- **75 percent of food stamp recipients perform at the lowest two literacy levels.**

- **50 percent of adults cannot read a book written at the eighth- grade level.**

- **50 percent of unemployed youth (16-21 years old) are functionally illiterate.**

- The U.S. is the only free market economy where the current generation is less educated than the previous one.

- The U.S. ranks 12 out of 20 in literacy among high-income countries.

- 90 percent of high school dropouts are on welfare.

Literacy is a learned phenomenon that is passed on by parents. Children in illiterate families are unlikely to ever develop good reading habits. Most adults need to be able to read basic texts, understand legal and financial documents and navigate technology. Those who cannot do so miss out on job opportunities. If employed they earn an average of $230 to $245 a week and work for less than 20 weeks a year. Not-surprisingly, illiterate people are more likely to pass on gossip and misinformation to their friends.

It is not easy to motivate a reluctant reader for to do so requires a close and trusting relationship. It demands flexibility and being in tune with the psychological or physical blocks that impeded learning in the first place. Patience, compassion and persistence are called for. Happily, once the student experiences success, self-motivation often takes over. Eyes light up, understanding occurs and confidence builds. Mentors have told me that they receive as much as they give.

Betty Hart. and Todd Risely, both with doctorates, discovered a startling phenomenon while conducting research at the University of Kansas.[109] In their book *The Early Catastrophe: The 30 Million Word Gap by age 3 (2003,)* they write that there is a direct link between a child's academic performance in the third grade and the amount of words spoken in their home from birth to age three. Kids from a lower economic status are likely to hear 30 million fewer words than wealthier parents who communicate freely to their young ones. Yet, those parents of lower socioeconomic status who did talk to their children were equally successful. It is not race, ethnicity or socioeconomic status that influences success but rather constant talk that starts with *goo-goo* and *bye-bye* and continues by paying attention to the words and sounds their youngsters use when trying to communicate. "In four years, an average child in a professional family would accumulate experience with almost 45 million words, an average child in a working-class family 26 million words, and an average child in a welfare family 13 million words."

Children raised in poor and traumatized households are not likely to get the attention needed to develop language skills. It is rare that they are read to at bedtime or encouraged to share their thoughts over dinner and express their needs in conversation. Those who learn how to communicate with ease have an edge. Hart and Risley advise, "So if you have little ones at home, talk to them. Talk a lot. It may seem silly to gab incessantly, but it can make a big difference. And your third-grader will thank you."

You might easily imagine the handicaps that plague children who are raised in poverty, live on the streets or barely survive in their dysfunctional homes. It is no wonder that as teens they drop out and runaway without hope or thought of a future.

STAGES OF CHANGE

Change is never easy. Just ask an addict or person trying to shed a few pounds. There are systems counselors employ to understand the recovery process. One documents how clients move through a series of stages to adopt healthy behaviors. I found the analysis fascinating because it explained a lot about my own reluctant behaviors when trying to change.

Based on more than two decades of research, the *Stages of Change* model proposed in 1992 suggests that most people who want to heal, start tentatively with only a bit of thought before moving to more active contemplation.[110] Eventually, whirling thoughts move on to a stage of preparation or determination. The person becomes ready to take action and give their end goal a try. The process is rarely straight without occasional relapses, but over a period of time, it settles down to a maintenance level. The client is considered cured when he or she is unlikely to relapse. It becomes time to terminate counseling. The length of time a person stays in a particular stage may vary but the tasks necessary to move to the next level do not.

At the onset, most people don't intend to take action in the foreseeable future. They don't see the problem, so are not looking for a solution. They may be uninformed about the consequences of their behavior or demoralized by false starts they undertook in the past. Traditional programs do not work at this stage. It is only when entering the contemplation stage and there is intention to change within the next six months that the pros and cons of remaining stuck are considered. As the problem begins to make itself understood, the person wonders about possible solutions. They enter a procrastinating stage of should I or shouldn't I, that may take a long time before they are willing to act. Slowly, their thoughts turn more to the future than the past.

Once a decision is made to proceed, lingering ambivalence has to be resolved before they are ready to continue. Taking action is an indication that change is welcome. The person may see a counselor, join a gym, or reduce their use of cigarettes at this stage. This is when clients can be enticed to participate in an action-oriented program.

Change takes a great commitment of time and energy but by this time in the process, people are motivated to do so. Taking action now is equated with a sufficient reduction of risk of disease or unhealthy lifestyle, and a professional can look at the person and note their progress. For instance, moving from fewer, low-tar cigarettes to eliminating them altogether counts as action. Action, however, is not enough if the person is secretive about what they are doing. Making a public commitment, as weight loss programs and drug and alcohol rehab centers do, is helpful. Having as cheerleaders those who already have been through similar situations can be motivating, since over time, success breeds success. When Zach was at Job Corp his instructors handed out awards in the form of certificates and coupons for food and clothing. But the best thing they did was to announce his accomplishment before the group. He was very proud of the small steps acknowledged on the way to successfully completing his program. Hope and self-confidence continued to develop with benefits that snowballed over the years.

Maintenance involves a strong commitment to lifestyle change and can last from six months to five years. There is often a relapse that put people back to the precontemplation stage so counselors try to arm their clients with ways to avoid backslides by being shown where to get help to restart the process when needed. It is not unusual for people go through the various stages several times before they make it all the way to the end and counseling can be terminated. Ultimate success means that there is little fear of relapse.

Knowledge of this behavioral cycle can be useful to parents as well as those working with homeless and runaway youths. Caregivers who analyze risks and benefits of behavior often point out how the youth's reluctance will affect his or her future. They help the teen acknowledge his rebelliousness and that he rationalized his behavior. So many homeless youths do not understand that there are consequences to their behavior. A great deal of patience is needed, for relapses are the norm rather than the exception.

LOVE?

Numerous studies show early intervention as being the most effective time to establish healthy emotional patterns. I previously mentioned the importance of touch, love and compassion to newborn infants. But what happens when children spend their infancy deprived of love and attention? What if they are rarely touched? Sadly, they are likely to become one of the children found sleeping in doorways, couch surfing in hovels, or assigned to juvenile detention homes.

Psychologist Philip Fisher at the University of Oregon says

that abnormalities are a result of stress and that contributing factors must be reduced before there can be a positive outcome.[111] Disturbed youths can not be dealt with in isolation. Fisher suggests that training be given to care parents to help them understand that they are not dealing with a normal brain. Once the facts are accepted, it is easier to grasp the difficulties their child faces. They become better able to learn coping mechanisms that address the dysfunctional behaviors displayed at home. When a child repeatedly makes the same mistake, frustrated caregivers are taught that it is not unusual behavior and they must be patient. Children sense if their parents bthink they're beyond help and have given up on them. Recognizing how difficult it is to help a needy child when under duress, Fisher also suggests that caregivers learn to reduce their own stress.

It helps when behavior modification programs and support groups are organized for children and caregivers.Targeted interventions, such as computer-based brain training games are also used to help youth tune into social cues they are not used to seeing. These programs are fun and known to have positive results, especially when the entire family joins together to improve the home atmosphere. Unfortunately, many parents have so many problems of their own that they are not willing or able to spend the time to help their disturbed child.

Child psychologist, Alan Sroufe, is an internationally recognized expert on early attachment relationships, emotional development and developmental psychopathology. While studying mother-infant attachment, Sroufe recognized that once a dysfunctional pattern of interaction is established it is difficult (though not impossible) to break.[112] He was one of the first to set up a program in the United States to teach parenting skills and to monitor results. In his classes, mothers were taught the meaning of their child's behavior and shown ways of responding appropriately. As the women changed their attitudes over the weeks, they were rewarded by positive improvements in their children's behaviors. Sroufe also discovered that it is not enough to teach mothers when the father is not on board. A supportive partner is extremely important if therapy is to work for without the father's agreement, the mother's participation is undermined.

Many of the women sampled were not only neglected as children but also had been victims of sexual abuse. "Mothers fail in part," he says, "because they do not know how to be nurturing. Since they did not learn the skill from their own parents they are likely to bring dysfunctional practices to the next generation. A great many mothers look to their children for the love and care that they lacked when they were young."

Once the youth's safety is secured, caseworkers put together intervention plans. Most assume that children do best when surrounded by family so whenever possible, their goal is to reestablish ties with parents or caregivers who are more likely to provide a loving atmosphere than strangers. As Kevin Donegan from Janus Youth Services Programs said, "By the time kids are in their thirties they all want to go home for the holidays." Parents may need help in overcoming past prejudices and resentments they are harboring before they begin to appreciate their child's strengths. A surprising number of adults need to be taught how to express love and positive feelings. Once a parent understands their child's needs, they are more likely to be supportive and nurturing than abusive.

No counselor wants to send a youth back to the same situation that caused flight to the streets in the first place. But there are times when a less than desirable home life is a better solution than foster care or a residence where drugs, alcohol and prostitution abound. Unfortunately, it may take years to effect change and funding is limited for ongoing family counseling. Yet, without the family's commitment to their child, success rates are marginal.

There are times when the state intervenes and takes a child away from the home to be placed in foster care. All too often the placement backfires and the child's problems are compounded by abusive foster parents. Some difficulties caused by a child's continuing misconduct are the result of ignorance, for many substitute parents don't understand the survival reactions of traumatized children. They expect their foster child to be docile and appreciative of being fed and housed. When a youth misbehaves, the caregiver may react negatively with anger. Some go a step further and become physically or verbally abusive. Foster parents need skills similar to those of a child psychologist before they are trusted with an abused youth, for their job is not going to be an easy one. They would benefit greatly by training.

⊷••••••••••⊷

THE CURRENT STATE OF FOSTER CARE
SYSTEM NUMBERS AND TRENDS

In 2015, there were an estimated 670,000 children who spent time in foster care.[113] Here are a few more statistics:

- Most children remained in care for nearly two years.

- More than half of the children were of color

- The average age was nearly 9 years old.

- More than 62,000 children were waiting to be adopted because their parents' rights had been legally terminated.

- Twenty thousand aged out without having anywhere to go.

Being placed in the "safety" of foster care does not always guarantee that the child is safe from abuse—28 percent of the children in foster care are abused.[114] Many caseworkers are young and do not pick up on abuse in family homes. They often turn a blind eye and rarely ask probing questions. Group homes also have problems, in part, because children are moved around based on a system of levels. The child then is faced with new teachers, therapists, classmates, roommates and home life. Abuse, including beatings with paddle or razor strap, is not uncommon. One foster family required their children to memorize the Bible or be subject to a beating. Once placed in an abusive individual or group home it is not unusual for the child to start to distrust authority figures. As a protective measure they may become emotionally detached.

After age 18, foster children face tough times. For 30,000 youths the cutoff of funding is abrupt. They are asked to move out and are on their own in finding a job, obtaining housing or applying to college. They have lost their lifeline to parents, adults, and home. One study of foster children conducted in Iowa, Wisconsin and Illinois showed what happened to them by the of ages of 23 and 24.[115]

- Less than half were employed.

- Almost 25 percent had been homeless since exiting foster care.

- More than 75 percent of young women had been pregnant since leaving foster care.

- Nearly 60 percent of young men had been convicted of a crime, and more than 80 percent had been arrested.

- Only 6 percent had a two- or four-year college degree.

Love contributes to a sense of belonging, something all people need. When not provided by family, children seek out love and friendship elsewhere. Once on the streets, they immediately identify with other homeless kids and embrace their morality. Zach's story demonstrates how he transitioned through several stages of attachment. He first identified with the teens he met, accepting their rudderless mores. Those values were superseded when he enrolled in Job Corps and found a more focused affinity group, one that had goals and foresaw a future. Upon graduation, Zach moved into a relationship with brothers in the International Union of Painters and Allied Trades (IUPAT). Through these transitions, my partner and I provided Zach with security and let him know that we believed in him. We told him how much we enjoyed his company and provided warmth and love as best we could.

Kanoe Egleston fof NAYA mentioned how important her heritage was as a young Hawaiian surrounded by a loving family and shared what happened when she came to the United States to study and lost the security of belonging. Jimmy James's accounting is presented in a future chapter. It demonstrates how acceptance by the Native-American community gave him the grounding he sorely needed. Knowing the importance of identifying with a group, NAYA encourages Native youths to participate in community activities and take pride in being a "First American."

MENTAL ILLNESS

My early training in mental heath was during the time large state hospitals were emptied of their patients. Simultaneously, government subsidies were cut. Community health centers, were inadequate to care for the needs of so many seriously ill people, ushering in an era of increased homelessness. As a young counselor, I was traumatized when my 21-year-old client committed suicide. This football player was devastated when a knee injury dashed his dreams of playing for a professional team. He became severely depressed and needed an extended stay in a mental institution to see him through a rough time. Instead, after a three-day hospital stay, he was sent home to parents who were inadequately prepared to care for him.

The Canadian Journal of Adolescent Psychiatry conducted a random study of 60 youth in homeless shelters and found 50 percent of them to be clinically symptomatic or with a drug addiction problem.[116] The study, one among many, provides evidence that mental illness undermines problem-solving abilities needed for survival. Only recently have social agencies for the homeless started addressing psychiatric diseases, but it is a growing area of concern. The Canadian teen population mirrors that of the United States, so I include the following information as an approach to combat *hopelessness*.

There is conflicting evidence about whether lack of shelter undermines hope. Therapists say that without optimism, there is suffering, which in severe cases can lead to suicide. Youths with stable housing are more likely to feel hopeful and able to perceive themselves as resilient, are less lonely, and engage in fewer life-threatening behaviors. Those in unstable living situations are more likely to have bleak, hopeless attitudes, becoming easily depressed and in need of psychiatric intervention. Counselors face a conundrum, for unless a mentally ill youth walks into their clinic seeking help, there is not much that can be done for a disturbed adolescent wandering the streets.

Homeless adolescents never use fee-based services and only rarely use those that are free. Hospital emergency rooms are the path of least resistance when health concerns are serious. Since most teens consider themselves to be more mentally stable than they actually are, the burden falls on emergency room and clinic practitioners to identify those who are unstable and offer services beyond the presenting illness.

The majority of youths in the Canadian study left home because of a traumatic incident though most did remain in contact with their family. As a whole, they were poorly educated (without a high school degree), yet there were some among them who were previously good students. Because of variations, researchers recommended not categorizing mentally ill street youths by statistical averages. Each adolescent carried unique and horrific experiences onto the streets and needed an individualized service plan to prevent them from taking extreme life-ending measures.

Several suggestions came out of the study:

1. The need for mentors to assist in navigating the health system

2. Nonjudgmental providers working in an environment with flexible policies

3. Attention to culturally diverse and psychologically challenged populations

4. The need for the provider to establish immediate trust

5. A person on staff who shares the same ethnic background as the client

U. S. statistics report that 20 to 25 percent of people who live on the streets suffer from severe mental illness as compared to 6 percent of the general population. Psychological problems contribute to an inability to develop stable relationships, and the youths often push away caregivers, family members and friends willing to assist.

Emotional problems often lead to physical disease because of neglectful health practices and inadequate hygiene. Skin diseases, exposure to tuberculosis or HIV, and respiratory diseases are among those commonly seen in emergency room settings. Minorities are especially vulnerable. Those who are mentally ill are prone to self-medicate by using readily available street drugs.

Contrary to popular belief, once identified and contacted by a health provider, mentally ill adolescents tend to accept treatment willingly. Housing, though a first concern of runaways and caseworkers, does not give adequate care for emotionally challenged teens in need of a trusting counselor. Those from impoverished backgrounds also require lessons in personal hygiene, finances and how to navigate the health care system. Emotional problems are not easily mended and require treatment and supportive services over many years. Education, employment, money management and peer support need to be integrated into medical and psychological treatment plans.

The U.S. Department of Housing and Urban Development, Projects for Assistance in Transition from Homelessness (PATH), the American Recovery and Reinvestment Act (ARRA) and the National Alliance to End Homelessness are charged with serving mentally ill youths. However, they are underfunded and unable to meet the demand for service.[117] Between 2005 and 2010, approximately 2 million adolescents between the ages of 12 and 17 were diagnosed with a mental disease, with suicide being the second leading cause of death. Numbers are especially high among distressed kids living near or under the federal poverty line. Those affected are more likely to be girls than boys and twice as likely be white non-Latino than Mexican-American. These statistics are helpful but inadequate when accounting for African-American and Mexican-American adolescents who are less inclined to report mental distress.

The reason mental disease is rising is attributed to the use of illicit drugs, alcohol abuse, cigarette dependence and environmental factors such as industrial pollutants. Changes in school and family environments also have been contributing factors. Single-parent households, low-wage earners, drugs and gang infested neighborhoods have contributed to the growth of mental problems among youths. A high percentage of children raised up in poor neighborhoods without access to nutritious food develop weak bodies and have emotional problems. Further stress from being homeless and perpetually in poverty exacerbates mental issues. The situation can create problems where none previously existed. Since they don't have healthcare, disturbed youths are likely to be counted as adults where they are viewed as chronically homeless and therefore not offered treatment.

Mental problems tend to accelerate in the late teens and early 20s, causing impulsive acts and irrationality.[118] But oftentimes, symptoms are visible earlier, well before the youth gets into serious trouble and leaves home. Family physicians and parents need to intervene when distress is first suspected, for once the teen has left home it's harder to get help. Homeless youth are wary and tend to distrust the medical system because they don't think they will be taken seriously. They believe adult solutions are likely to involve pills being thrown at them rather than helping them understand the root cause of their problems. When sent to mental wards that serve a mixed-age group, they don't feel free to discuss their problems. Adolescents need to be in environments among their peers, and not with mature adults.

It is important to remember that treatment only works if the person is ready and not compelled. Culturally specific counseling of a nontraditional nature that prepares them to go through the stages of change has a better chance of succeeding. For instance, a depressed LGBTQ youth might need peer mentors who are encouraging, while an anorexic teen might be aided by someone who overcame an eating disorder. A learning disabled child might benefit from tutoring. In each case, the counseling goal is to motivate the youth to want to overcome their dysfunction and develop a personalized action plan.

DRUGS AND ALCOHOL

There are wide variations of treatment and a great many facilities helping drug and alcohol abusers. Both behavioral and pharmacological approaches are used when dealing with complex disorders that affect every aspect of the person's functional life. Family, employment, school and community are impacted by the user as well as the supplier.

Drug addiction is commonly treated as a chronic disorder with occasional relapses expected. Short-term, one-time treatment is rarely enough to overcome addiction, and long-term treatment involves many types of interventions along with regular monitoring.[119] Detoxification does little to change the outcome of long-term drug abuse, though it is the first step— along with medical care— that an addict has to take. For those dependent on opioids, drugs like methadone, buprenorphine and naltrexone are prescribed while nicotine addicts are given patches, gum, lozenges and nasal spray. Alcoholics may be treated with disulfiram, acamprosate or naltrexone. It is not uncommon for users to have more than one addiction, which further complicates treatment and tests their livers.

Those taking prescription drugs are affected in similar ways to street addicts in that its use affects their brains. I knew a cancer patient who, while undergoing chemotherapy, became permanently mentally ill after her third session. Drugs of all types can have dangerous side effects.

To help addicts, physicians prefer prescribing nonaddictive drugs for medical conditions along with behavioral therapies. They hope to motivate the patient to participate in his or her own treatment, to stay on course, and to develop strategies to prevent relapses.

Group therapies are useful because they provide social reinforcement from peers. Those suffering from a multitude of health and personal problems, however, usually need individualized counseling as well. It is not unusual to see mentally ill addicts have issues caused by HIV, legal problems, occupational difficulties or myriad family issues. Psychiatrists may prescribe antidepressants and mood stabilizers in hopes that the person will be better able to face his or her problems in the counseling office. Each patient requires a thorough assessment before the right combination of therapies is employed.

The Office of National Drug Control Policy suggests a number of ways communities can improve the way they deal with the nation's growing problems with drug addiction.[120] The strategies are easy to list but difficult to implement.

- Prevent drug use in communities;

- Seek early intervention opportunities in health care;

- Integrate treatment for substance use disorders into health care and supporting recovery;

- Break the cycle of drug use, crime and incarceration;

- Disrupt domestic drug trafficking and production;

- Strengthen international partnerships; and

- Improve information systems to better address drug use and its consequences.

Drug courts are an especially effective strategy that have been adopted for use in every state.[121] They originally were set up to target nonviolent offenders with substance-abuse problems. Their goal is to break the cycle of substance abuse, addiction and crime by offering offenders in-depth help. Participants who voluntarily agree to be involved in treatment rather than incarceration are provided with intensive court supervision, mandatory drug testing, substance-abuse treatment, and other social services such as job-training, employment, education and housing assistance.

The effectiveness of drug courts is state-dependent for they require adequate funding and support of follow-up programs. Recently, 27 evaluations were combined, compared and analyzed to look at recidivism, relapse, program completion, costs and benefits. The assessment found a statistically significant reduction in recidivism since the drug courts were instituted. However, when looking at relapses, the story is less clear, with mixed results. Program completion rates ran from 66 percent to 27 percent, again dependent on state resources. The study concluded that overall, society benefits from reductions in drug use, crime, medical services and from having more users become employed.

EMERGENCY PREPAREDNESS

It is during times of crisis caused by natural or manmade disasters that the most vulnerable among us suffer greatly. The slightest setbacks can have disastrous consequences for children and adolescents. For example, in January 2017, Portland, Oregon had an unusual storm that dumped 14 inches of snow on city streets. In general, Portland winters are mild, but that year, below-freezing temperatures plagued the city for many days.

Shut-ins and those living in poverty suffered. Four homeless people died of exposure and many children went hungry. When schools close for inclement weather, children in low-income families often go without food. In Portland, where over 50 percent of the students participate in federally subsidized breakfast and lunch programs, cancelled school days mean lots of hungry bellies.

Portland's mayor declared a state of emergency during the storm, asking drivers to stay home so the plows could do their work unencumbered by stranded cars. His directive impacted Meals on Wheels recipients who went hungry, since most vehicles were unable to navigate unplowed streets. It took two days before enough shelters were able to get the homeless off the streets. It was a massive undertaking coordinated by the city and county that included the fire bureau, police department, bureaus of emergency communications, transportation and water, human services, a mobile mental health crisis team and the Bureau of Emergency Management. These good people worked day and night in committees to acquire warm coats, boots, mittens and quilts. Volunteers were dispersed to vulnerable neighbors to ask whether help was needed.

Though most Oregon communities are involved in emergency planning, the most vulnerable are usually the last to receive services. For example, a recommendation for earthquake preparedness is that each person set aside 14 gallons of water in their home or apartment. Homeless people most certainly have no way of doing so. Imagine an earthquake, hurricane, tornado or tsunami hitting your town. Emergency responders and hospital staff will attend to the most drastic situations first. Those who have bank accounts, stocked pantries, vehicles, neighbors and relatives will be better able to survive than poor and homeless people who will have to endure days, weeks or even months of added trauma.

Portland's snowstorm was a wake-up call for community leaders. The mayor did an excellent job of coordinating emergency personnel to deal with the situation. Though the event lasted only a few days there was recognition that there needs to be a plan in place for those without shelter. Puerto Rico's Hurricane Maria of 2017 is another example of what happens when people are left stranded. With limited transportation and no electricity, the Bureau of Emergency Management was incapable of giving special attention to those unable to care for their own needs. Advanced preparation for emergency situations that considers housing, communication and food for the poor, homeless, mentally ill and homebound seniors is a must if humanitarian crises are to be averted. A trained network of volunteers who know what to do and where to go for on-the-spot instructions is part of the solution.

Emergency preparedness and the ethics of helping one's neighbors should be introduced in the elementary grades. Friends should be directed to call one another to see if they are OK or need food or clothing. Families need up-to-date first-aid kits, extra food, water, easily accessible clothing, and an identified meeting spot to go to in case of separation. Homeless youth also need instructions in what to do and where to go in case of an emergency. Shelters could play a role in teaching their clients.

SECTION V
WHAT MAKES HOPE?

T HE FOLLOWING TWO STORIES DEMONSTRATE ways youths can be helped to overcome their dysfunctional childhoods. The story of *Young Scholar* demonstrates the importance of mentoring programs. *Jimmy James'* story shows how spirituality and cultural identity can aide in overcoming years of trauma.

THE TALE OF YOUNG SCHOLAR

Jeff Gottfried, former director of education at the Oregon Museum of Science and Industry (OMSI), initiated and received National Science Foundation (NSF) funding to conduct an innovative Young Scholars program. High school students were selected from a national pool of teens interested in working alongside research scientists during their summer vacation. There was never difficulty in finding applicants with a 4.0-grade-point average who wanted to take advantage of the opportunity. Most came from middle- and upper-class families who encouraged their children to exceed. Jeff looked beyond the obvious to find children with talent but who, for reasons of poverty or family dysfunction, were not high achievers. He asked teachers to make suggestions of those who might fit into the category of unrecognized talent.

Sure enough, one of the local high school teachers mentioned a boy whose family moved annually because of nonpayment evictions. The father was a Vietnam vet who, if entering treatment today, would be diagnosed with post-traumatic stress disorder (PTSD). His mother, suffering from a variety of mental and physical illnesses, also was incapacitated. If the police had not picked up the neglected boy one fall while roaming the beach he never would have started school. There were numerous occasions when the family spent the night sleeping in their car.

Teachers encouraged the teen to apply for the summer research position despite having poor grades. Young Scholar's appearance and manner of speaking was mismatched to his knowledge but they saw through superficial attributes to a spark of genius. His grades were low Bs and Cs and his command of English was marginal. His clothes were shabby, indicative of his poverty, yet his application essay was compelling as he wrote of his life with its challenges, so Jeff decided to take a risk on the young man. His intuition was good, and I named the boy "Young Scholar," for throughout the summer he became energized, hopeful and more studious.

His research was focused on an environmental study of water quality of rivers in eastern Oregon. During a site visit, Jeff noticed that Young Scholar was not present during dinner. Inquiring about his whereabouts, he was told that the boy was so wrapped up in his research that he didn't like to stop what he was doing until it became too dark to see. Later that evening, Jeff overheard Young Scholar asking another youth if ther e was a possibility of living with the boy's family the following school year since his parents were planning to move once again. Jeff immediately discussed the situation with his wife and they decided to invite the boy to stay in their home during the following academic year.

Jeff drove Young Scholar to his apartment, loaded a few belongings into his car, and brought him home to caring, creative people who applauded learning. The following year, Young Scholar never missed a day of school, earned a 4.0-grade-point average, and won a Bausch and Lomb Science Award upon graduation. This prestigious award included a four-year full scholarship to Rochester University. It was quite an achievement and shows what can happen when a caring adult recognizes the potential of a struggling youth and does something about it.

Young Scholar accepted the scholarship and went off to study science while cleaning dorms to augment his stipend. He returned to Jeff's house for vacations where he was respected and loved as a member of the family. Upon graduation, Young Scholar accepted a job as a teacher in a private school in New Orleans, returning to Oregon several years later to obtain a master's degree in environmental science with a focus on sedimentology. With diploma in hand, he went on to enter a doctoral program at Tulane University.

When Tulane suffered hurricane Katrina's force, the student thought he lost his doctoral dissertation. Instead, understanding adversity, he did not remain still but rescued his thesis from the floodwates even though the campus was closed. Defending his thesis, however, was difficult because his committee scattered to various locations throughout the country. He undertook the arduous task of reassembling his dissertation committee in order to graduate. Today Young Scholar is a married man with two children and supports himself as a college professor. Because of astute teachers who recognized his brilliance, inspiration gained by participating in museum-sponsored research, and a dedicated museum educator willing to go the extra mile, Young Scholar became a contributing member of society.

JIMMY JAMES - A SPIRITUAL LIGHT

Jimmy's story is insightful because it demonstrates how a spiritual connection can overcome despair. Surviving an abusive childhood and bereft of stable role models, Jimmy was able to move from childhood trauma to become a productive adult, giving back to the community that helped him succeed. Youth homelessness is identified as a governmentally recognized problem for those between the ages of 14 and 25. Unfortunately, mental anguish does not come to an end on the 26th birthday when funding ends. It may continue for years into adulthood. Jimmy is an insightful man who portrayed with clarity the agony of his long journey. To share his tale, names and places were altered.

The 1966 book by Richard Farina, *Been Down So Long It Looks Like Up To Me*, parallels Jimmy's life in that he hit rock bottom to crawl in the muck before he could stand to see the truth of his traumatized childhood and consider possibilities for his future. He gives hope to all who are down and out and demonstrates what it takes to overcome years of abuse. Jimmy's story demonstrates how moments of success are all too often followed by setbacks. There is no such thing as a straight path to successful healing. Lastly, Jimmy's insights tell of the power of belonging and identifying with a group of people willing to help you change.

Climbing over or going around the *Peanut Fence* is a prickly affair that counselors alone cannot accomplish no matter how competent they are. Mending and then moving on takes internal willpower and stamina.

———————

"The blows kept coming. The enraged gorilla that charged me had no intention of stopping to listen to reason. Certain I was going to die, I defended myself as best I could, but though an athlete, I didn't have the strength or will to hit back. It was when his boot came crashing down on my head that my mother finally sprang to action and for the first time rushed to my defense, throwing herself between our bodies. Two brothers and my sister watched in horror as my father's anger turned toward Mom. He first grabbed and threw her across the room, but as soon as he realized what he had done, his rage seemed to fizzle out. Dad was in a daze. H looked around, turned and walked out of the room without another word. Fortunately, the younger kids had been spared.

"I knew then, at the age of 15, that I had to leave home. Dad was a full-blown alcoholic and drug abuser turned psychopath, and my survival depended on escaping his erratic behavior. I had had enough.

"What caused his angry outburst? Money had gone missing from the top of his dresser and he immediately assumed one of us kids was the culprit. He lined us up for questioning, but when no one admitted to the crime, out came the hardwood paddle he always grabbed when preparing to do damage. As the oldest, I was first to be told to pull down my pants. Knowing I was innocent I refused, thus provoking Dad's uncontrolled reaction. He did not tolerate "no" for an answer. It is ironic that several days later the missing cash was discovered behind his bedroom bureau where it accidentally had fallen from its resting place. There was no apology. There never was.

"My childhood was not easy. I came from a long line of abusive, unstable adults raised on discipline derived from military upbringings. My parents grew up on bases surrounded by soldiering killers who gave their lives to the services. Their fathers were both bird colonels in the army which meant that their families lived with privileges. They had servants to ease the way as they traveled from one base to another. Though the men often were absent from home, their strict upbringing infused my parents with authoritarian values. Kids in military families did as told and never talked back.

"My parents first met in Boston and fortuitously, a second time at college in L.A. where they fell in love. Mom arrived one day to model for Dad's drawing class and he was instantly smitten. She was an attractive fashion design student who shared his creative interests. It wasn't long before she became pregnant which in those days meant immediate marriage. Dad eventually graduated as a draftsman, but after a few years he became more interested in design engineering. Though self-taught, he became capable and respected for his many accomplishments. In those early days, before his total inebriation, Dad was a good provider, which enabled Mom to stay home. She kept herself busy as a mother of four and caring for a large Victorian house.

"When I was 12, Dad decided that it was time to move and try a different lifestyle. He took our family to a small cottage in the wings of a redneck town in Oregon. It was quite a change from our large house and the big city amenities we were used to in L.A. At the end of the year, though, we did move into better quarters and bought another large Victorian house near the center of town.

"Life for us kids was filled with fear, for we were often slapped around and never knew when the next outrage would occur. Being subjected to both psychological and physical abuse made us insecure and belligerent. Though both parents enjoyed the bottle, Dad took addiction one step further by taking and selling drugs. He started associating with gangsters and developed an executive clientele that let him to support our family well.

"Thankfully, my parents divorced while in their thirties, though upon leaving, Dad left Mom with few resources for our care. But once gone, the danger from his uncontrolled anger was no longer a daily threat. Mom was now the one we had to watch out for, but at least she was not physically abusive.

"No matter how horrendous parents are, there is a conflict between what we think is love and the desire to be loved. Terror and fear are always laced with wishful thinking. Dad was a psychopath unable to feel remorse, yet he could justify his cruel actions in his own mind. I did not know until years later that he had been sexually abused by his mother when he ws a child. It obviously scarred him for life. Eventually he, too, became a predator involved in sexual acts against children. Though my sister once pressed charges against him for molestation, nothing came of it. It wasn't until his late thirties that he was caught and sent to prison for life.

"I was a mess as a teen, mentally unstable even then. My first drugs were given to me by well meaning doctors. In those days,Valium was the preferred way of handling out-of-control kids, and I certainly was one of them. It was about the same time, at the age of 13, that I also started drinking. With role models like my parents, it was the natural thing to do.

"Dad was out of the house, but my worries were not over. As a good Catholic, I attended parochial schools, became an altar boy and was surrounded by priests, nuns and seminarians who often were invited to the house. Though not a good student, my abilities were great, with intelligence tests showing that I was well above average.

"The first sick encounter I had with a priest was when I was only eight. We were in his car when the man started fondling me. I was too afraid to say anything. A number of years later it was a college-bound seminarian who pinned me down on the ground and dry-humped me. That time I did complain but was told by his superiors that I must have been mistaken and just didn't understand what was happening. They were convinced I was a troubled child — which I was but . . . "I understood, all right, that nothing was going to happen to the man. Where was God? Boy, was I happy when years later the Catholic Church was raked over the coals for concealing sexual abuses. I did not put in a legal claim, but my soul went out to the hapless victims. Yet, despite being abused, in general, I liked the theologians. Many of the nuns and priests were stellar people who, unfortunately, were mixed in with troubled ones.

"After confirmation, I went on an angry rampage. I lit every candle in the church, robbed the charity boxes, and grabbed a bottle of wine before sitting down to have a conversation with God where I called on the devil. I shouted that the world was fucked up, that it's not a good place to be and it was his responsibility to show me something. 'Are you real or not?' I screamed. 'Show me what you got.'

"In my push to leave home, I enlisted in the Marines at 16, though I had to wait a year before I was eligible to go. If it was not for the military keeping me occupied for a few years, I would have been on the streets. However, after serving for only 18 months, my childhood and service traumas came tumbling down around me. With this first mental collapse, I was medically discharged. Leaving the military with benefits enabled me to register for college under the the GI bill. A period of on again and off again stints as a student, involvement with drugs and living on the streets was interspersed with an occasional mental breakdown.

"On the positive side, the community college I attended reframed my idea of education. I took wonderful classes in the arts, athletics, social sciences and writing. Since I loved sports and exercise my goal was to become a health education instructor. At the same time I used my skill on the guitar to join a band that got gigs before wild college audiences. We were pretty good — even had occasional standing ovations.

"Nevertheless, each time I moved ahead I was held back by

my addictions. I dropped out of college and went to work for a company that made garage doors. With speed as an aid, I proved to be a dedicated employee and was promoted to a full-time metal worker. It was while working in that position that I foolishly took a short cut moving between two dangerous machines and I lost my hand above the wrist. I was lucky that it was a warm time of year that called for short-sleeve shirts or I could have been pulled further into the machine.

"Until that moment, despite being emotionally broken, I had always felt bulletproof. I was still young and believed I could not get hurt from any of my reckless escapades. All of that bravado changed in my mid-twenties, with the loss of my hand. My mind snapped. I could do nothing but become a homeless youth prowling the streets.

"Workers comp, counseling and therapy were not enough to deal with the sickness that took over my soul. The following years I lived on and off the streets, couch surfing at times with acquaintances and in other instances living with women who propped me up through a series of rotating relationships. I was still a good-looking guy and found it easy to attract women. Though life on the pavement was social and at times fun, it also could be brutal. You might think that there was no place further to slide, but there was, until I finally hit bottom.

"I lived in a culture revolving around drugs and alcohol that was similar to the one my father engaged in before he was put away. As my addictions continued to worsen, I had to find a way to pay for drugs and feed myself, which meant I had to do something. Selling drugs was the logical and only way I knew to survive. In the end, I was busted for growing pot in the basement of a house I was sharing. In my early thirties and facing my first felony, I luckily I had a good lawyer who knew the judge and convinced him that I was an OK guy. My four-year sentence was knocked down to two, and even though I showed up at court drunk, it was further reduced. I was given a six-month penalty in a work-release program. After one month in county jail and four months working, I was let go for good behavior.

"That experience was a turning point, for after meeting quite a few desperate characters in jail, I realized that I didn't want incarceration to be my life. For the first time in ages, I was clean and did not have to look over my shoulder in fear of being caught. I was given alcohol and drug counseling, attended AA and welding school, and for a while even got into real estate training. I didn't finish anything I started, but as I matured, I began to realize there is some goodness in everyone and accepted that there was a "little Jimmy" inside me that wanted to be good too. "During that period of renewal, a Native-American counselor invited me to a sweat lodge. The experience was overwhelmingly positive, changing my outlook on life by giving me a sense of belonging. At about the the same time my sister got interested in our family's genealogy and discovered that we had a small amount of native lineage from the Matis, a Canadian tribe. Our ancestors had been buffalo hunters and tradespeople in the Midwest at one time. I became curious and wanted to know more about them. For the first time in ages I became hopeful.

"Native culture is spiritual, communal and puts emphasis on care of the environment and the world. It talked to me and so I became active in the Sundance family of the Lakota tribe, participating fully and as a dancer.

"Finally settling into a respectable and honest career, I worked for a local taxi company and loved it enough to stay seventeen years. Driving a taxi took energy, for I had to learn nuances of the road. I also was a bit of a psychologist and tuned into the needs of my customers. I enjoyed meeting people so much that a reporter picked up on my gift and wrote a three-page article about me for the local newspaper.

My guiding principle today is to view the world respectfully and gratefully. The mission statement I live by is, "In service, we find purpose, community and healing. In joy, we find ourselves." It is printed on my website.

"Since leaving my job with the taxi company I've been involved in a great many community projects. For years I raised money for a nonprofit that helps women discharged from prison. I became the manager and executive director for a Native -American music group, scheduling gigs in bars and at festivals. They performed all over the Northwest, including prisons, at powwows and blues festivals.

"I also became active with the Native American Youth Agency (NAYA) by helping them with such things as their annual gala. The organization is located some distance from town, but I respect their desire for privacy, for many First People just want to be left alone. They want the white culture to stop trying to turn them into something they are not. Troubled Native-American youths fear and avoid the city-center scene, preferring to be with their own kind." Jimmy concluded, "I am a result of generations of dysfunctional relatives. American society made my grandparents and parents sick. Thankfully, I overcame that part of my background and have found my way to joy. Getting involved with spiritual communities was my way forward. I continue to be an activist, though my path now includes writing, filming documentaries and promoting music to build foundations for improving lives."

SECTION VI
SEARCH FOR SOLUTIONS

FINAL THOUGHTS

T HE QUESTION REMAINS: IS THERE hope for eliminating youth homelessness? Despite many difficulties, I believe the answer is yes—that is if, as a nation, we have the will to do what needs to be done. Over the past ten years, more effective interventions have been designed to help traumatized youths. We now know that adolescent brains are malleable and capable of lifelong growth.

Educators, responding to No Child Left Behind initiatives, now reach out to failing children well before high school. Teens are no longer forced to leave school due to pregnancy but are encouraged to enroll in parenting classes and finish their education. Those who do drop out have access to GED programs run by hospitals, community colleges, and youth agencies.

More effective, simple advice for new parents is now available. For instance, the importance of reading. With documentation clearly showing that infants born into welfare households are likely to hear 30 million fewer words during their first three years than those born into middle- and upper-income families, welfare advocates now give parents books to read to their infants. Readily available parenting classes include topics about brain development and stress the importance of reading and talking to infants and toddlers.[122]

I also am optimistic because of the many compassionate people I met in the course of writing this book. They are making a difference in the lives of youths who were dealt a bad deal.

Thousands of staff and volunteers are willingly giving their time to build a mountain of success stories, one child at a time.

Many people mistakenly think that street kids do not have a social conscience, are unappreciative and therefore undeserving, but that conclusion is far from the truth. Not feeling empowered or knowing how to direct their own future, they operate within guidelines set up by street communities. They do care and willingly adhere to strict rules of behavior that promote group loyalty, even though anti-social to the population at large.

Take the example of a young man who was given an apartment. He invited his street friends to a party and proudly let them stay overnight. Within his moral code it was the right thing to do, since he had been similarly helped from time to time. Neighboring tenants were not as understanding and didn't appreciate the loud music or kids showing up at odd hours reeking of marijuana. The boy was evicted and became angry at all landlords. He thought he had been behaving well. His compassion for friends bodes well for his future if he can be taught how to accommodate society's expectations.

In small towns in the early 20th century, where neighbors knew one another, it was common for communities to assist those in need. Barns, churches and public buildings were often built communally. Participation created public pride, a sense of belonging, and an obligation to others.

Perhaps our youths could be taught similar attitudes. Volunteering to keep streets clean, pull ivy, assist the disabled, maintain park paths and aid teachers are but few ways they might get involved. Unfortunately, such activities tend to be seen as punishment in lieu of going to prison rather than as positive contributions to society. Why not turn this thinking around and make community contributions an expectation starting in the elementary grades?

Some high schools require seniors to participate in a community service project before graduation. Teens often have their eyes and hearts opened by these experiences and continue to volunteer when their assignment is complete. Awakened adolescents give me hope. Imagine what our communities would be like if they started earlier.

Street kids may not know how to manage money, yet are surprisingly generous. When Zach received his first paycheck, he gave most of it away by visiting old hangouts and dispersing $20 bills and cigarettes. He bragged about his earnings and wanted to share his good fortune even though he could not meet his own obligations for rent, past debts and current needs. He even signed up to support a needy child in Thailand with a contract that automatically took monthly deductions from his bank account. This admirable desire to give could easily have landed him back on the streets. He was fortunate to have mentors who taught to him to care for himself and stay within a budget, donating his time until he had enough money to give it away to others.

At the core of poverty is a lack of jobs for untrained workers. Over ten years, 29.4 million dropouts with high illiteracy rates lack job-ready skills and motivation. When employed, many arrive late to work and don't apply themselves to the task at hand. A friend from China once said, "you have to start young to develop a willingness to work." Work ethics could be nudged along if more youths participated in mentorship and vocational training programs. Internships are excellent ways to be taught hands-on practices and work-ready attitudes. My partner recently mentored a 13-year-old boy, teaching him how to carve totem poles. It was a learning experience for both the youth and Cory — a skill was passed on to a student and an adult gained an understanding of the problems facing young people today.

The move from rural America to cities in search of family-wage jobs continues, though robots, self-driving cars, delivery drones and computerized factories indicate that fewer workers will be needed in the future. Working less than 30 hours a week may become the new norm. Long hours passed in unproductive pursuits is a formula for trouble, so it behooves us to prepare the next generation to participate in productive leisure activities. Educating the whole person should be the goal of schools. This means that exercise and hobbies need to be the type that will continue into maturity. It means inspiring healthy eating and promoting activities that build feelings of self-worth. It also means building a sense of community and not just of self. I was pleased to discover that youth agencies promote enjoyment through sports, dance, music and crafts.

Many wonderful model programs have come and gone that were aimed at instilling job readiness skills. The wheel does not need to be reinvented and more studies are not required if we learn from the past. The Youth Conservation Corp and CETA, numerous vocational programs, alternative schools and Job Corps have demonstrated the way to effective learning. What is necessary is the community will to strengthen these programs by providing adequate funds. Why spend $30,000 a year or more to incarcerate one criminal when that money could prevent the crime from happening in the first place? Why waste taxpayer dollars? Why waste a life? The situation is hopeful but we need understanding and a desire to act appropriately.

CREATIVE TEACHING

Not every child is destined for college but each can be productive. High school curriculums primarily are designed for the visually and linguistically talented with the average student in mind. Those more physically and tactilely astute also need to be educated, but with a different approach. When the No Child Left Behind initiative was implemented, rampant testing spread across the country forcing educators to teach to tests designed for the average linguistic learner. But no child lies statistically in the middle. Intelligence takes multiple paths and to accommodate all types of learners, teaching methods have to follow many roads to accommodate them. Tapping into individual learning styles takes time and effort, and that means smaller student-to -teacher ratios in elementary grades.

Over the past fifty years, interactive science centers developed ways to reach diverse learners. They build open-ended exhibits and offer education classes that employ each of the senses. In my book, *Lives of Museum Junkies: The Story of America's Hands-On Education Movement,* I explain how philosophers such as Jean Piaget, Maria Montessori, Howard Gardener, John Holt, Frank Oppenheimer, and A.S. Neil influenced contemporary hands-on museums. Their ideas turned science centers into the "free schools" of today, in that they allow visitors to choose what, how and when they learn. Exhibits start with basic concepts, giving visitors time to build confidence before moving to the next challenge. Visual cues, sound, touch, smell and taste are incorporated into designs to appeal to different ways of digesting information. Graphics accompany explanatory words on signs for those attuned to visual cues, and sound devices disperse information to auditory learners. Nonreaders experience success through tactile experimentation at interactive stations. This approach can be used successfully in public schools by reorganizing classrooms with learning stations rather than desks.

High school students are certainly job-worthy and deserve to be given responsibilities. Two hundred years ago, 14-year-olds received commissions as sea captains and set off to sail the oceans for years at a time. Most adults I know don't trust their teens to make sound decisions. What happened? Perhaps if adolescents are given more freedom along with responsibility they will stop acting as children well into their twenties.

Vocational opportunities need to be expanded so noncollege-bound-youths will be prepared to take jobs in manufacturing, agribusiness and technology. Apprenticeships could be organized with electricians, plumbers, carpenters, roofers, drywallers and glaziers. Chefs, teachers and healthcare providers might let youths job shadow in order to understandworkplace expectations. Nurseries, organic gardens, forestry and landscaping businesses could provide students with experiences in working the land.

Teaching the skills for independent living should be at the heart of every education program. At one time this information was taught by family members, but with both parents employed there often is no one at home to act as educator. Financial management, parenting, nutrition, cooking, automobile care and use of simple tools are important to know. If parents are not available, then schools need to step in. When I was a teen, home economic classes taught us about nutrition and how to cook. We even were taught how to take care of a sick person. In Oklahoma, schools teach money management skills. Transitioning to adulthood would be easier if more schools followed their lead and even went further by including more life-skills subjects in the curriculum.

Zach is a good example of what happens to a child ignorant of practical know-how. At the time he moved into our house, he knew nothing about grocery shopping, cooking, car maintenance or simple repairs. He had spent four years eating in fast-food restaurants that offer high-carb and expensive alternatives to a home-cooked meal. My partner and I insisted he cook once a week, a task he was not happy to do and one that was hard on me since it took time to teach him the most rudimentary tasks. He didn't know how to cook and flavor something as easy to make as rice. Though he complained, he eventually improved and diversified his diet to include salads and vegetables. His meals became more flavorful. Coming from a family that hid cash under the mattress and in holes carved into the wall, Zach had to learn to trust banks. Since his work was seasonal, a savings account was imperative to managing finances year-round. It would have been easier if he previously had learned how to budget, establish a bank account and pay bills. When I was in first grade, a local bank came to our elementary school and gave each child a passbook for a savings account. I loved seeing my pennies add up over time. I am not sure why the practice stopped.

These stories explain why it is difficult for neglected youths to climb over or around fences put in their way. Moving from rags to riches involves more than just job readiness. Obstacles are many, yet they are not insurmountable if dissected and tackled in small increments. It takes understanding, time, patience and one-on-one involvement to build a ladder that can scale a fence. In areas where basic economic and social skills are lacking, educators or mentors are needed to take up the slack. School may be the only available socializing institution in which to practice common courtesy and to learn the communication skills needed for independent living.

Bullying and verbal and physical exploitation have dire consequences that stay with children for years. Teachers identifying such abuse have an obligation to do something about it other than just passing the information on to welfare workers. In Finland, educators put social needs on an equal footing with academic achievement, especially in the early years. Children are taught how to engage in nondestructive interactions that encourage communication. They learn to get along. Finnish teachers are highly respected and trusted to do whatever it takes to ensure that their children are successful. Social workers, nurses and psychologists form a team of specialists who assist the teacher when needed. When solving problems, emotions, cultural differences and social relationships are all taken into account. If one method fails, then they are free to get help and try something different. Teachers brag that they are preparing students for life.

In the United States, The Center for Non-Violent Communication has course material to help children express themselves without using violence. Training programs for teachers greatly benefit students who are poor communicators.[124]

Replacing years of bad habits and impulsive behavior takes time. Adolescents who eventually find counseling too often are seen under severe budgetary constraints. Funders expect instant results while overcoming a traumatized childhood may take years. Just because a youth has been "rescued" doesn't mean that he or she will be grateful and immediately change their ways.

It took five years of one-on-one intervention for Zach to overcome his dysfunctional childhood. He kept falling down and needed to be propped up. When stressed and frustrated, he needed help calming down before he could analyze the problem. We helped him financially so he could pay for security deposits, transportation, health services, and unexpected auto repairs.

Adolescents are taken advantage of because they are poor and young. First-time car buyers like Zach, lacking a credit history, are frequently charged 34 percent interest for an auto loan for a used vehicle that requires costly repairs. It is no wonder that those without assistance commonly return to the streets rather than a job they love.

Twenty years ago, programs like Job Corps provided financial aid to graduates during their first year of employment. A staff advisor was on call for twelve months, and a yearlong stipend was given that enabled the newly employed youth to save for a car and security deposit for his next apartment. If we want to end youth homelessness, benefits need to be provided that are similar to those given to middle-class children by their parents.

Zach's Job Corps instructor, Dewey Taylor, suggests establishing group homes for graduates. He envisions a low-rent communal-living situations with adult mentors in attendance to teach shopping, meal preparation, budgeting, banking, and car maintenance. To ensure habits get well established, he plans to provide transportation for on-time arrival at worksites. Participants would be encouraged to save enough money to purchase a car by year's end.

Though Dewey's dream is laudable, we do not need to wait for it to materialize. Much can be accomplished by establishing a mentor system of those willing to help high school graduates solve problems as they occur over the following several years.

UNIVERSITIES

Colleges and universities are faced with homeless issues among their own students, many of whom lack shelter.[125] As tuition climbs, the number of hungry and homeless enrollees grows. Many students wind up living in shelters, sleeping in cars, residing in tents or couch surfing. Those with a part-time job do not earn enough to cover rent, tuition, food, and transportation. And 13 percent of matriculating students complain of hunger even though they receive food stamps. They are faced with reductions in Pell grants, which peaked in 2010-11 and have declined every year since. Though many work and borrow, they can wind up with so much debt that it impacts their lives for years to come. My relative is a case in point. He accumulated nearly $100,000 in debt in order to acquire a doctorate in a declining social service field.

Students need assistance if society is to meet predictions calling for a trained, educated workforce. Several states are considering making state colleges and universities tuition-free. It seems strange that we cannot figure out how to create an educated workforce when developingcountries like Cuba can.

Another way for universities to impact homelessness is to establish multidisciplinary degree programs with a strong research component. There is a need to collect better data and point the way to better interventions. When interviewing Vailey Oehlke, director of the Multnomah County Library system, I was told libraries do not ask personal questions of patrons. Nevertheless, statistical information could help them plan targeted programs and they welcomed the idea of university-sponsored researchers taking the lead.

To the best of my knowledge, there are no comprehensive degree programs in the United States, though I did discover a few in Canada and Great Britain. Social work programs do offer courses in homelessness and individual students who focus on the subject take some multidisciplinary classes, especially in urban affairs. However, impacting homelessness is a broad subject that needs to include more options. Social work, sociology, education, urban affairs, neuropsychology, health, human services, child psychology, government affairs, fundraising, management, statistics, financial management and marketing need to work together. That may be a mouthful but these disciplines depend on one another.

Issues are complex and not easily resolved, and I fear that traditional departmental approaches are not enough to influence society's will. Knowing how to work with the homeless population is not enough. Students interested in bringing about change need to learn ways to influence taxpayers and politicians. And they need to learn how to increase, train and keep volunteers. And they need to develop skills in fundraising and nonprofit public relations, subjects not usually covered in traditional courses.

Community colleges have an opportunity to play a greater role training government employees, volunteers and agency personnel. Workshops provide an intellectual grounding and camaraderie that many staff and volunteers crave. Since most employees learn on the job, refresher courses are a way to keep them up to date with the latest medical research and intervention ideas. Fee-based offerings for parents of troubled youths could be offered to help them learn ways of helping their own children.

VOLUNTEERS

Volunteers are important assets in the fight against youth homelessness, and there are not enough of them. Now is the time to recruit retiring baby boomers to fill the gap. I know many retirees who are bored after a few months of travel and fixing up the house. They crave ways to find meaning, look for worthwhile causes to get involved in, and seek camaraderie with like-minded individuals. Intellectually stimulating training programs that are cause-driven address all three desires. Social opportunities that encourage friendships between volunteers create loyalty.

CASA operates one of the most organized volunteer programs of its type that I came across. In over 900 centers, thousands of volunteers participate in 30-hour training programs and monthly meetings. In return, volunteers are asked to commit to helping a child for at least two years. Ongoing classes, supervision and social events keep volunteers involved for years.

Arts organizations also have model programs that develop educated, loyal and devoted helpers. The Metropolitan Museum of Art in New York requires docents to take a multi-year art history course before they are permitted to lead groups through the museum. Their model has a win-win approach, education and camaraderie in exchange for volunteering. As a young mother, I participated in a program at a Boston-area mental hospital. A dozen young mothers attended weekly training sessions for a year before being assigned a patient. We enjoyed one another's company when not in class, rarely missed session, and were happy to think of something else besides our children. Many compassionate people are ready to give back to society, but they do not always know how. Volunteers will pay for training when they believe what they are getting in return is worthwhile.

Volunteers are needed to help adolescents communicate their needs to officials. They are needed to serve on boards, raise funds, teach and engage in public relations. Opportunities of every type abound for willing participants. A few suggestions follow:

a) The foster care system poses an especially difficult conundrum for graduating teens. At the age of 18, children are dropped from public rolls and left on their own with inadequate resources. As a result, 40 percent wind up living on the streets. Theses youths need mentors and financial help after they are discharged from foster care. It's surprising that a welfare program designed to help young people operates in such a way as to invite failure for graduates. Let's put an end to shortsightedness and encourage volunteers to become involved for a year or two. In Portland, a complex is under construction to house seniors who will serve as mentors to foster youth living in the same complex. People are ingenious when they have a mind to be.

b) Missionaries working with youth on foreign soil have model programs that could be adapted to fit the needs of our own communities. For instance, Adopt-A-Child, raises funds to support foreign aid workers in outreach sites serving impoverished families. Various levels of giving are solicited to pay for school supplies, clothing, a bicycle or other form of transportation, counseling or a few month's get-started rent. Donors are encouraged to communicate with the child they adopt and establish a bond. As the child ages, some donors become invested in their child's well-being and willingly pay school tuition.

Adopt-A-Child has a way for those who want to give money rather than time to do so. They have a clever way of marketing so the donor feels personally involved and supportive.

c) The role of education parent could be legally expanded. Traditionally, the court appointed position was reserved for children with disabilities. By broadening the concept to include homeless and neglected youths, volunteers would be trained to interact with teachers, parents, relatives and student to ensure that the child's educational needs are met. They would stay abreast of truancy issues, oversee course selections, look at homework, meet with teachers, review special-needs plans, and offer emotional support. Education parents might read to younger children, look at report cards, listen to the child's concerns and applaud successes. Knowing that someone cares can build confidence, self-esteem and a desire to succeed.

d) Poor children want the same opportunities as their wealthier friends. Hikes in the woods, visits to the beach, afternoons in museums, swimming, snowboarding, children's theater, and backyard ball are American activities that neglected youth don't get to experience. Volunteers can bridge the gap to a middle-class existence.

e) Affordable housing is at the crux of homelessness, for without it the situation will not change. Twenty-year-olds need to earn an adequate salary to cover shelter, clothing, food and transportation. Most likely they'll need to be subsidized during their first few years of college or employment, for without adequate backing they are likely to have trouble making ends meet. Volunteers and donors can ease the situation by stepping up to raise funds to subsidize poor youths in transition from school to work. Big business can play an additional role in ending youth homelessness by lending talented employees to participate in think tanks.

A Community Voice

Many people have little idea of the scope of the problem or the interventions needed to overcome youth homelessness. Instead they see loitering truants and it makes them angry. Care providers know a great deal about how to help these youths, but are stretched by demand and are not marketers with time to engage in public discussions. It took several years of research before I understood that by acting together and sharing knowledge it is possible to develop a synergistic movement to solve youth homelessness.

Americans are a caring and generous people in times of crises. It is when a long-term solution is called for that confusion, frustration and partisan politics get in the way, leading to inaction. Cost is a huge factor, but there are no shortcuts to solving a situation that has been long in the making. It takes years to overcome a poor education, trauma and bad parenting practices. Change requires a political will that goes beyond Democratic or Republican politics.

We cannot afford to wait and watch the number of street youths grow. Personal involvement is needed to form a groundswell of concerned citizens willing to expand programs and support for agencies engaged in this mission. Without a way to inform the public, we will continue to walk around sidewalk tents and pass huddled bodies in doorways.

A message of urgency along with stories of hope can be presented to the media. Police officers, church leaders, community groups and medical practitioners might share their success stories to show hope rather than discouragement. It is uplifting to hear favorable outcomes and tales that inspire others to see that change is possible. Chambers of commerce, city clubs, libraries and social organizations are perfect venues for dissemination and discussion.

School programs can help parents recognize signs of abuse and where to go for help. Prevention is always easier than trying to clean up after damage has occurred.

In some states, before a divorce is finalized, separating adults are required to attend classes to discuss ways of making the transition easier on their children? Why not require similar attendance for parents of at-risk children? Sessions could include nonviolent communication, financial management, and how to be an education parent. Learning how negative behavior affects their children's brain and learning to engage in meaningful discussions will develop cooperation and harmony. Learning to listen attentively and value their offspring's ideas are likely to keep thoughts of running away far from the child's mind.

The following is a summary of ways to organize community interventions:

- Once children hit the street they need immediate intervention. Agencies that send a web of volunteers and staff out each night looking for new runaways need to be well supported as the first line of defense. When a youth learns street survival, gets hooked on drugs or is sexually exploited, it is more difficult to get them back to school, with their families, or into foster care.

- Reuniting a child with his or her parents is an important priority as long as safety is not an issue. But parents need to be helped, trained and supported while learning new ways of interacting with their child. Parenting classes and family counseling are necessary.

- Health services, tattoo removal, pregnancy care, education, and contraceptives services must be accessible and free.

- Temporary overnight shelters for youths must be separate from those that house adults. Having sufficient overnight beds for every runaway is imperative, for the streets are dangerous. Shelters need to be coordinated with counseling and social services. Day shelters and not just overnight accommodations are needed. Most of all, permanent affordable housing needs to be available.

- All schools should teach communication skills, decision-making, acceptable ways of interacting socially, financial management, leadership and healthcare at every grade level. High schools should prepare students for independent living.

- Alternative high schools and GED programs need to be incentivized. Poor youths may have to be paid a salary to go to school. These children need clothes, food and an allowance, in addition to shelter.

- Teen pregnancy programs need to locate affordable housing and child-care facilities that enable young mothers to work or remain in school.

- Programs in mindfulness, meditation and yoga should start in elementary school. These programs will benefit all children, but especially will help those coming from dysfunctional backgrounds. Traumatized brains need to be calmed in order to give the cerebral cortex a chance to think.

- Teen literacy programs should include material that relates to their lives. Reading readiness programs need to be expanded and incentives in the form of social activities and training need to be provided for volunteers.

- Vocational education, job readiness, computer literacy, volunteerism, common courtesy and manners and courses in independent living should be included in high school curriculums.

- Sports activities, crafts, dances, trips, hikes, hobbies, camps, trips to museums, homework, visits to various worksites, etc., should be available to all children, not just the wealthy. Poor children especially need exposure to the greater community since they are constrained by their neighborhood and exposed to so much hopelessness. They need introductions to possibilities outside of their home situation.

- Racism and bullying need to be addressed starting in elementary school. More jobs need to be available for minority and LGBTQ youths.

Central to all of these recommendations is a need for consistent one-on-one interaction between youths and mentors. Foster parents need increased emotional support, training, supervision and financial compensation for the children assigned to them. Lives are best changed with consistent, caring involvement. Volunteers also need ongoing emotional support and, in some cases, money that they can use to help the children they serve.

MOVING ON

A great many organizations put their emphasis on shelter and health care, but that's not enough. Youths need social, mental, and educational services for many years. I served on the board of The Giving Tree, an organization that helps homeless people after they are given a secure place to live. They often lack the necessary skills to maintain their new residence. We saw many apartments become ant and rodent infested due to lack of cleanliness. In one situation, the owner planned to kick everyone out of the building. We intervened, fumigated the apartments, and taught the residents how to maintain them.

The isolation and boredom that newly housed residents experience often leads to depression. Some became suicidal after losing contact with their street buddies. Others invite friends to their apartments, party, play loud music and are surprised when evicted. The newly housed need to learn commonly accepted societal norms and adjust to living behind a closed door. Cooking, cleaning, computer use, crafts and social activities are the types of programs The Giving Tree engages in to supplement counseling.

Drug treatment centers offering inpatient and outpatient accommodations are readily available as well.

Observing teens wandering aimlessly in parks and on street corners is a concern to everyone. Let's change this scene before there are communities of roaming youths acting as they do in *Lord of the Flies*. Let's not become a country with beggars on every corner and gang shootings the norm. There is reason for hope, but change has a price tag, and all of us must pay our fair share, for we are part of the reason this situation exists in the first place and so must be part of the solution.

PUBLIC SERVICE

The time has come to institute a public service option for all high school graduates. There are not enough meaningful jobs to employ untrained teens, so rather than have them sit bored at home, why not engage them in pursuits that develop readiness skills? A one or two-year obligation in civil defense, the military, or in a community service organization like Vista Corps or the Peace Corps will contribute to a better society, add experience to a résumé, encourage team building, and allow time for the youth to mature. Since they will be helping the country, enrollees should be compensated for their time and provided with housing.

Mixing youths from diverse backgrounds will forge understanding between races and soften the political divisions that plagues our country. When people work side by side and learn to depend on one another, differences in race, wealth, religion, and gender are mitigated. Public service provides opportunities to interact across class lines and a way to reduce the bullying and bigotry that plagues our nation.

This type of short-term public employment can be especially useful for those who have a difficult time with academic studies. The military has shown that learning to follow directions and being given leadership opportunities builds self-esteem. Public service can be exciting, challenging and developmentally significant when expanding the participant's worldview. A few ideas for service jobs include disaster relief, forestry, fire suppression, agriculture, child development, park maintenance, housing, assisting food banks, and helping the poor.

Public service might be the inspiration for a young person to want to continue toward an advanced degree. The Amish have shown how working for community can be an uplifting and empowering experience that builds compassion.

National Dialogue

Homelessness needs to be elevated to a campaign issue, especially at the local level and, once elected politicians have to be held to their promises. A national dialogue would provide a base from which action could grow. Since treatment of the homeless has been politically divisive it must be addressed by both parties and independent people willing to work on a roadmap for change. Surely, there is a forum in which we can get together. Suggestions for discussion follows:

1. How many people can our communities support?

2. How do we balance the needs of rural areas losing population with cities becoming overcrowded?

3. What problems are raised by overcrowding?

4. As industrialization becomes robotized and mechanized, requiring fewer workers, what will people do to fill their time? Should they learn leisure pursuits?

5. Who will pay for affordable housing?

6. Is a single payer healthcare system feasible?

7. How can an education system that supports multiple learning styles be implement ed?

8. How do we inspire pride in protecting the environment?

9. What should a child's responsibility be toward family and community?

10. How should those with disabilities be supported?

11. What is our responsibility to our citizens? The rest of the world?

12. Do we insure that there is a job for everyone? A living wage for everyone?

It is my hope that this book will help people realize that homeless youths are ordinary children who have been subjected to extreme difficulties. They are not a hopeless cause, and solving their problems will help society. Imagine living in a place where everyone has a chance to climb to the top of Maslow's pyramid.

ADDENDUM

T HE AMERICAN PSYCHOLOGICAL ASSOCIATION'S *REPORT of the 2009 Presidential Task Force on Psychology's Contribution to End Homelessness*[126] defined homelessness to exist when people lack safe, stable and appropriate places to live, including sheltered and unsheltered people, and those in overcrowded and doubled-up situations. The report includes information from 2014 taken from government statistics on various agencies.

WHO ARE THE HOMELESS?

According to the National Alliance to End Homelessness, in 2009, an estimated 656,129 people experienced homelessness in the United States on a given night. As of 2015, that number declined to 564,708 showing some progress has been made. The number of unaccompanied homeless youths and children was relatively unchanged at 45,205. There was a 3 percent decrease in those who went unsheltered though some people dispute this number and believe the Department of Housing and Urban Development is not counting accurately.[127]

An estimated 2.3 million to 3.5 million Americans experience homelessness at least once a year. Homelessness affects people of all ages, geographic areas, occupations, and ethnicities, but occurs disproportionately among people of color.

Access to permanent and adequate shelter is a basic human need; however, the Great Recession of 2008 (composed of the foreclosure crisis, spiking unemployment, worsening poverty rates and inadequate low-cost housing) increased rates of homelessness. Even though the economy has improved, poor and uneducated people have a difficult time finding employment.

The Center for Homeless Education's Federal Data Summary reports that during the 2013-14 school year, 1,301,239 homeless youths were enrolled in public schools, a significant increase over the past two years. Of these, 42,003 are unsheltered, 989,844 were doubled up living with others, 187,265 are awaiting foster care or shelters, and 80,124 were living in motels.[128] The data is underestimated since it does not reflect pre-school age children, toddlers and infants.

In 2013 approximately 48 percent of children in homeless families were black, although black children make up just 14 percent of the U.S. families with children (Child Trends Databank, 2012).[129] On the other hand, although white children make up 54 percent of the child population, they account for 23% of homeless children. Hispanics comprised 23 percent of families with children and made up children make up 22 percent of the sheltered homeless population. Native-Americans and Pacific Islanders are overrepresented in the homeless population, while Asians are underrepresented.

In "Runaway and Homeless Youth: Demographics and Programs,"[130] a congressional research report written in 2013, we learn that 51percent of funds serve the white population, 32.2 percent help blacks, 2.4 percent go to Native -American, .7 percent to Asians, and 4.4 percent go to other multi-racial groups. Homeless single mothers often have histories of violent victimization with over one-third having post-traumatic stress disorder (PTSD) and over half experiencing major depression while homeless. An estimated 41 percent develop a dependency on alcohol and drugs and often are in poor physical health. Maternal depression and parental substance abuse create a series of negative outcomes for children.

Runaway youths number between 575,000 to 1.6 million annually and range from ages 16 to 22. The major causes for leaving home are mental illness, substance abuse, poverty and lack of affordable housing. Since 2011 there's been a decline in available public assistance.[131]

Family conflict is the primary trigger of their homelessness with 46 percent having experienced abuse and an estimated 20-40 percent identifying as lesbian, gay, bisexual, transgendered or questioning (LGBTQ).

Homelessness is traumatic for children who experience frequent moves, family separations, or living in crowded places or homeless shelters. (National Center on Family Homelessness, 2011).

South and Southwest states, where poverty is more prevalent, have more homeless children than those in the North and Northeast. Homelessness affects children's health and well-being, their brain development, causes stress, and hinders readiness for school.

THE GREATEST RISKS

Extreme poverty is the strongest predictor of homelessness. Families struggling for survival often are forced to choose between housing and other necessities. At least 11 percent of American children living in poverty have no home. Female-headed households (those led by women with limited education or job skills) are particularly vulnerable. Even with a high school diploma it is difficult to get a job in the current economic climate. Those who find work are likely to be paid at the minimum wage which is not enough to support a family. Teen parents are especially at risk since they lack the education and income of those who choose to become parents in later life.

Limited affordable housing looms as a monster impediment to families. Often more than 50 percent of their household income goes toward rent or mortgage payments causing them to become delinquent. Those who own homes may have tenants who then become vulnerable to being evicted.

Substance abuse and having physically violent parents or step-parents are the major drivers for runaway youths. Those identifying as lesbian or gay are often are forced from their homes.

Living Without Shelter

Homelessness causes hunger, poor physical and mental health, limited social interactions, and missed educational opportunities. Youth grow up without stability. Annually, 97 percent move at least once, leading to disruptions in education and negatively impacting academic achievement. When schooling is interrupted and delayed the child is twice as likely to develop a learning disability, repeat a grade or to be suspended from school.

A quarter of homeless children have witnessed violence and 22 percent are separated from their families. Exposure to violence causes both emotionally (depression, anxiety, withdrawal) and behaviorally (aggression, acting out) psychosocial difficulties. Half of destitute schoolchildren experience depression and anxiety and one in five preschoolers have emotional problems that require professional care.

Itinerant lives are linked to poor physical health. A low birth weight, malnutrition, ear infections, exposure to environmental toxins and chronic illness (e.g., asthma) are some of the outcomes. The homeless are less likely to have adequate access to medical and dental care. Wandering adolescents wind up with mental health (depression, anxiety and PTSD) and substance abuse problems.

Because many runaways engage in sexually risky behaviors (sometimes for their own survival), they are at risk for HIV, other sexually transmitted diseases and unintended pregnancies. Emerging research shows that LGBTQ youths are seven times more likely to be victims of violent crime.

Risk of Injury

The National Institutes of Health reports an increased risk of injury associated with attention-deficit/hyperactivity disorder (ADHD).[132] Though most injuries are minor, there are indirect expenses to the workplace due to absence and healthcare costs. Since the limbic system (fight and flight) of traumatized youths is well developed while the frontal cortex (critical thinking) is not, these youths find it difficult to concentrate. Their first reaction is to act quickly without thinking.

Zach is an example of what can happen to such a youth. Six months after becoming a journeyman he fell from scaffolding while painting. Unfortunately, his injury was quite serious, leaving him a quadriplegic. Zach's life trajectory changed once again. His year long rehabilitation therapy cost well over $1 million. But, Zach is a survivor. He uses the skills he learned to overcome homelessness and works tirelessly to heal both body and mind. Zach maintains a positive attitude and is actively involved in redirecting his future.

REFERENCES:

1. Busse, P. (2014) The Truth about Hobo Teens. Portland Mercury. retrieved from www.portlandmercury.com/portland/the-truth-about-hobo-teens/Content?oid=31543

2. Griffin, A. (2015) Our Homeless Crisis, Oregon Live. retrieved from www.oregonlive.com/portland-homeless/

3. Youth Homelessness (2017). National Coalition for the Homeless. retrieved from website: http://nationalhomeless.org/issues/youth/

4. Illiteracy (2014) The U.S. Illiteracy Rate Hasn't Changed in 10 Years. Huffington Post. retrieved www.huffingtonpost.com/2013/09/06/illiteracy-rate_n_3880355.html

5. Luscombe, B. (2014). How the American Family Has Changed Dramatically. Time Magazine. Retrieved from, http://time.com/3624827/how-the-american-family-has-changed-dramatically/

6. Hussung, T. (2015) The Evolution of American Family Structure. Concordia College. retrieved from http://online.csp.edu/blog/family-science/the-evolution-of-american-family-structure

7. Pew Research (2015), *The American Family Today. Pew Research Center Report. retrieved from* www.pewsocialtrends.org/2015/12/17/1-the-american-family-today/

8. U.S. Bureau of Labor Statistics (2017). Employment Characteristics of Families. retrieved from https://data.bls.gov/search/query/results?cx=013738036195919377644%3A6ih0hfrgl50&q=number+of+unmarried+working+mothers

REFERENCES:

9. Burton N. MD (2017) Our Hierarchy of Needs. Psychology Today. retrieved from https://www.psychologytoday.com/blog/hide-and-seek/201205/our-hierarchy-needs

10. Child Poverty (2010) National Center for Children in Poverty based on 2010 Census Data. retrieved 2017 from http://nccp.org/topics/childpoverty.html

11. Wight, Vanessa, PhD; Nov. 4, 2011 Impact of Poverty on Youth: www.prweb.com/releases/2011/11/prweb8948552.htm

12. LGBTQ Homeless Youth Fact Sheet. National Alliance to End Homelessness. retrieved 2017 from www.safeschoolscoalition.org/LGBTQhomelessFactSheetbyNAEH.pdf

13. Davis, J. (2017) Trump's Budget Cuts Deeply into Medicaid and Anti-Poverty Efforts. New York Times. retrieved from www.nytimes.com/2017/05/22/us/politics/trump-budget-cuts.html

14. Olivet,J. (2016) Homelessness is a Symptom of Racism. Huffington Post. retrieved from http://www.huffingtonpost.com/jeff-olivet/homelessness-is-a-symptom_b_8409582.html

15. Hahn, S. (2012). Political Racism in the Age of Obama. Huffington Post. retrieved from www.nytimes.com/2012/11/11/opinion/sunday/political-racism-in-the-age-of-obama.html

16. Berman, M. & Lowery,W. (2015) The 12 Key Highlights from the DOJ's Scathing Ferguson REport. Washington Post. retrieved from www.washingtonpost.com/news/post-nation/wp/2015/03/04/the-12-key-highlights-from-the-dojs-scathing-ferguson-report/?utm_term=.5d1965c9b13f

17. Sommers,N. (2016) White People Think Racism is Getting Worse Against White People.Washington Post. retrieved from www.washingtonpost.com/posteverything/wp/2016/07/21/white-people-think-racism-is-getting-worse-against-white-people/?utm_term=.e59682e3d854

18. Child Welfare Information Gateway. (2013) What is Child Abuse and Neglect? retrieved 2017 from website https://www.childwelfare. gov/pubPDFs/whatiscan.pdf#page=3&view=What%20Are%20 the%20Major%20Types%20of%20Child%20Abuse%20and%20 Neglect?

19. Urban Child Institute. (2011) Nutrition and Early Brain Development. retrieved 2017 from http://www.urbanchildinstitute.org/articles/ updates/nutrition-and-early-brain-development

20. Nutrition and Growth. Facts for Life. retrieved 2017 from website www. factsforlifeglobal.org/05/

21. Brody, Jane E., December (1983) NYTimes, Science : www.nytimes. com/1983/12/20/science/emotional-deprivation-seen-as-devastating-form-of-child-abuse.html?pagewanted=all

22. Larson,S.(1997)TeenageRebellion.CultureandYouthStudies.retrievedfrom http://cultureandyouth.org/troubled-youth/articles-troubled -youth/teenage-rebellion/

23. Justice Policy Institute (2017) Calculating the Full Price Tag for Youth Incarceration. retrieved from http://www.justicepolicy.org/ uploads/justicepolicy/documents/sticker_shock_final_v2.pdf

24. Cunningham. R . MD (2016) Violent Reinjury and Mortality Among Youth Seeking Emergency Department Care for Assault-Related Injury. US National Library of Medicine, NIH. retrieved fromhttps:// www.ncbi.nlm.nih.gov/pmc/articles/PMC4306452/

25. Gill,D. (1973) (reprinted 2014) Violence Against Children, Harvard University Press. ISBN 978-0-674-18791-7

26. Childhelp (2017) Child Abuse Statistics and Facts.retrieved from website www.childhelp.org/child-abuse-statistics/

27. Nelson, C. & Fox, N. & Zeanah, C. (2014) Romania's Abandoned Children, Deprivation, Brain Development, and the Struggle for Recovery, Harvard University Press.

REFERENCES:

28. Parks, G. (2000) The High/Scope Perry Preschool Project. U.S. Department of Justice; Office of Juvenile Justice and Delinquency Prevention. retrieved from www.ncjrs.gov/pdffiles1/ojjdp/181725.pdf also Rand Published Study www.rand.org/pubs/research_briefs/RB9145.html

29. Bergland, C. (2013) Parental Warmth is crucial for a Child's Well-being. Psychology Today. retrieved from www.psychologytoday.com/blog/the-athletes-way/201310/parental-warmth-is-crucial-child-s-well-being

30. Weir, Ki. (2014). Lasting Effect of Love Deprivation. American Psychological Association, Vol.45. No.6. retrieved from www.apa.org/monitor/2014/06/neglect.aspx

31. Castro, J. (2012). How a Mother's Love Changes a Child's Brain. LiveScience. retrieved from www.livescience.com/18196-maternal-support-child-brain.html

32. Centers for Disease Control and Prevention (2017) Essentials for Childhood, Steps to Create Safe, Stable, Nurturing environments for all Children. Division of Violence Prevention. retrieved from www.cdc.gov/violenceprevention/childmaltreatment/essentials.html

33. Youth Ending Slavery (2017) Slavery Today. retrieved from website www.youthendingslavery.org

34. Human Rights Report on Ending Human Trafficking in Oregon (2010) International Human Rights Clinic at Willamette University College of Law. retrieved from www.mwvcaa.org/HYRC/documents/Human_Trafficking_&_Homeless_Youth.pdf

35. UNICEF (2017) Child Protection from Violence, Exploitation, Abuse. retrieved from www.unicef.org/protection/57929_58006.html

36. Kadlec, G. (2016) Child Slavery: America's Hidden CrimeChild's World America: retrieved from http://childsworldamerica.org/child-slavery-americas-hidden-crime/

37. National Alliance to End Homelessness (2017). LGBTQ Homeless Youth Fact Sheet. www.safeschoolscoalition.org/LGBTQhomelessFact SheetbyNAEH.pdf

38. Durso,L. & Gates, G. (2012) Ninety-Four percent of Homeless Youth Service Providers Report Serving LGBT Youth. The Williams Institute, UCLA School of Law. retrieved from http://williamsinstitute.law. ucla.edu/headlines/lgbt-homeless-youth/

39. National Institute on Drug Abuse (2016) Monitoring the Future Survey Results. retrieved from www.drugabuse.gov/related-topics/ trends-statistics/infographics/monitoring-future-2016-survey-results

40. NN4Y Issue Brief (2017) Consequences of Youth Homelessness. retrieved from www.nn4youth.org/wp-content/uploads/IssueBrief_Youth_ Homelessness.pdf

41. Wyman, J. (1997) Drug Abuse Among Runaway and Homeless Youths calls for Focused Outreach Solutions. NIDA Notes. retrieved from www.nn4youth.org/wp-content/uploads/IssueBrief_Youth_ Homelessness.pdf

42. Government Substance Abuse Prevention web sites for Youth. (2018) retrieved from http://youth.gov/youth-topics/substance-abuse and https://archives.drugabuse.gov/NIDA_Notes/NNVol12N3/ Runaway.html

43. Center for Disease Control (2017) Reproductive Health: Teen Pregnancy. www.cdc.gov/teenpregnancy/about/index.htm

44. Chuck,E. (2017) Trump Administration Abruptly Cuts funding to Teen Pregnancy Prevention Programs, U.S.News. retrieved from www. nbcnews.com/news/us-news/trump-administration-abruptly-cuts-funding-teen-pregnancy-prevention-programs-n795321

45. Howell, J, U.S. Department of Justice, Office of Juvenile Justice and Delinquency, 1997 Prevention. retrieved fromwww.ncjrs.gov/ pdffiles/fs-9772.pdf

References:

46. Carlie,M. (2017) Into the Abyss: The Structure of Gangs. Missouri State University. retrieved from https://people.missouristate.edu/michaelcarlie/what_i_learned_about/gangs/recruitment_techniques.htm

47. Frieden,T. (2011) FBI report: Gang Membership. CNN. retrieved from www.cnn.com/2011/10/21/justice/gang-membership-increase/index.html

48. Petering,R.(2015). Why Homeless Youth Become Involved in Gangs. UCLA School of Social Work. retrieved from http://ncfy.acf.hhs.gov/news/2015/01/qa-robin-petering-homeless-youth-and-gangs?utm_source=FindYouthInfo.gov&utm_medium=Federal%20Links&utm_campaign=Reports-and-Resources

49. Complaining of the Youth. The Literature Network. retrieved 2017 from www.online-literature.com/forums/showthread.php?17788-Socrates-Plato-Complaining-of-the-Youth

50. Rumspringa. Amish Studies, the Young Center. retrieved from home page 2017 http://groups.etown.edu/amishstudies/cultural-practices/rumspringa/

51. Larson,J.(1997).Teenage Rebellion. Culture+Youth Studies. retrieved from http://cultureandyouth.org/troubled-youth/articles-troubled-youth/teenage-rebellion/

52. Dryfoos, J. (1990) Adolescents at Risk, Prevalence And Prevention:. Oxford University Press.

53. Flores, T. &, Griffith, S. (2002) ,Oregon History Project, Oregon Historical Society

54. Rector, E. (2010) Looking Back in Order to Move Forward. Coaching for Educational Equity. retrieved from www.portlandoregon.gov/bps/article/412697 - Oregon State Information

55. Mesh, A. (2014) Bring the Noise. Willamette Week. retrieved from www.wweek.com/portland/article-23657-bring_the_noise.html

56. United States Department of Labor, Employment and Training Administration, Job Corps Fact Sheet (2017) www.doleta.gov/ programs/factsht/jobcorps.cfm

57. Job Corps (2017) retrieved from website at www.allgov.com/departments/ department-of-labor/job-corps?agencyid=7169

58. Janus Youth Services (2017) retrieved from website at www.janusyouth.org

59. Friends of the Children (2018) retrieved from website at http://friendspdx. org

60. Court Appointed Special Advocates For Children (2017) retrieved from CASA website at www.casaforchildren.org/site/c.mtJSJ7MPIsE/ b.5301295/k.BE9A/Home.htm

61. Basic Rights Oregon (2017) retrieved from website a www.basicrights. org/about/our-history

62. Outside In (2018) retrieved from website at http://outsidein.org/index. php/about-us/

63. Building place, Permanence and Purpose for Foster youth, adoptive parents, and Alders (2017) Bridge Meadows. retrieved from website at www.bridgemeadows.org.

64. New Avenues for Youth (2018) retrieved from website at http:// newavenues.org/about-us/

65. Foster Care Basics. (2017) . Foster Club/ National Network for Youth in Foster Care. Retrieved from www.fosterclub.com

66. Six Problems with the Foster Care System. (2017). Washable. retrieved from http://mashable.com/2016/06/04/foster-care-problems/#boS JxnIxCqqJ

67. Cross,T. (1997) Relational Worldview Model. Presentation Pathways Practice Digest, vol. 12, No.468.

68. Native American Youth and Family Services (2018) retrieved from website at http://nayapdx.org/about/

References:

69. William, Walter L, The Two-Spirit People of Indigenous North America, www.firstpeople.us/articles/the-two-spirit-people-of-indigenous-north-americans.html

70. Portland Oregon Government (2017) retrIeved from website at www.portlandoregon.gov/oni/article/505489

71. Transforming the Lives of People Experiencing Homelessness (2017) Future in Humanity. retrieved from website at www.futureinhumanity.org/about-2

72. Building a Movement to End Homelessness. National homeless.org. retrieved 2017 from website at nationalhomeless.org

73. Macomb Homeless Coalition (2017) retrieved from website at www.macombhomelesscoalition.com

74. Portland Opportunities Industrialization Center + Rosemary Anderson High School. retrieved 2017 from website at www.portlandoic.org/

75. POIC (2018) Community Haling Initiative. retrieved from website at www.portlandoic.org/families/community-healing-initiative/

76. Ifill, G, (2015) Library social worker helps homeless seeking quite refuge. PBS Newshour. retrieved from www.pbs.org/newshour/bb/library-social-worker-helps-homeless-seeking-quiet-refuge/

77. Goldberg, E. (2016) Library Offers Homeless People Mental Health Services, And It's Working. HuffPost. retrieved from www.huffingtonpost.com/entry/a-library-is-often-the-safest-place-for-homeless-people-thats-why-this-one-hired-a-social-worker_us_56fbf43ee4b083f5c6063b0d

78. San Jose Public Library (2017) Lawyers in the Library. retrieved website at from https://events.sjpl.org/event/lawyers_in_the_library_2017

79. Barbieus, K. (2017) Tips and Tools from the American Library Association's Social Responsibilities Round Table and Office for Literacy and Outreach Services. American Library Association. retrieved from www.ala.org/aboutala/offices/diversity/resources

80. Poor and/or Homeless Library Patrons/ American Library Association. retrieved from web site www.ala.org/tools/atoz/poor-and-or-homeless-library-patrons

81. American Academy of Child & Adolescent Psychiatry (2016) The Teen Brain:Behavior,ProblemSolving,andDecisionMaking.retrievedfrom www.aacap.org/aacap/families_and_youth/facts_for_families/ FFF-Guide/The-Teen-Brain-Behavior-Problem-Solving-and-Decision-Making-095.aspx

82. Spinks, S. (2000) Adolescent Brains are Works in Progress: Here's Why. Frontline. retrieved from www.pbs.org/wgbh/pages/frontline/ shows/teenbrain/work/adolescent.html

83. The Teen Brain: 6 Things to Know.National Institute of Mental Health. retrieved in 2017 from www.nimh.nih.gov/health/publications/ the-teen-brain-still-under-construction/index.shtml

84. Wu, S. (2015) USC scientists Arthur toga, Paul Thompson are on the cutting edge of brain mapping. USC News. retrieved from https://news. usc.edu/77654/77654-usc-scientists-arthur-toga-paul-thompson-are-on-the-cutting-edge-of-brain-mapping/

85. Spinks, S. (2000) Adolescent Brains are Works in Progress: Here's Why. Frontline. retrieved from www.pbs.org/wgbh/pages/frontline/ shows/teenbrain/work/adolescent.html

86. Olson, S. (2013) Men Mature After Women Medical Daily. retrieved from www.medicaldaily.com/men-mature-after-women-11-years-after-be-exact-british-study-reveals-246716

87. Bergland, C. (2013) Scientists Identify why girls often Mature Faster than Boys. Psychology today. retrieved from www.psychologytoday. com/blog/the-athletes-way/201312/scientists-identify-why-girls-often-mature-faster-boys

REFERENCES:

88. Lopez, M. & Gonzalez, A. (2014) Women's college enrollment gains leave men behind. Pew Research Center. retrieved from www.pewresearch. org/fact-tank/2014/03/06/womens-college-enrollment-gains-leave-men-behind/

89. Robb, P, (2009) Cross Crawl: Neurological Disorganisation. Head Back to Health. retrieved from www.headbacktohealth.com/Cross_crawl. html

90. Murrell, M. Psy.D. (2013) Understanding our Fight or Flight Response" of our Limbic System. Morrell Counseling Service, LLC. retrieved from www.murrellpsychologicalservice.com/blog/2013/03/09/The-Good-and-Bad-News-about-Anxiety.aspx

91. Matrix Repatterning (2018) What is Matrix Repatterning? retrieved from website at www.matrixrepatterning.com/Pa_MR_what

92. EMDR Institute, Inc. (2018) What is EMDR? retrieved from website at www.emdr.com/what-is-emdr/

93. (2018) Is Luminosity an Effective Braining training? MD health.com. retrieved from web site http://www.md-health.com/Does-Lumosity-Work. html

94. Science Daily (2014) Regular marijuana use bad for teens' brains, study finds. retrieved from www.sciencedaily.com/releases/2014/08/ 140809141436.htm

95. Ghose, T. (2012) smoking Pot in Teen Years Lowers IQ Later. Live Science. retrieved from www.livescience.com/22711-smoking-marijuana-lowers-iq.html

96. The Doors (1971.) Been Down So Long Lyrics. Lyrics Depot. retrieved from www.lyricsdepot.com/the-doors/been-down-so-long.html

97. Zimmerman, M. (2014) Resiliency Theory: A Strengths-Based Approach to research and Practice for Adolescent Health. US National Library of Medicine, NIH. retrieved from www.ncbi.nlm.nih.gov/pmc/ articles/PMC3966565/

98. Fleming, J & Ledogar, R. (2010) Resilience, an Evolving Concept. US National Library of Medicine, National Institute of Health. retrieved from www.ncbi.nlm.nih.gov/pmc/articles/PMC2956753/

99. Leonard, L. (2008) The Relationship Between Navajo Adolescents' Knowledge and Attitude of Navajo Culture and their Self-Esteem and Resiliency. Dissertation at Arizona State University.

100. Zimmerman, M. PhD. (2013) Resiliency Theory. National Institution of Healthy Public Access. retrieved from www.ncbi.nlm.nih.gov/pmc/articles/PMC3966565/

101. Alban,D. (2016) Overstimulation: Taming A Modern Problem That Leads to Anxiety. reset.me. retrieved from http://reset.me/story/overstimulation-taming-a-modern-problem-that-leads-to-anxiety/

102. TBTEN, K (2014) Processing Disorders: The Understimulated Brain. Hub Pages. retrieved from https://hubpages.com/health/processing-disorders-under-stimulated-brain

103. Kabat-Zinn, J. (2017) Practices with Jon Kabat-Zinn. Guided Mindfulness Meditation. retrieved from website www.mindfulnesscds.com/pages/about-the-author

104. Benefits of Yoga & Mindfulness Programming for Youth.(2017) Street Yoga. retrieved from website http://streetyoga.org/benefits-of-yoga-mindfulness-programming-for-youth/ -About benefits

105. Howard Garner's Theory of Multiple Intelligences, - Northern Illinois University. Faculty Development and Instructional Design Center. retrieved 2017 from www.niu.edu/facdev/_pdf/guide/learning/howard_gardner_theory_multiple_intelligences.pdf

106. Finkel, M. (2013). Aboriginal Australians. National Geographic Magazine. retrievedfromwww.nationalgeographic.com/magazine/2013/06/australia-aboriginals-tradition-cultural-preservation/

107. Illiteracy Statistics (2016) U.S. Illiteracy Statistics. retrieved from www.statisticbrain.com/number-of-american-adults-who-cant-read/

REFERENCES:

108. Lake, Rebecca, May 2016 - 23 Statistics on Illiteracy in America. Literacy facts and education. Credit Donkey. retrieved from www.creditdonkey.com /illiteracy-in-america.html

109. Wood, D.. Nov, 2009 for Education.com http://www.education.com/ magazine/article/30000_words/ about the work of art and Risely

110. Grohol,J Psy.D., M. (2006) Stages of Change. Psych Central. https:// psychcentral.com/lib/stages-of-change/

111. Fisher,P. (2017) Department of Psychology, University of Oregon. retrieved from website http://psychology.uoregon.edu/profile/ philf/ Also, Stress Neurobiology. University of Oregon. retrieved 2017 from http://snaplab.uoregon.edu

112. Srouge,A. (2000) Early Relationships and the Development of Children. University of Minnesota. retrieved from www.cpsccares. org/system/files/Early%20Relationships%20and%20the%20 Development%20of%20Young%20Children.pdf

113. Foster Care. Children's Rights. retrieved 2017 from web site. www. childrensrights.org/newsroom/fact-sheets/foster-care/

114. Babbel,S,Ph.D. (2012) The Foster Care System and Its Victims. Psychology Today. /www.psychologytoday.com/blog/somatic-psychology/ 201201/the-foster-care-system-and-its-victims-part-2

115. Fessler,P NPR, 2010, Report: Foster Kids Face Tough Times After Age 18.

116. Blue Knot Foundation- Wealth of information df studies of abuse and the brain-www.blueknot.org.au/Resources/General-Information/ Impact-on-brain

117. National Coalition for the homeless information: McKinney-Vento Act. http://www.nationalhomeless.org/publications/facts/McKinney. pdf http://homelesswithhomework.nycitynewsservice.com/2010 /05/04/mental-health-2/

118. Healy, M. (2013) Mental illness in Youth: a Common Struggle. Los Angeles Times.retrieved from http://articles.latimes.com/2013/may/17/science/la-sci-mental-illness-youth-20130516

119. National Institute on Drug Abuse, www.drugabuse.gov/publications/principles-drug-addiction-treatment-research-based-guide-third-edition/frequently-asked-questions/what-drug-addiction-treatment

120. Office of National Drug Control Policy - 2015 - National Drug Control Strategy - https://obamawhitehouse.archives.gov/ondcp/policy-and-research/ndcs

121. Franco,C. CRS Report for Congress about Drug Courts, Oct. 2010 : https://fas.org/sgp/crs/misc/R41448.pdf

122. Child Development and Early Learning (2018) Facts for Life, fourth edition. retrieved from website at www.factsforlifeglobal.org/03/1.html

123. Burkes, Paula, Oklahoma schools required to teach high school students to manage money, 2014, Newsok, http://newsok.com/article/3936334

124. Non-Violent Communication (2018) retrieved from website at www.cnvc.org

125. Carapezza, K, (2/8,2017) All Things Considered,NPR , The number of Hungry and Homeless Students Rises Along with College Costs;. retrieved from onlinelibrary.wiley.com/doi/abs/10.1002/%28SICI%291097-0355%28200001/04%2921%3A1/2%3C67%3A%3AAID-IMHJ8%3E3.0.CO%3B2-2

126. American Psychological Association, Report of the 2009 Presidential Task Force. www.apa.org/pi/ses/resources/publications/end-homelessness.aspx

127. State of Homelessness in America (2016) National Alliance to End Homelessness. retrieved from web site https://endhomelessness. org/homelessness-in-america/homelessness-statistics/state-of-homelessness-report/

128. National Center for Homeless Education (2018) Statistics. Retrieved from website at the:http://nche.ed.gov

129. Child trends Data Bank, 2012 : http://www.childtrends.org/databank -indicators/databank-by-life-stage/

130. Fernandes-Alcantara, Adrienne L. (2013) Runaway and Homeless Youth: Demographics and Programs. Congressional Research Service. retrieved from http://www.nchcw.org/uploads/7/5/3/3/7533556/ crs_2013_rhya_history_and_lit_review.pdf

131. National Alliance to End Homelessness (2018) retrieved from website at https://endhomelessness.org/

132. Primary Care Companion (2011) Risk of Injury Associated With Attention-Deficit/Hyperactivity Disorder in Adults Enrolled in Employer-Sponsored Health Plans: A Retrospective Analysis. US National Library of Medicine & National Institutes of Health. retrieved from www.ncbi.nlm.nih.gov/pmc/articles/PMC3184594/

ABOUT THE AUTHOR

Marilynne Eichinger has been an active supporter of hands-on learning throughout her career as both a mother and museum professional. Graduating magna culaude from Boston University with an emphasis on anthropology, she went on to receive a master's degree in counseling psychology from Michigan State University. In 1972, Marilynne founded Impression 5 Science Center in Lansing, Michigan in order to share the wonders of science that she was introduced to as a child at the Franklin Institute in Philadelphia.

After thirteen years she left Impression 5 to become president of the Oregon Museum of Science and Industry, one of the nation's oldest and most renowned science centers. There she spearheaded a new 250,000-square-foot facility and workshop on the Willamette River in Center City Portland, acquired a submarine from the Navy, and installed an IMAX theater. Under her presidency she cultivated a traveling exhibit service developing displays that circulated internationally. She oversaw science classes, camps and education programs that serviced a five-state region.

Throughout her career, Marilynne worked with children from all economic backgrounds, including those who were handicapped by poverty. She initiated special educational programs in ghetto areas of Cambridge, Massachusetts, Lansing, Michigan, and Portland, Oregon, working with the Urban League, Boys and Girls Clubs, and area churches. She helped rid pockets of drug dealers that impeded children from entering museum-sponsored events. While at OMSI she also oversaw programs held in conjunction with Native-American populations.

In 1995, Marilynne's concern for children propelled her to the national stage where she started a company to provide hands-on educational materials to the home. With the involvement of 22 museums and private investors, she established the Museum Tour Catalog, distributed annually to 2 million households. Her company adopted a low-income elementary school and assisted teachers by providing needed books and equipment. The business was sold in 2014. Marilynne remains an active painter, blogger and traveler. She is the author of books that benefit the education of young children.

Lives of Museum Junkies: The Story of America's Hands-On Education Movement was published in fall 2016. Marilynne's talks at bookstores, museums and clubs throughout the country are well received.

In 2010 she and her partner, Ray Losey, adopted a twenty-year-old homeless boy. His story, both personal and poignant inspired Marilynne's interest in disadvantaged youths. For the past three years she researched the topic of homeless youths in order to present a comprehensive accounting that will entice the general public to get involved. *Over the Peanut Fence* is the result of her efforts.

A FEW WORDS OF THANKS

In 2013, my partner, Ray Losey, and I invited a homeless youth to live with us. Helping him evolve into a productive, well-adjusted person was not easy, making me cognizant of the affects poverty and abuse have on children. This book is dedicated to my unofficial sixth child, whom I call Zach, and the many people who aid troubled youth in their fight to reach maturity.

Much of who I am is because of my five children. Not only are they the loves of my life, but they inspired me to want to be a super mom who challenged them to self-sufficiency while maintaining humanity. Due to their own ambitions, not mine, they attained adulthood being everything I hoped for and today work passionately to bring about positive societal changes. As president of the Oregon Museum of Science and Industry and later when operating my own company, Informal Education Products, I was involved with children born into poor and dysfunctional families. Building enthusiasm became a passion that remains with me today.

Writers work in isolation, not worrying about the opinions of others, but once feedback is requested, comments have to be ingested with a strong heart. I appreciate the hours Karen Segal spent listening to Zach's story. She kept pushing me to share what I learned about youth homelessness and the thousands of children who fall prey to predators. Editing is a large part of bringing a book to fruition and I appreciate Mary Rita Mitchell and Denise Szott for reaching out across half a nation to help. Thanks also goes to the Reverend Kate Lore, a Unitarian minister dedicated to social justice. Kate was a great help in identifying issues of public ignorance and areas that need to be addressed.

BOOK CLUB QUESTIONS

1. Did your understanding of youth homelessness change by reading this book? If so how?

2. What do you feel when passing a homeless youth on the streets asking for a hand out?

3. What do you think volunteers can do to improve the situation?

4. What should the role of schools be in helping those who come from traumatic family backgrounds? Should money be directed toward these kids?

5. What is your opinion of expanding vocational training and apprenticeship programs?

6. What do you think about broadening education practice to encompass a multitude of intelligence styles?

7. Should shop and home economics classes be reintroduced in middle and high school curriculums?

8. How do you think technology is affecting the poor?

READ ON

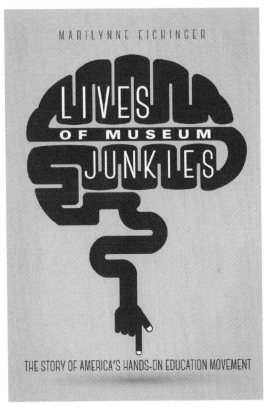

Former OMSI President Reveals the Good, the Bad, and the Ugly History Behind the Hands-On Education Movement

"...will help you see science museums in a new light."

– David Ucko, Museums+More llc

In this lively, behind-the-scenes look at the evolution of interactive science museums, discover:

> How the NY Hall of Science saved the Brooklyn Museum of Art from being closed by Mayor Rudolph Guiliani for showing a Chris Ofili painting of the Virgin Mary that contains elephant dung.

> How OMSI talked the navy out of a submarine.

> Who kept "NOVA" from being canceled when Congress did not agree with their investigative reporting style that explored sensitive subjects like nuclear energy.

> What inspired a poor Appalachian orphan to go from rags to riches to become a museum president who later rented an entire cruise ship to see a global eclipse on the Amazon.

> Why executives at the top are subject to sexual abuse and find it nearly impossible to manage.

> The outcry caused by the Playboy Bunnies playing basketball with business executives to raise funds for a museum.

"recommended for those who care about
museums, libraries and society today."

– Ginnie Cooper, Former director of library systems
in Washington D.C., Brooklyn, and Portland.

CHAPTER 1

CREATING AN INTERACTIVE MUSEUM: NAÏVE BEGINNINGS

"STOP RUNNING AND MAKING SO much noise!" I shouted to five rambunctious children playing hide-and-seek in closets throughout the house. It was a cold day and my friend Dee Pumplin was visiting with her son. She and I were having a difficult time hearing each other as we chatted animatedly in the kitchen. It was during this conversation that my homemaker days started to end, when over coffee in my suburban house we brewed up the idea of a hands-on museum that emphasized science. Children are not always polite, studious little creatures set on this planet to impress and please their parents. Instead they are balls of energy who love to run, scream and create bedlam. In short they can drive a parent crazy, especially on a rainy day. As Dee and I talked, her one and my four children shouted and squealed, ignoring the storm roaring outside. The increasing noise level was like a drum roll announcing a new idea. We started imagining what it would be like to take our kids to an indoor playground. "Wouldn't it be magnificent to have a great big barn," we fantasized, "and fill it floor to ceiling with ramps, poles, and climbing apparatus? What fun it would be for the children and their friends. They would get rid of their energy away from home and our houses would be preserved." Dee and I started to wonder where we could find a barn and even took the next step of contacting a realtor.

As we learned more, the vision for an indoor play structure grew. The immense dimensions of a working barn inspired our ideas to expand to include interactive learning activities inserted into climbing areas. We imagined children swooping down a sliding board and finding a light table, colored filters, and projectors to use for experimentation. The colored light could be projected on the next child speeding down the slide. We embraced the idea of physical play being integrated with academic challenges in a never-ending cycle of learning.

After months of talk and concept development we finally located a barn, but it wasn't long before we faced a dose of reality. The cost to acquire the property was more than we anticipated and building the inside play structure seemed monumental. The barn needed to be heated, insulated, electrified, bathroomed and water sprinkled and once it was upgraded, ongoing utilities would be astronomical. The permitting process was overwhelming to two inexperienced women who began to wonder if the city would even allow this type of play-barn to exist. Insurance was bound to be phenomenal, not only because we were dealing with a wooden structure but because we were planning to let children run throughout. We especially liked the idea of fire poles descending from one level to the next. Sound safe? Costs mounted, reaching an enormous number before we even considered the price of exhibits and staffing.

We did not give up, though, but started to change direction. The more Dee and I chatted the more we talked ourselves out of a play-barn and into a more permanent facility. During these early discussions our enthusiasm increased, and we came up with the concept for an inquiry- based science and art museum. It would be a "yes, you can touch" kind of place. We created an an opportunity to turn the books we had read about self-directed schooling and learning through sensory experimentation into our own institutional brand.

Our first assignment was to select a name. In front of a fire with an open bottle of wine, Dee and I lay on the floor giggling while throwing out possibilities. We wanted the center to be open-ended, exploratory and adventurous. The word museum sounded "fuddy-duddy old world" to our way of thinking so we eliminated it from our vocabulary. Though Dee and I both loved classical art and history museums they were not the type of institutions most young children enjoy. We were not interested in amassing a collection of objects but rather in developing interactive challenges. Finally the word Impression emerged. Our new center would make an impression on our visitors, and our visitors would be invited to leave an impression with us. The name seemed perfect, though we discovered later that it was difficult to brand Impression as a hands-on science center. To others it sounded more like a place to go for embossing paper. However, upon making our first decision in the warmth of the fire, Dee and I felt like proud parents giving birth to a concept and had a strong sense of accomplishment during those drinking hours. Impression was going to be fun! Developing it would be easy.

At the time, few national museums had branched out beyond being a collection of antiquities and artifacts. They tended to be filled with industrial displays that permitted a modicum of interaction rather than just passive viewings of objects placed behind glass. These museums, or centers of science and industry as they were often called, dabbled with sensory approaches to exhibitions. Pioneering institutions, such as Chicago's Museum of Science and Industry, The Franklin Institute, and the Los Angeles Science Center were supported in part by big businesses that controlled the messages presented in their exhibitions. In essence what was on display were advertisements in support of their industry. Visitors made push button selections to view automated procedures that took place behind glass. A few expensive immersion exhibits included a coal mine in Chicago, a steam locomotive in Philadelphia, and a walk through heart in Portland, Oregon. There were even a sprinkling of hands-on physics experiments though they were the exception rather than the rule.

Thus when we started Impression there were few models for the type of institution Dee and I were interested in promoting, so we mulled through ideas in a vacuum. We were focused on basic science and art activities and wanted children involved in a comprehensive way. During this early brainstorming stage we were open to ideas from anyone who would listen to us. Many suggestions came from our science and engineering friends.

Dee's and my initial goal was not to operate Impression ourselves but to establish it as a community organization complete with board of trustees and managing director. At the time both of us were pursuing other career paths. Dee was looking for a job as a paralegal and I, afraid to work, was enrolled as a graduate student in counseling psychology. We felt confident that university parents in East Lansing would jump to embrace the science center concept so we set about identifying our first tasks. Dee's assignment was to develop a logo, print business cards and create stationery. With donated services of our newly acquired attorney we were sure that we would be ready to operate successfully in a few months with a paid managing director.

Marilynne's Lesson #1: Nothing ever occurs as you might imagine.